FATHERING IN CULTURAL CONTEXTS

How do men think about fathering? How does this differ across different regions of the world? And what effect does this have on child development? *Fathering in Cultural Contexts: Developmental and Clinical Issues* answers these questions by considering a broad range of theoretical and conceptual models on fathering and childhood development, including attachment theory, developmental psychopathology, masculinity and parenting typologies.

Roopnarine and Yildirim provide a comprehensive view of fatherhood and fathering in diverse cultural communities at various stages of economic development, including fathers' involvement in different family structures, from two-parent heterosexual families to community fathering. This book's interdisciplinary approach highlights the changing nature of fathering, drawing connections with child development and well-being, and evaluates the effectiveness of a range of father interventions.

Fathering in Cultural Contexts will appeal to upper level undergraduate and graduate students in human development, psychology, sociology, anthropology, social work, and allied health disciplines, and professionals working with families and children in non-profit and social service agencies across the world.

Jaipaul L. Roopnarine is Pearl S. Falk Professor of Human Development and Family Science, Syracuse University, New York, USA, and Professor Extraordinary of Developmental Psychology, Anton de Kom University of Suriname, South America.

Elif Dede Yildirim is Assistant Professor of Human Development and Family Studies, Auburn University, Alabama, USA.

International Texts in Developmental Psychology

Series editor: Peter K. Smith

Goldsmiths College, University of London, UK

This volume is one of a rapidly developing series in *International Texts in Developmental Psychology*, published by Routledge. The books in this series are selected to be state-of-the-art, high level introductions to major topic areas in developmental psychology. The series conceives of developmental psychology in broad terms and covers such areas as social development, cognitive development, developmental neuropsychology and neuroscience, language development, learning difficulties, developmental psychopathology and applied issues. Each volume is written by a specialist (or specialists), combining empirical data and a synthesis of recent global research to deliver cutting-edge science in a format accessible to students and researchers alike. The books may be used as textbooks that match on to upper level developmental psychology modules, but many will also have cross-disciplinary appeal.

Each volume in the series is published in hardback, paperback and eBook formats. More information about the series is available on the official website at: www.routledge.com/International-Texts-in-Developmental-Psychology/book-series/DEVP, including details of all the titles published to date.

Published Titles

An Introduction to Mathematical Cognition
Camilla Gilmore, Silke M. Göbel, and Matthew Inglis

Developmental Transitions
Exploring Stability and Change through the Lifespan
Sarah Crafter, Rachel Maunder, Laura Soulsby

Fathering in Cultural Contexts
Developmental and Clinical Issues
Jaipaul L. Roopnarine and Elif Dede Yildirim

FATHERING IN CULTURAL CONTEXTS

Developmental and Clinical Issues

Jaipaul L. Roopnarine and
Elif Dede Yildirim

Routledge
Taylor & Francis Group

LONDON AND NEW YORK

First published 2019
by Routledge
2 Park Square, Milton Park, Abingdon, Oxon OX14 4RN

and by Routledge
52 Vanderbilt Avenue, New York, NY 10017

Routledge is an imprint of the Taylor & Francis Group, an informa business

British Library Cataloguing-in-Publication Data
A catalogue record for this book is available from the British Library

Library of Congress Cataloging-in-Publication Data
A catalog record for this book has been requested

ISBN: 978-1-138-69107-0 (hbk)
ISBN: 978-1-138-69108-7 (pbk)
ISBN: 978-1-315-53617-0 (ebk)

Typeset in Bembo
by Apex CoVantage, LLC

CONTENTS

ILLUSTRATIONS

Figures

Tables

ACKNOWLEDGEMENTS

We sincerely thank Professor Ziarat Hossain for his feedback on the manuscript and for his valuable insights into the cultural aspects of fathering, especially in Islamic-based societies. The first author owes a life-long debt of gratitude to Michael E. Lamb, who introduced him to fathering research years ago. We are grateful to our colleagues across the world for sharing their research findings with us. India L. Roopnarine and Maya L. Roopnarine assisted with editing portions of the manuscript. Finally, we thank our respective families for their patience during the preparation of this book.

1

FATHERING

The global picture

Simply put, fathers matter to children. Regardless of the cultural community, the physical and psychological presence of fathers can make a significant difference in children's lives. Fathers provide resources and enable access to health care, offer protection from exploitation, and contribute to children's overall development. Evidence from different social science and health disciplines points to the importance of optimal levels of developmentally appropriate, sensitively-attuned paternal involvement for advancing the social and cognitive development of children in different family constellations and cultural communities across the world (Cabrera & Tamis-LeMonda, 2013; Gray & Anderson, 2010; Pattnaik, 2013; Roopnarine, 2015; Shwalb, Shwalb, & Lamb, 2013; Sriram, 2019). Fathers too seem to benefit from quality involvement with children; they enjoy greater happiness and appear healthier than other men (Chereji, Gatz, Pedersen & Prescott, 2013; Knoester, Petts, & Eggebeen, 2006).

Regardless of whether they reside with them or not, there are familial and societal expectations that fathers become fully engaged in the multiple aspects of caring for and nurturing their children in responsible ways (Carvalho, Moriera, & Gosso, 2015; Plantin, 2015). Having said that, there is considerable variation in the ways in which men approach fatherhood and fulfill their parenting and other responsibilities toward children. In some cultural communities (e.g., in North America and Europe), fathers have risen to the challenge of becoming more engaged caregivers, whereas in others such as in the Arab, Asian, African, Latin American and Caribbean countries men continue to embrace traditional conceptions of masculinity and most remain perfunctory to the everyday care of children (see Roopnarine, 2015). Our sole purpose in this volume is to capture these wide variations in fathering and their meaning for different dimensions of childhood development in an ever-changing technological and interconnected global community.

The global picture

Noting the complexity of the construct, fathering has received increased attention within different academic disciplines, governmental and non-governmental organizations, civil society groups, and policy think-tanks across the world (Heilman, Levtov, van der Gaag, Hassink, & Barker, 2017; Levtov, van der Gaag, Greene, Kaufman, & Barker, 2015; Yogman & Garfield, the Committee on the Psychological Aspects of Child and Family Health, 2016). For instance, the United Nations (www.un.org/en/index.html), and other international agencies (e.g., Promundo) have emphasized the need to provide support to families in order to make fathers more informed about their responsibilities and roles as caregivers and nurturers to children. For now, promoting the care, social, intellectual, and economic responsibilities of men toward children has become a priority issue for different countries, and a number have devised policies and implemented legislation that defines the responsibilities of men toward children within a rights perspective (Levtov et al., 2015). Related efforts at social policy development can also be seen in the areas of interpartner violence, discrepancies in women's and men's wages, and the harsh treatment of children worldwide, all issues affecting fathering (El Feki, Heilman, & Barker, 2017; Levtov et al., 2015).

Accompanying this global push for men to become more involved in their children's lives is greater recognition of the diverse family configurations in which fathering occurs in different regions of the world. Men become fathers and rear children in marriage, visiting, common-law, co-habiting, male-male, multiple-partner fertility, re-partnered, and other family living arrangements (Anderson & Daley, 2015; Makusha & Richter, 2015). In some of these diverse relationship constellations, non-resident fatherhood and fathering are not uncommon, and employment patterns, educational attainment, relationship with partner/spouse, and economic conditions tend to determine men's investment and involvement with children. It is prudent to point out that other family members such as uncles and grandfathers in extended family units may assume instrumental roles in rearing children in different family constellations (Clark, Cotton, & Marteleto, 2015; Marlowe, 2005; Shwalb & Hossain, 2018). An advantage is that in the absence of the biological father or limited father care, other male kinship and nonkinship members may serve as surrogate caregivers or community fathers.

Few would question that the changes in women's roles across societies have also had significant influences on men's involvement with children. Although it should come as no surprise that most women still assume major responsibility in caring for young children around the world, maternal employment in economic systems with different modes of production has forced men to re-examine their roles as husbands/partners and as fathers (El Feki et al., 2017; Roopnarine, 2015). As traditional masculine ideologies are being revised in the context of gender equality, the nexus of work and family life is in a state of constant flux. Because gender equality remains elusive in most cultural communities, especially in the developing world, the work–caregiving balance can be tenuous for most couples/partners.

Achieving such a balance becomes more difficult to accomplish when men shirk caregiving and economic responsibilities toward children and eschew morally intelligible fathering. For responsible fathering to flourish, childrearing and caring for offspring must be on equal footing with work responsibilities (see Bjork, 2013).

To encourage men to be more involved in care work, a number of societies have introduced paternal leave policies. There are active campaigns in the developed countries for men to take advantage of these opportunities so that they can become more involved in their children's cognitive and social lives (Heilman et al., 2017; Levtov et al., 2015; Plantin, 2015). These policies explicitly acknowledge the importance of fathers in the family socialization equation and are meant to stimulate change in traditional patterns of paternal investment and involvement in meeting children's needs. Nowhere are the paternal leave policies more prevalent than in the European countries (e.g., Sweden, Finland, Iceland, Norway; see Chapter 7). So far they have met with mixed success but some changes have been documented in fathers' attitudes toward caregiving and in their physical and emotional availability to their children in Europe and North America. By comparison, patriarchal traditions prevail in developing countries and traditional gender ideologies continue to impede attempts to usher in new approaches to the equitable and fair distribution of childcare and household responsibilities (Anderson & Daley, 2015; Promundo, 2015; Roopnarine, Krishnakumar, & Vadgama, 2013). Though modest, signs of change in developing countries are visible in men's internal working models about masculinity and in their involvement with children.

As stated already, perhaps the most compelling reason for the increased focus on fathers across cultural communities is that their presence and quality of involvement matters for the health and safety, the nutritional status, and the socio-emotional and cognitive development of children. Paternal involvement matters from the time of conception and may have lasting effects over different periods of the life cycle (Caragata & Miller, 2008). From both developed and developing societies, there is a rich and growing body of scientific work on fathers in diverse family constellations (e.g., monocare fathers, visiting unions, same-sex, and dual-earner) across the world. As examples, studies have documented men's involvement in such diverse areas as prenatal care, pregnancy and labor, basic caregiving, joint cognitive and social activities, family rituals, schooling and school-related activities, and have also determined the salience of these different modes of involvement and engagement for the overall development and well-being of children. On a related front, there is increased emphasis on the benefits of paternal intervention programs for fathers' intra-personal and inter-personal functioning and different aspects of children's development.

This volume documents the diverse roles of men as fathers within different family constellations, taking into account the changing dynamics of childrearing patterns and the ethos of childhood across cultural communities. Fathering is broadly conceived as any male or males, committed to providing consistent and reliable care with the goal of enhancing the welfare and development of children, irrespective of biological relationship, union status, and residential pattern. These male caregivers can be biological fathers, grandfathers, mother's/father's partner, or male surrogates in the community (Yogman & Garfield, the Committee on the Psychological Aspects of Child and Family Health, 2016). Drawing on research conducted in the fields of psychology, human development and family science, sociology, social work, anthropology, demography, pediatrics, nursing, ethnic studies, early childhood education, and other adjacent disciplines, we attempt to construct a portrait of the different modes of paternal involvement and their connections to childhood development across cultural communities. Throughout this volume we use the term paternal involvement to reflect basic care offered to children as well as the qualitative aspects of engagement (e.g., warmth and sensitivity, cognitive and social activities) with children (see Pleck 2010, chapter 2).

With the aforementioned in mind, the six chapters that follow focus on: theoretical perspectives and models that have been employed in constructing fathering research; mating and marital systems in which fatherhood is realized and fathering takes place; conceptions of men's roles as fathers; the levels and quality of different dimensions of fathers' involvement with young children; connections between paternal involvement and children's cognitive and social-emotional development; primary and secondary intervention programs for fathers; and social policies for fathers. It is our hope that the material covered in these chapters will lead to a broad appreciation for the diverse ways in which men contribute to childrearing and childhood development, and will simultaneously serve as a springboard to more general discussions about research and policy issues regarding men as caregivers across the world.

Overview of chapters and organization of the volume

Following this brief introduction to the volume, Chapter 2 lays bare some of the tenets of prominent theories and models that have guided much of the work on father involvement with children to date. In most instances, early research on father–child relationships was mainly grounded in established sociological (e.g., structural-functional) and psychological theories (e.g., ethological theory of attachment, psychodynamic). These established theories held mother-centric views of childhood development that relegated fathers to a minimal role in caregiving or described them as secondary caregivers. The impact of father involvement on children's development was inferred from what men did not do in families and by their peripheral role as caregivers. To be fair, thinking about fathers' roles within and external to the family matched traditional sociological norms about family structure and functions that existed during most of the last century. It was not until the 1970s that researchers began in earnest to systematically document fathers' actual involvement with children. Prior to this time, models of father absence dominated the limited fathering literature. Men were pathologized more than they were recognized for their contributions to rearing children.

Both established theories and parenting frameworks that have been utilized to explore fathering across cultures are featured in Chapter 2. Three that are discussed include attachment theory that emphasizes the quality of the emotional bond between fathers and children, Baumrind's typologies of authoritative, authoritarian, and permissive parenting that articulate levels of warmth and demandingness and control, and interpersonal acceptance-rejection theory that considers paternal acceptance and rejection along a care continuum (Ainsworth, 1989; Baumrind, 1967, 1996; Bowlby, 1969; Lamb, 2010; Rohner & Khaleque, 2005). Together, these frameworks stress the underlying function of parental warmth and sensitivity for optimal childhood development across cultural communities.

A popular model of paternal involvement developed by Lamb and his colleagues focuses on fathers' engagement, accessibility, and responsibility to children (Lamb, Pleck, Charnov, & Levine, 1985; Pleck, 2010). This model dominated research in the 1980s and 1990s and continues to be a force in fathering research. During these two decades, there was tremendous fervor to demonstrate that men were actually involved in caregiving. Father time investment studies were popular and researchers quickly established the obvious, that men did far less caregiving than women. Pleck (2010) later revised this model to include the qualitative aspects of engagement patterns by fathers. Unquestionably, other frameworks such as generative fathering, men as resource providers, masculine identity, and co-parenting gained traction in research on fathering, but the Lamb model had broad appeal to researchers across academic disciplines. It was not until the latter part of the 1990s that conceptual models on fathering began to explore the associations between father involvement and childhood outcomes and factors that mediate and moderate the associations between paternal involvement and childhood development. Process models of human development along with the biosocial perspective, cultural ecological models, individualism and collectivism, developmental psychopathology, and perspectives on immigrant adjustment are considered as well in Chapter 2.

In Chapter 3, discussion turns to the diverse family constellations within which fatherhood is realized and in which men share responsibilities in providing and caring for children. Whereas marriage is a basis for becoming parents in most cultural communities, men become fathers in diverse family configurations, such as non-marital heterosexual and same-sex relationships, visiting, and common-law unions. In visiting and temporary common-law unions and in part-time cohabiting relationships, it is often difficult for men to engage in optimal levels of caregiving. Likewise, multiple-partner fertility presents unique challenges for men who leave children behind to enter other nonmarital relationships in which they have new offspring. These diverse relationship configurations are evident in the developed and developing societies and are often described as fragile (Carlson & McLanahan, 2010; Makusha & Richter, 2015; Roopnarine & Jin, 2016). Besides the transient nature of these non-marital relationships that can result in nonresidential fatherhood, other potential barriers to engaged fathering include interpersonal difficulties with previous and current partners, gendered ideologies, and economic instability. Men may also become estranged from prior families when they repartner or migrate to find employment within country or externally from their home country for extended periods.

Across marital and mating systems, men express multiple views about what it means to be a man and father. Beliefs or internal working models about masculinity range from the traditional hegemonic orientations in Islamic-based Arab and non-Arab societies and in other traditionally-based patriarchal societies such as India, Pakistan, Bangladesh, Malaysia, and Indonesia that are steeped in religious belief systems (e.g., Adat, Laws of Manu; Islamic laws) and the biological basis of father-hood, to more egalitarian views of men's and women's roles in socially engineered developed societies (e.g., Sweden, Finland, Norway, Iceland). Intergenerational shifts in men's conceptions about traditional roles are discussed in terms of change and continuity, negotiations within families, and institutional structures across cultures. It is not unusual for change and continuity in men's mental scripts about roles in the family to occupy the same psychological and cultural space, and this can present interesting paradoxes for fathers. Children's views about fathers are introduced in Chapter 3.

After a discussion of different mating and marital systems and men's conceptions of fatherhood and fathering, Chapter 4 provides select accounts of what we know about the levels and quality of different dimensions of fathers' involvement with children: prenatal care and pregnancy, the birthing process, feeding and holding, warmth and affection, discipline, playing, and cognitive, educational, and techno-logical activities. Data from a wide spectrum of societies and cultural groups form the basis of this discussion: North America and Europe, Middle Eastern societies, Asian societies, foraging and indigenous groups, and countries in Africa, the Latin American and Caribbean regions, and immigrant groups in developed societies. Where possible both fathers' and children's accounts of paternal involvement are provided. This is in keeping with the child's rights perspective to encourage dis-courses regarding the necessity for engaged fathering.

In the developed world, fathers have increased their time investment and qual-ity of involvement with children. The numbers of primary caregiver, stay-at-home dads, and "hands on" fathers have also inched up a bit. With the exception of groups of fathers in communities in Europe and North America, paternal involvement in caregiving and in social and cognitive activities with children lags noticeably behind those of mothers across the world. What fathers should do "in principle" does not match what they claim to do and what they actually do in terms of childcare and household work. Nevertheless, there is some indication that the affectional distance between fathers and children in some developing societies may be narrowing and that men across developed and developing societies are less likely to be seen primar-ily as playmates to young children.

Factors that influence men's involvement with children are woven into Chapter 4. Economic resources, educational attainment, gender ideologies, the availability of other caregivers in the family, social support, family structural arrangements, residential patterns, personal and interpersonal functioning, parenting competence, and how men were fathered, among a host of other factors, seem to influence paternal involvement with children. Among these, income and education, men's personal functioning, their relationship with the spouse/partner and ex-partner, gendered ideologies, family structural arrangements, and residential patterns seem key in influencing the levels and quality of fathers' involvement with children and, as such, they are given more attention in our discussion than other factors (Cabrera, Fitzgerald, Bradley, & Roggman, 2007; Roopnarine & Jin, 2016).

How do fathers' diverse levels and quality of involvement influence childhood development across cultural communities? Chapter 5 outlines some of what we know about the connections between paternal involvement and children's cognitive and social-emotional development. Although much of the work in this area is based on data collected on European and European-heritage families, studies on childhood outcomes in other recently developed societies (e.g., China), Islamic-based societies in the Middle East (Egypt, Saudi Arabia), and developing societies in Africa, and Latin America and the Caribbean help to punctuate the importance of paternal involvement and to ascertain the local and particular from pan-cultural trends on fathering and childhood outcomes. Depending on the purpose of the study, care is taken to delineate direct and indirect associations between paternal involvement and childhood outcomes in different family constellations.

It will become readily apparent that there are similar patterns of associations between paternal involvement and childhood cognitive and social outcomes in the developed societies, with less consistent associations in the developing ones. This may be attributed, in part, to the lower levels of paternal involvement with children in the developing world when compared to developed societies. Furthermore, a lacuna exists on systematic assessments of the qualitative aspects of paternal involvement in developing societies, which makes it difficult to make inferences about the associations between fathering and childhood development in many of the most populated countries in the world (e.g., India, Indonesia).

With increasing emphasis on the importance of paternal involvement in reducing psychological and cognitive risks during childhood and in promoting positive developmental outcomes in children at the earliest stages of the life cycle, Chapter 6 examines primary and secondary fatherhood intervention programs (e.g., Skin to Skin, Involvement in Early Childhood Education, Parent Training Programs, Relationship Education and Co-parenting, Mental Health, Triple P) and their beneficial effects on fathering and childhood development. In addition to intervention programs implemented in North America, Europe, and Australia, emerging and established programs in the developing world are also covered (e.g., ACEV in Turkey, REAL in Uganda). The stated goals and objectives of the different fathering intervention programs, their curricula, and their developmental and clinical impact on fathers and children are outlined. The effect sizes of these programs tend to be low, but their importance and practical significance for enhancing paternal involvement and childhood development, fathers' own functioning, and women's well-being and mental health should not be taken lightly.

A number of societies have implemented paternal leave policies (e.g., Sweden, Norway, Finland), have attempted to address paternity and paternal responsibilities in non-marital relationships (e.g., Brazil), and have devised different family policies that speak to paternal rights and responsibilities, domestic violence, and gender equality. The length of time and compensation permitted for paternal leave across European and other countries are discussed in the final chapter of this volume. Established provisions for parental leave policies are far from ideal in developed and developing societies alike. Men who make use of paternal leave opportunities are often better educated, have stable jobs, and embrace the notion that caring for children is equally their responsibility as well.

To recap, fathering research across cultural communities has grown at a steady pace (see volumes by Cabrera & Tamis-LeMonda, 2013; Gray & Anderson, 2010; Lamb, 2010; Roopnarine, 2015; Pattnaik, 2013; Shwalb et al., 2013; Sriram, 2019) revealing both the variability and commonality that exist in fathers' involvement with children and their implications for childhood and family development across societies. A few of the distinguishing features of this volume are:

- Fathering within a global perspective in which pan-cultural and local patterns of involvement and engagement with children are organizing principles
- Diverse conceptual frameworks for studying and interpreting father–child relationships and childhood outcomes
- Father–child relationships in the context of new definitions of men's roles within diverse caregiving constellations, and the changing ethos of parenting and childhood
- Different dimensions of paternal involvement and their links to children's social and cognitive development in developed and developing countries are presented side by side
- Intervention programs for fathers across societies and their impact on fathers' personal and interpersonal functioning and childhood development
- Social policies for fathers across developed and developing countries.

2

THEORIES AND CONCEPTUAL MODELS

From Bowlby's ethological theory of attachment (Ainsworth, 1989; Bowlby, 1969, 1973) and Freud's theory of psycho-sexual development (Freud, 1963) to established parenting frameworks (e.g., Baumrind, 1967), mother-centric views of childhood development held center stage in popular psychological theories and models in the developed world way into the latter part of the last century. In the realm of sociology, structural-functional theory emphasized the father's role as the economic provider and as a window to the external world, while the mother was cast in the light of nurturer, providing intimate care and emotional sustenance to children (Parsons & Bales, 1955). Likewise, early cultural ecological models based in anthropology (e.g., Whiting & Whiting, 1975) also failed to fully recognize the father's role in the cognitive and social development of children.

Things were no different in the developing world. Across social science and related disciplines, early analyses of men's roles largely portrayed fathers as psychologically absent or simply abrogating their responsibilities as husbands/partners and fathers. When present, men were seen mainly as economic providers to families, displaying little interest in the day-to-day care of children. For example, in Edith Clarke's classic book on Jamaican families, *My Mother Who Fathered Me* (Clarke, 1957), men were described as irresponsible and emotionally distant from children. Low-income Jamaican families were characterized as "denuded" seemingly because of the lack of male investment in children's lives. In a parallel manner, Sudhir Kakar's *The Inner World: A Psychoanalytic Study of Childhood and Society in India* anointed the Indian mother as the central figure in the development of the young child (Kakar, 1992). Driven by principles in the psychodynamic perspective of human development and indigenous religious principles, it was intimated that the father was minimally involved in the Indian child's life during the preschool years (Kakar, 1992). Mothers and other female caregivers were the ones who ushered the Indian child into the larger social world (Kakar, 1992; Kurtz, 1992). In Brazil, the patriarchal role of men and the decline of their ultimate control over family members are described in different literary canons of family life (Carvalho et al., 2015; Filgueiras & Petrini, 2010). For most of Brazil's history, the traditional *rua* (street) and *casa* (house) dichotomy aptly captured the roles of men in Brazil and elsewhere in Latin America. Along the lines of the structural-functional conceptual framework, men were responsible for economic issues and matters outside of the home and women were in charge of caregiving and affairs inside the home (Rebhun, 2005).

Obviously, a lot has changed since the emergence of these characterizations and conceptual formulations of men's roles within and external to the family across cultural communities. For one thing, the structural dynamics of families and the economic and social lives of men and women have been modified noticeably in developed and developing societies over the last 40 years. Dramatic increases in the number of women who work outside of the home worldwide, along with societal challenges to traditional conceptions of masculinity and gendered ideologies, have pushed men in different cultural communities to examine and revise their internal working models or mental scripts about what it means to be a man and father. As a result, gender equity in the workplace, family and childcare roles, women's and children's rights, and general family health and well-being have come to the forefront of the world community (Heilman et al., 2017; Levtov et al., 2015; UNICEF, 2016). This has led to greater scrutiny of men's involvement in families and to concomitant changes in how we conceptualize and assess fathering roles and responsibilities, father–child relationships, and childhood development.

For the most part, existing research on fathering has been framed and guided by theoretical propositions and frameworks that emerged out of the sub-disciplines of developmental psychology and human developmental science. Theories and models in the adjacent fields of sociology, demography, anthropology, and evolutionary biology have also been instrumental in conceptualizing fathering research in diverse cultural communities (Gray & Anderson, 2010; Hewlett & Macfarlan, 2010; Marlowe, 2005). This chapter discusses the tenets and propositions of some of the major theories and models that have shaped fathering research thus far. Emphasis is on those that offer greater explanatory power to what we currently know about continuity and change in fathering and father–child relationships and developmental outcomes in children and fathers themselves. The theories and models discussed next provide a basis for defining and articulating different dimensions of what fathers do in families and the influence of their investment in and involvement on childhood development. These theories and models serve as a useful platform for interpreting the findings of the studies on fathers discussed in subsequent chapters.

Father–child attachment

Built on the groundbreaking work of Bowlby (1969) and Ainsworth (Ainsworth, 1962; Ainsworth, Blehar, Waters, & Wall, 1978), attachment theory has wide application for interpreting father–child relationships across cultures. At the heart of attachment theory is the development of close emotional ties to particular individuals. The formation and development of these emotional bonds are contingent upon caregiver sensitivity (Ainsworth, 1989; Bowlby, 1969). Sensitivity entails the ability of fathers to read children's social cues accurately and to respond to them promptly in the context of warmth. Thus, sensitively attuned caregivers respond to their children's social and cognitive needs in a non-intrusive, appropriate manner. Through consistently sensitive care, children develop secure relationships with their primary caregivers between 7 and 9 months of age (Bowlby, 1969, 1982). Securely attached children use their caregivers effectively as a base from which to explore the social and object world. As they mature, children develop representations or "internal working models" of the nature of the care they receive from their primary caregivers, which then serve as the foundation for the development of trust (Ainsworth, 1989; Bowlby, 1969).

On the basis of extensive laboratory observations of mother–infant interactions in the United States using the "Strange Situation" procedure that consists of a series of separation and reunion episodes, Ainsworth and her colleagues (Ainsworth et al., 1978) classified infants as: securely attached (B – these children greet their parents after separation and are comforted by them after which they return to exploration), insecure resistant (C – difficult to comfort and their exploration curtailed because of distress), and insecure avoidant (A – do not show much distress upon separation and do not seek the comfort of and may avoid the parent upon reunion). Later, another category labelled disorganized-disoriented (D – acting in a contradictory manner seeking comfort from the parent but at the same time rejecting it; exploration is somewhat disoriented) was identified (Main & Cassidy, 1988; Main & Solomon, 1990). In the United States and Western Europe, roughly two-thirds of infants are classified as securely attached to mothers (see van IJzendoorn & Sagi-Schwartz, 2008).

Assessments of mother–infant attachment in cultural settings outside of the United States (Africa, Israel, Germany, Japan, Arabs in Israel) show comparable percentages of securely attached infants but variations do exist in different categories across cultural settings (Sagi, Koren-Karie, Gini, Ziv, & Joels, 2002; True, Pisani, & Oumar, 2001; Zreik, Oppenheim, & Sagi-Schwartz, 2017). For instance, among the Dogan of Mali, 25% of infants (True et al., 2001) and among families living in Cape Town, South Africa, 25.8% of infants were classified as disorganized-disoriented (Tomlinson, Cooper & Murray, 2005). Higher percentages of avoidant insecure infants were observed in Germany, whereas higher percentages of anxious-insecure infants were observed in Japan and Indonesia relative to infants in the United States (Miyake, Chen, & Campos, 1985; Zevalkink, Riksen-Walraven, & Van Lieshout, 1999). Two primary reasons were offered for the variations in the number of infants in the insecure attachment categories: childrearing beliefs and practices and the procedures used to assess parent–child attachment across cultures (see Fraley & Spieker, 2003; van IJzendoorn & Sagi, 1999).

During the early conceptualization of attachment theory, fathers received very little attention. Perhaps of interest is that during her naturalistic observations of parent–infant interactions in Uganda, Ainsworth (1962) indicated that a few infants around six months of age preferred the father over the mother as an attachment figure. Furthermore, it was observed that a few Ugandan fathers comforted infants when the mother was not present (Bretherton, 2010). It was also determined that for a sub-sample of Scottish infants the father was the "principal object" figure at 18 months (Schaffer & Emerson, 1964). Despite these observations, fathers remained a second-ary figure to the proponents of attachment theory. It was not until the mid-1970s that Lamb (1976, 1977) and others (e.g., Belsky, 1979; Clarke-Stewart, 1978) would begin the task of describing patterns of interactions between mothers and infants and fathers and infants. Lamb's findings not only introduced a new era of studies on father–child attachment, but they also challenged existing conceptions about the primacy of the mother–child attachment relationship.

In a series of observational studies on European American families, Lamb (1976, 1977) found that infants were equally as likely to approach and seek contact with mothers and fathers but extended more social affiliative behaviors (e.g., smiling, vocalizing) to fathers than to mothers. This all changed when a stranger joined the parents in a laboratory setting; infants showed a preference for the mother over the father, suggesting that in a more stressful situation, infants clearly turned to their mothers. Qualitative differences were also noted in the interaction patterns of mothers and fathers; mothers engaged in more sedentary activities (e.g., put-ting a puzzle together, reading) than did fathers, while fathers engaged in more bouts of rough stimulating play than did mothers. In view of these engagement patterns with infants, it was presumed that mothers held infants for caregiving and that fathers held infants to engage in playful activities. Ultimately, this led to ques-tions about whether there were different mechanisms and pathways through which infants form attachments to fathers and mothers.

As interest in father–child attachment grew toward the latter part of the last cen-tury, the research focus expanded to assessments of the differences in mother–infant and father–infant attachment classifications. Contrary to previous claims (Ain-sworth, 1967), infants who were determined insecurely attached to their mothers at 12 months were securely attached to their fathers. The reverse was also true (Lamb, 2002; Main & Weston, 1981). A comparative analysis of infant–parent attachment showed that 64% of infants in the Netherlands and 65% of infants in Israel were securely attached to their fathers (van IJzendoorn, Sagi, & Lamberman, 1992). Within a predominantly European American sample of father–infant dyads, Brown, Mangelsdorf, and Neff (2012) found that 65.7% of infants were securely attached to their fathers, 6.7% were insecure-avoidant, 13.3% were insecure-resistant, and 14.3% were disorganized; and in another study (Umemura, Jacobvitz, Messina, & Hazen, 2013) 58% (32% insecure) of infants were classified as securely attached to their mothers and 56% (44% insecure) as securely attached to their fathers.

Later, the development of the Adult Attachment Interview (AAI) permitted interpretations of adults' perceptions of their relationships with their parents when they were children and the quality of attachment relationships they developed with their own children. Four categories emerged from the transcripts of the adult inter-views: secure-autonomous (mother's or father's accounts of family of origin attach-ments were logical, emotionally open, and thoughtful; noted the importance of early attachment relationships); dismissing (presented parents' behaviors in a very positive light but could not provide specific examples of such behaviors, and they minimized the importance of early attachments for later development); preoccupied (provided changing, incoherent accounts of conflicted relationships with their parents); and unresolved disorganized (displayed noticeable lapses when describing traumatic experiences during childhood). Infants of secure-autonomous parents were likely to be securely attached, those of dismissing parents were likely to be classified as avoidant, those of preoccupied parents were likely to be classified as ambivalent, and those of unresolved disorganized parents were likely to be classified as disorganized as assessed by the Strange Situation procedure (see Bretherton, 2010; George, Kaplan & Main, 1985). Data from the Turku study of Finnish families revealed that approximately 63% of fathers had autonomous, 33% had dismissing, and 4% had preoccupied representation of their attachment figures (Kouvo, Voeten, & Silven, 2015). It should be made clear that the adult classification system reflects a "person's state of mind" about the attachment relationship (Main, 1995).

Researchers have used other methods to assess parent–child attachment relationships. For example, the "Attachment Story Completion Task" has been employed to assess the affective relationship between mothers and children and fathers and children in Spain (Portu-Zapirain, 2013), the Q-set was developed to further assess the secure base in the home setting and the different classifications determined by the Strange Situation procedure in the United States and elsewhere (Waters, 1987), and the "Risky Situation" laboratory procedure has been used to further examine the nature of early father–child relationships in Montreal, Canada. The "Risky Situation" deserves some consideration because it assesses risk-taking behavior and exploration. Paquette (Paquette, 2004a, 2004b; Paquette & Bigras, 2010; Paquette & Dumont, 2013) developed the Risky Situation procedure based on his "activation relationship" theory of the development of a close relationship with the father. Meant to add to what we already know about early father–child attachment, the theory focuses on paternal stimulation of risk-taking and control while children engage in exploration.

To substantiate his theoretical propositions, Paquette and colleagues (Paquette, 2004a, 2004b; Paquette & Bigras, 2010; Paquette & Dumont, 2013) observed fathers and infants 12–18 months of age during the Risky Situation (RS) procedure (20 minutes in duration and occurs in a strange room) to assess the "quality of the parent–child activation relationship". Whereas the Strange Situation assesses attachment security to mothers and fathers, the risky situation procedure determines the security of exploration. In the RS, the security of exploration is determined during six unstructured episodes. Initially, the child is presented with a social risk (an intrusive male stranger) followed by a physical risk (a set of stairs) during which the child is then prohibited from climbing the stairs by the parent. The goal is to put in motion the activation system whereby the child achieves a balance between exploring the object environment and honoring the limits imposed by the father.

Based on behaviors in the laboratory setting, children are classified as activated (shows confidence in exploration and obeys the parent's limit setting), overactivated (tends to be hasty and disobeys the parent's limit setting), and underactivated (engages in little exploration, is passive and withdrawn, and remains within close proximity to the parent). In one study (Paquette & Dumont, 2013) of father–toddler dyads that used both the Strange Situation and the Risky Situation, 63% of children were determined to be securely attached, 25.9% avoidant, and 11.1% resistant while 42.6% were classified as activated, 25.9% as underactivated, and 31.5% overactivated. Only 24.1% of children were classified as securely attached and activated, 18.5% were securely attached and underactivated, 20.4% were securely attached and over-activated, and 14.8% were avoidant and activated. As suggested by the authors, the activation and attachment relationships are quite separate.

In efforts to assess father–child and mother–child attachment relationship over the decades, establishing links between parental sensitivity and quality of attachment has been a major focus. Three meta-analyses (Fox, Kimmerly, & Schafer, 1991; Lucassen et al., 2011; De Wolff & van IJzendoorn, 1997) indicate that the association between paternal-sensitivity and infant–father attachment security was rather low (e.g., $r = .13$, $k = 8$, $N = 546$) when compared with the association between maternal sensitivity and infant–mother attachment security ($r = .24$; De Wolff & van IJzendoorn, 1997), and that little has changed in the relationship between paternal sensitivity and infant–father attachment over time ($r = .12$, $k = 16$, $N = 1355$; Lucassen et al., 2011). There was also a weak association between father–child attachment security and negative infant temperament, similar to what was found for mother–infant attachment security (Groh, Fearon, van IJzendoorn, Bakermans-Kranenburg, & Roisman, 2017). Research on the associations between father–child attachment and developmental outcomes in children has also grown over the last two decades (see meta-analysis by Ahnert, Pin-quart, & Lamb, 2006; Al-Yagon, 2011; Duchesne & Ratelle, 2014; Hoeve et al., 2012). Those associations are discussed in Chapter 5.

Early models of father involvement

An influential conceptual framework that laid the groundwork for a number of the early studies on father involvement with children consisted of three core compo-nents: engagement, accessibility, and responsibility (Lamb et al., 1985; Pleck, 2010). Engagement was conceived as direct father–child interactions through caregiving and joint activities with the child. Accessibility was described as being available to the child for interactions and being there for the child regardless of whether inter-actions occurred or not. Responsibility consisted of those non-direct involvement and accessibility activities such as providing resources to the child and making sure the child is cared for (e.g., making appointments for the child to see the doctor; childcare arrangements; assessing when the child needs new clothing). Factors that influence paternal involvement were also identified: motivation, skills and self-confidence, social support particularly from mothers, and institutional factors such as employment and employment-related issues.

A major impetus of some of the early fathering studies that used this model was to demonstrate that men were not only around but were variously involved in their children's lives (see Pleck, 2010, for a review). It is perhaps safe to say that maternal behaviors were largely used as a template to examine paternal involvement with children. When it was first conceived, the Lamb et al. (1985) model had wide appeal in that it enabled researchers to document men's time investment in care-giving activities as well as their engagement in childrearing overall relative to their wives or partners. It also permitted an examination of where mothers and fathers diverged and converged in the qualitative aspects of their involvement and engage-ment with children. An objective was to discern whether certain involvement and engagement activities were unique to fathers.

Much of the fathering research on time investment in care and household activities conducted in the 1980s and 1990s focused largely on European and European-heritage families. However, the Lamb et al. (1985) model was also used to document levels of paternal involvement in other cultural groups. In the United States, it brought to the fore levels of paternal involvement among African American men who at times were broadly stereotyped as distant and uninvolved (see Ahmeduzzaman & Roopnarine, 1992; Roopnarine, 2004; Roopnarine & Hos-sain, 2013) and among Hispanic American men who were characterized as author-itarian and controlling (Cabrera, Aldoney, & Tamis-LeMonda, 2013). It was also utilized in investigations of paternal involvement in other cultural communities in Jamaica, India, Taiwan, Malaysia, Brazil, and Thailand to tap into cultural variations in gender disparity in childcare (Benetti & Roopnarine, 2006; Hossain & Juhari, 2015; Roopnarine et al., 1995; Suppal & Roopnarine, 1999; Tulananda & Roop-narine, 2001).

As informative as these efforts were, recording levels of involvement did not fully account for the qualitative aspects of father–child activities. With the growing emphasis on the nature and quality of parental involvement and childhood out-comes in the child development field, the focus began to shift from substantiating what men did in families to delineating the developmental currency behind the quantity and quality of different dimensions of their parenting activities with chil-dren. As Pleck (2010) summarized, there was thin evidence that total paternal time involvement was associated with children's development. Accordingly, Pleck (2010) revised the father involvement framework in the direction of the qualitative aspects of fathering and father–child relationships. The reconceptualization was informed by constructs in other theories that emphasize the importance of different dimen-sions of warmth and sensitivity and control displayed by parents toward children across cultural communities (Baumrind, 1969; see meta-analyses by Khaleque & Rohner, 2013; Rohner & Khaleque, 2013; Rohner, 2016; and review by Sorkhabi, 2005). At this point it might be appropriate to state that before Pleck's reconcep-tualization of the original father involvement model, Palkovitz (2002) had already called attention to three interrelated domains of paternal involvement: cognitive, emotional, and behavioral. Fifteen different ways in which fathers were involved with children were identified: communicating, teaching, providing, protecting, monitoring, engaging in cognitive activities, caregiving, running errands, displaying affection, child-related maintenance, emotionally supportive, sharing interests, shar-ing activities, being available, and planning.

Staying close to the intent of the original framework to catalog fathers' day-to-day activities with children, the new iteration of the Lamb et al. (1985) model consists of positive engagement activities (e.g., social and cognitive play, reading, physical play), warmth and responsiveness, and control as forming the fundamental basis of paternal parenting. The term paternal involvement is now defined to capture the interrelation of its three main domains of "positive engagement activities," "warmth and responsiveness," and "control," and the two subdomains of "indirect care" and "process responsibility". Positive engagement refers to father–child activities that support favorable child development rather than total paternal engagement (Pleck, 2010). The warmth and responsiveness and control domains overlap with Baumrind's (1967) authoritative parenting style and refer to fathers' parenting behavior during interactions, such as showing affection, hugging, monitoring, and engagement in decision making (Pleck, 2010). Indirect care refers to "activities that parents do for the child but not with the child" (Pleck, 2010), and process responsibility addresses "taking initiative and monitoring what is needed" (Pleck, 2010, p. 66). Even though indirect care and process responsibility have received little explicit attention in the extant literature, Pleck (2010) suggested that material indirect care, which is defined as providing goods and services, has implications for children's development due to its direct connection to child life issues, and it should be distinguished from generating income.

This was a much-needed reconceptualization of the original Lamb et al. (1985) model. For over 60 years, parenting research has attempted to capture the core aspects of warmth and sensitivity and the control dimensions of parenting. In the process, parenting styles have been described in terms of nurturance and control, acceptance and rejection, warmth and hostility, demandingness and control, permissiveness and restrictiveness, detachment and involvement, and dominance and submission (Darling & Steinberg, 1993). Because of its qualitative properties and recognizing the need to determine cultural and scalar equivalence of parenting constructs, the utility of the new paternal involvement model will undoubtedly be more suitable for assessing fathering in cultural settings outside of the developed world.

Baumrind's parenting typologies and interpersonal acceptance-rejection theory

Not originally intended to examine fathering per se, two influential parenting frameworks, one developed by Baumrind (1967) and the other by Rohner (Rohner, 1986; Rohner & Khaleque, 2005) have found their way into discussions of father–child relationships. For over five decades, Baumrind's parenting style typologies have been utilized to assess childrearing practices in different cultural communities around the world (Sorkhabi, 2005). Basically, this parenting framework zeroes in on two overall constructs, warmth and responsiveness and demandingness or control, to assess authoritative (responsiveness, rule setting, and fostering autonomy), authoritarian (low responsiveness and high control) and permissive (responsiveness with limited control) parenting styles – the emotive qualities of parenting if you will (Darling &

Steinberg, 1993). A fourth category, neglectful (low responsiveness, low control) was later constructed by Maccoby and Martin (1983). High levels of warmth and responsiveness and appropriate levels of rule setting and guidance, characteristics of authoritative parenting, are associated with more desirable social and cognitive outcomes in children than the authoritarian, permissive, and neglectful styles.

There is good support for the links between parents' authoritative parenting style and childhood development in a number of cultural communities in the United States, Europe, and to a lesser extent Asia (Li & Lamb, 2015; Sorkhabi, 2005). Nevertheless, skepticism exists about the cultural validity of this framework for measuring fathers' and mothers' childrearing practices across cultural and ethnic groups (Chao, 1994; Roopnarine et al., 2013). For example, dimensions of high levels of warmth and high levels of harshness are used by fathers and mothers in combination during childrearing in some Caribbean cultural groups (Roopnarine & Jin, 2016) and control is viewed positively as a vehicle for managing children's behaviors in India (Saraswathi & Dutta, 2010) or governing (*guan*) childhood socialization in Chinese cultural communities (Chao, 1994; Li & Lamb, 2015).

Like Baumrind's parenting styles typology, interpersonal acceptance rejection theory, grounded in principles in personality sub-theory, coping-subtheory, and sociocultural systems sub-theory, proposes that varying levels of parental care and warmth and hostility define parenting practices across cultural communities (Rohner & Khaleque, 2005; Rohner, 2016). Acceptance is reflected in the display of warmth, affection, and adequate care and rejection in hostility and the withdrawal of love and affection (Rohner & Khaleque, 2005). Dimensions of warmth and rejection fall along a continuum from warmth at one end to rejection at the other. Just as in Baumrind's parenting typologies, optimal socialization practices are characterized by high levels of sensitive and attentive caregiving in the context of low levels of rejection and harshness. Physical control (physical punishment, physically restricting the child), psychological control (making the child feel guilty, worthless), and behavioral control (limit setting, restriction, structure, clear and consistent rules) have particular relevance for abusive parenting because of the maltreatment of children by fathers and mothers across the world (Cappa & Khan, 2011; Cyr, Michel, & Dumais, 2013). These dimensions of paternal control are yet to be explored fully in the developing world.

Adequate support has also been found for interpersonal acceptance-rejection theory. A meta-analysis that consisted of 66 studies in 22 cultural communities involving 19,511 participants in 5 continents (Khaleque & Rohner, 2012; Khaleque & Rohner, 2011) and a review of 120 studies conducted in Arab countries some of which involved fathers (Ahmed, Rohner, Khaleque, & Gielen, 2016) found good links between parental warmth and care and childhood adjustment. Other studies (e.g., Bornstein et al., 2014; Roopnarine et al., 2013) that have relied on the tenets of interpersonal acceptance-rejection theory to assess father–child relationships across cultures have generally indicated similar associations between the two constructs. In some instances (Khaleque & Rohner, 2012), a stronger association was found between paternal acceptance and children's social adjustment than between maternal acceptance and children's social adjustment.

Nevertheless, simply codifying fathers' and mothers' parenting behaviors along dimensions of warmth and sensitivity and control is not sufficient. An area in which parenting frameworks have improved a bit is in determining homogamy in parenting. That is, to what extent do fathers and mothers in different cultural communities engage in similar and different styles of parenting and how do their parenting behaviors change across time? Because so much of what mothers and fathers do within families occurs jointly, the focus has been on consistency/inconsistency in parenting practices between mothers and fathers. A handful of studies suggest that there is good stability in parental warmth but less stability in parental control over the middle childhood years in the United States (Holden & Miller, 1999) and that there is good agreement on the degree to which mothers and fathers use warmth and control in the early socialization of children in some cultural settings in the developing world (Roopnarine, Yang, Krishnakumar, & Davidson, 2013). Co-parenting models have also been used to assess the extent of cooperation and conflict between spouses/partners and ex-spouses/partners in attending to the needs of children in the United States. Maccoby and Mnookin (1992) proposed three typologies in this regard: cooperative (high cooperation, low conflict), conflicted (high conflict, low cooperation), and disengaged (low cooperation, low conflict). It is not unreasonable to expect more congruence in parenting among couples/partners who adopt the cooperative than the other two approaches. Much more needs to be done to assess stability and change in the nature of paternal involvement during the early-childhood, middle-childhood, and adolescent years in different cultural settings.

Process models of human development

Important advances have been made in specifying the diverse factors that influence father–child relationships over time. In the tradition of systems theory, Bronfenbrenner (1979; Bronfenbrenner & Morris, 2006) proposed the bioecological model of human development. Most would agree that systems theory as conceived by von Bertalanffy (1965, 1968, 1972) and elaborated on by others in sociology, psychiatry, and psychology has been used widely in family research (e.g., Bowen, 1974; Minuchin, Rosman, & Baker, 1978; Masten & Cicchetti, 2010). The bioecological model delineated a set of interrelated systems (microsystem, mesosystem, exosystem, macrosystem, and chronosystem) within which developmental processes unfold. An array of proximal and distal factors either directly or indirectly facilitate or undermine human developmental processes, and may have cascading effects on later development (see Masten & Cicchetti, 2010). As per later formulations of the bioecological model, major consideration is given to process, person, context, and time (Person-Process-Context-Time; PPCT). Human development is viewed within the perspective of "continuity and change in biopsychological characteristics." The impelling forces in human development are processes or direct interactions between the individual and different facets of the social environment.

In terms of fathering, the microsystem processes would normally include the activities that children encounter in the different systems, the nature and quality of relationships children have with different members, and the roles that children assume. The direct interactions between the child and members of the family (e.g., father reading to child, hugging child and displaying affection) and quality of spousal/partner relationship and how these influence children's social and cognitive functioning are good examples of microsystem processes. The mesosystem captures the connections between environments such as father–child ethnic/racial socialization at home and teacher–child ethnic/racial socialization in preschool settings, and the exosystem is comprised of experiences that are external to children but that may have an indirect influence on their development, such as fathers' employment experiences. The macrosystem includes the ideological and cultural belief systems of the community such as men's roles within the family and society and emphasis on particular childrearing practices. The chronosystem reflects the dynamic nature of changes that occur in children and the different systems that influence childhood development. Propositions within the bioecological model led to a sea change in how human developmental processes are conceptualized and investigated by different social scientists. In broad areas of human development, including fathering, studies have targeted diverse factors within (e.g., partner relationships, parent–child relationships) and external to the family (neighborhood cohesion and collective efficacy) that influence family functioning and childhood development in everyday settings. From its conception and through its several revisions, the bioecological model remains viable in guiding research on parent–child relationships across the lifespan in cultural communities across the world.

No doubt influenced by propositions within the bioecological model, process models of parenting have played a significant role in advancing research in the direction of the multiplicity of factors within and external to the family that shape fathering. Two good examples are Belsky's (1984) Parenting Process Model and the Heuristic Model of the Dynamics of Paternal Influences on Children over the Life Course (Cabrera et al., 2007, 2014). Belsky's (1984) parenting process model incorporates sources of stress and support in the study of parenting more broadly and, more specifically, fathering. In as much as earlier models focused on components of father–child involvement and engagement, Belsky's (1984) model made it feasible to assess determinants of fathering: the personal functioning of parents, childhood characteristics, and sources of stress and support. Factors that directly affect parenting stem from within fathers themselves, children, and the larger social context within which parenting occurs. The developmental histories of fathers, the quality of marital relations, social support, and job-related issues impact fathers' personal functioning and well-being which have a bearing on the quality of parenting, all of which have direct or indirect associations with children' social and cognitive skills. These multiple determinants exert differential influences on parenting. For instance, it is argued that developmental history and the personality characteristics of individuals influence parenting indirectly through the larger contextual issues of marital relations, social support, and employment. Other models (Cummings, Merrilees, & George, 2010) have elaborated on precisely how the quality of marital relationship (e.g., conflicts) affects fathering and childhood outcomes. While Belsky's model has guided large-scale efforts to investigate father–child relationships, such as the Fragile Families Study in the United States (see Carlson & McLanahan, 2010), a better delineation of the moderating and mediating role of different variables and childhood outcomes would have been helpful.

The Heuristic Model of the Dynamics of Paternal Influences on Children over the Life Course (Cabrera et al., 2007, 2014) did provide a greater level of specificity on moderators and mediators and the associations between paternal functioning and childhood outcomes over time. It is one of the few developmental models on paternal involvement and childhood development that considers the changing nature of structural, personal, and interpersonal functioning as families move through the life cycle. A few of the important predictors of paternal involvement are childrearing history (e.g., relationship with one's parents), cultural history (e.g., race, ethnicity), biological history (e.g., mental illness), personal characteristics of the father (fertility, employment patterns, parenting beliefs, practices, and styles, personal functioning), maternal characteristics (e.g., fertility, health, employment), contextual factors (e.g., mother–father relationship, community ties, economics), and child characteristics (e.g., gender, temperament). These factors work collectively to influence paternal involvement and childhood outcomes across the life course. The model allows for the specificity of factors that have direct and indirect influences on paternal involvement. This is significant because the model stresses multiple pathways of influences on paternal involvement and, in turn, childhood development across time (see Figure 2.1).

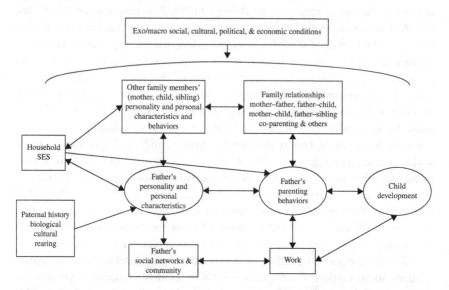

FIGURE 2.1 Heuristic model of the dynamics of parental behavior and influence on children over time

Source: Cabrera et al., 2014.

It is worth stating that other propositions within models of the competencies of children from underrepresented groups (indigenous groups, First Nation People, African Americans) in North America (Garcia Coll et al., 1996), the colorism framework, critical race theory (Burton, Bonilla-Silva, Ray, Buckelew, & Hordge Freeman, 2010), and anti-colonial theory (see Escayg, 2014) have proposed a deeper look at the associations between current experiences with different forms of oppression, residential and economic segregation, promoting and inhibiting environments in communities and schools, personal and interpersonal factors, and developmental outcomes in children. Still others (Roopnarine & Jin, 2016) have urged us to consider the retentionist and creolization theses, both of which stress the power structure that existed during the social and economic domination of different ethnic and cultural groups across different regions of the world, and the resistance and adaptations families display to cope with inequality and loss of cultural practices. These latter perspectives have relevance for men who have experienced apartheid (e.g., South Africa), or whose predecessors experienced long periods of colonialism (e.g., Brazil, the Caribbean), and slavery and oppression (e.g., Brazil, the Caribbean, and the United States).

With the advent of more sophisticated research methodologies and data analytical techniques (e.g., structural equation modeling, Bayesian, Complier Average Causal Effect) in the psychological sciences, studies have built and tested increasingly complex models involving different modes of paternal involvement, mediators and moderators, and childhood outcomes. For example, one study (see Figure 2.2) examined the mediating role of paternal warmth and avoidance of destructive conflict behavior on the associations between paternal depressive symptoms and interpartner violence when children were 15 months old, and their internalizing

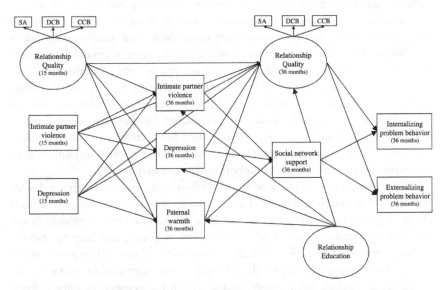

FIGURE 2.2 Paternal risk factors, mediators and childhood behavioral difficulties

Note: SA: Support and Affection, DCB: Destructive Conflict Behavior, CCB: Constructive Conflict Behavior

Source: Roopnarine & Dede Yildirim, 2017.

and externalizing behaviors at 36 months of age, in Hispanic American, African American, and European American families, controlling for economic hardship and residential stability (Roopnarine & Dede Yildirim, 2017). In this model, it was expected that protective factors such as warmth and appropriate conflict resolution strategies might influence the relationships between paternal risk factors and childhood behavioral difficulties over time. These types of studies have become common in the fathering literature.

Biosocial model of father involvement and investment

Just how far back did paternal care emerge in our evolutionary history? Gray and Anderson (2010) in their book on *Fatherhood: Evolution and Human Paternal Behavior* suggest that pair bonds may have approximated contemporary patterns roughly about 150,000 years ago. The contribution of resources by men, the development of pair bonds, length of life span and mortality, and the emergence of the sexual division of labor all had a role in the evolution of paternal investment in and the care of children. For a more detailed discussion of these issues, the reader is referred to Gray and Anderson (2010) and Marlowe (2005). We point out a few core elements of the biosocial perspective that is rooted in evolutionary biology.

The biosocial perspective provides a wider lens for interpreting men's investment and involvement with biological and nonbiological offspring. This perspective considers how "biological or evolutionary factors influence and interact with socio-cultural factors" in explaining male investment and involvement with children (Hewlett, 1992, p. xv; Hewlett & Macfarlan, 2010). Evolutionary biologists prefer the term male paternal investment because it encompasses the diverse ways in which fathers provide material resources and care to biological and non-biological offspring that will ensure their survival and, in turn, reflect the man's own reproductive success. Across the world, fathers may have similar interests around the paternal role when it comes to the health, safety, and survival of children in the context of reproductive success (Hewlett, 1992). Evolutionary biologists focus on the adaptive strategies that men use to attract and keep a mate, produce offspring, and the resources and care provided to ensure offspring survival and maturity across cultures (Hewlett, 1992). Typically, the focus is on direct (e.g., activities related to the survival of the offspring such as food, holding) and indirect paternal investment (e.g., provision of economic and social support to the mother/partner).

Evolutionary theorists speak of somatic effort (risks and costs associated with staying alive) and reproductive effort (replicating one's genes). According to Hewlett (1992), reproductive effort has three components: parental effort (investing in the care and socialization of children), mating effort (acquiring and keeping spouse/partner), and nepotistic effort (offering resources to relatives). The allocation of resources and energy toward growth and development, mating, and parenting varies across groups (Belsky, Steinberg, & Draper, 1991). Fathers/men in some cultural communities may expend more energy and resources toward mating than parenting. The life effort model has been used to characterize male care in the Caribbean (e.g., Flinn, 1992), in groups in Central Africa (see Hewlett & Macfarlan, 2010), and in low-income nonresidential fathers in the United States (e.g., Carlson & McLanahan, 2010). Others have used evolutionary ecological models to examine the "show-off hypothesis" to determine mating opportunities and the distribution of resources and paternal care to biological and nonbiological offspring among the Hadza of Tanzania (Marlowe, 1999, 2005). Paternity certainty and male investment in the care of children has also received some attention (see Marlowe, 1999, 2005).

Eco-cultural models

Until fairly recently, the cultural basis of fathering received limited attention in the mainstream developmental psychology literature. This is not to suggest that fathering in cultural context has been totally ignored. Anthropologists such as Hewlett (1987), Flinn (1992), Marlowe (1999) and others (e.g., Fouts, 2013) have conducted systematic observations of paternal investment and caregiving among fathers in developing societies for decades. Largely ethnographic in their methodology, these studies have employed adaptationist and the biosocial perspective to examine father–child relationships within cultural communities in Africa, South America, and Asia (Hewlett & Lamb, 2005). At times, anthropologists have also leaned on parenting frameworks and attachment theory from within developmental psychology to interpret their ethnographic work in foraging groups (e.g., Hewlett, 1987, 1992).

A framework for understanding cultural variations in childrearing was proposed decades ago in the Six Cultures Study of Socialization (SCSS) (Whiting & Whiting, 1963). Factors that have an influence on childhood development are the environment and history, maintenance systems (e.g., subsistence patterns, modes of production, etc.), learning environment of the child (e.g., settings, caregivers), the behavioral tendencies and beliefs of the adults, and projective-expressive systems (e.g. religion and ideology). Among these, it is believed that the learning environment exerts the most influence on behavioral patterns exhibited by children (Whiting & Whiting, 1975). Through detailed field observations in Khalapur (India), Okinawa (Japan), western Kenya, Tarong (Philippines), New England (USA), and Juxtlahuaca (Mexico), Whiting and Whiting (1975) recorded the wide variations in interaction patterns between parents and children and the contextual factors that impart influences on them within and across cultural settings. At the time of this groundbreaking study, levels of father involvement in the early socialization of children were seemingly low across the communities. This may have contributed to the cursory attention that fathers received.

Emanating from the work of Whiting and Whiting (1963), the developmental niche model (Super & Harkness, 1997, 2002) has identified parental psychology or ethno-theories about childrearing (e.g., beliefs about physical punishment, play), customs and practices (e.g., co-sleeping, prolonged weaning), and the setting (e.g., opportunities and hazards) as key features in determining cultural pathways to human development. It was proposed that the child shapes and is shaped by factors within the developmental niche. In a subsequent overview of socialization processes in context, Greenfield, Keller, Fuilgni, and Maynard (2003) offered interpretations of cultural developmental pathways via the ecocultural approach, the values approach, and the co-construction approach. In brief terms, the cultural values approach focuses on the role of ethnotheories or internal working models in the socialization of children, the ecocultural approach stresses economic and environmental conditions as having significant influences on developmental pathways, and the sociohistorical approach emphasizes social construction (co-construction) in the acquisition of competence. All three approaches have been used to discern cultural-developmental patterns of childrearing and socialization in developed and developing countries, but with limited focus on fathering.

A strong aspect of contemporary cultural ecological frameworks is their focus on alloparenting and allocare. These practices are prevalent across African, Asian, and Latin American and Caribbean cultural communities. Notably, caregiving is shared by several individuals – grandparents, siblings, aunts, uncles and other kinship members and in some cases these other caregivers eclipse fathers' involvement with young children. The role of these other caregivers has received some attention in fathering research in northern Trinidad and Tobago (e.g., Flinn, 1992), among the Hadza in Tanzania (Marlowe, 2005), in South Africa (Madhavan & Roy, 2012; Swartz & Bahana, 2009), and in India (Roopnarine, Krishnakumar, & Vadgama, 2013), but have not been fully integrated into conceptual models that assess fathering and childhood outcomes. Dyadic models of father–child relationships are still more commonly used in fathering research across the world.

To further understand paternal parenting practices and childhood outcomes in cultural context, some researchers have used the tenets of collectivism–individualism in their work on fathering in western and non-western cultural communities (see Hyun, Nakazawa, Shwalb, & Shwalb, 2016 for a review). Cultural communities in North America and Europe are categorized as more individualistic (value autonomy, personal responsibility, freedom of choice) (Hofstede, 1980; Waterman, 1984) than those in Asia and some Middle Eastern countries. Asian societies are viewed as embedded in more collectivistic practices (interpersonal harmony, in-group orientation, obligation) (Oyserman, Coon, & Kemmelmeier, 2002). Although, the collectivism–individualism framework has been used to describe parent–child relationships in Asian societies (e.g., China and India), Turkey and elsewhere, this dichotomy may not fully account for the changes that are occurring in childrearing across the world. For example, it has been suggested that urban families in Turkey value both elements of individualism and collectivism and choose to rear their children toward what Kağıtçıbaşı (2005, 2007) termed the autonomous-relational self – the desire to nurture autonomy and interdependence in children. Individualistic aspirations are also evident in Chinese families. Once driven by collectivistic principles and Confucian beliefs, Chinese society as a whole is witnessing rapid socioeconomic and family structural transformations that signal movement toward individual pursuits (Li & Lamb, 2015). With these types of changes occurring worldwide, it is likely that childrearing practices among fathers may fall along different points on the individualistic–collectivistic continuum for societies in transition.

From what has been said so far, ecocultural models have been central to advancing research on cultural pathways to family socialization practices and childhood development. Nevertheless, there has been a call for more indigenous constructions of models of human development (Berry, 2013, 2016). Research on father–child relationships in many of the world's most populous and religiously complex regions is conspicuously absent from the current fathering literature. This has restricted attempts to discern the universal from the culture-specific in the area of fathering and childhood development. Strides have been made to both test some theories (interpersonal acceptance-rejection) as they apply to father–child relationships in diverse cultural settings (Rohner, 2016) and to integrate components of fathers' cultural history into models of father involvement as is clear from the Heuristic Model of the Dynamics of Paternal Influences on Children over the Life Course (Cabrera et al., 2007). These meager attempts to determine the role of cultural practices on fathering are far from sufficient in laying the foundation for understanding men's parenting behaviors in different regions of the world.

Developmental psychopathology

Developmental psychopathology is a fruitful framework for understanding adaptive and maladaptive patterns of individual functioning in fathers and their links to childhood development at specific periods across the life cycle. In accordance with Sroufe and Rutter (1984), the aim is to uncover the onset, course, causes, and transformations in the individual behaviors of fathers and children across developmental periods. Because developmental psychopathology is also concerned with successful developmental adaptations, attention is given to those factors that serve a protective function against risk to fathers and children.

How fathers influence childhood development at any given point in time or later in the child's life is tied to several considerations: their own developmental history, ideologies about gender roles and childrearing, the changing nature of family social, structural, and economic circumstances, residential patterns, child characteristics, susceptibility to stressful life events, coping mechanisms, and neighborhood and community characteristics, among others (Belsky, 1984; Cabrera et al., 2007; Masten & Cicchetti, 2010). This complex array of factors at the individual, family, and community levels seem to work in related and particular ways within and across developmental periods to directly or indirectly influence paternal involvement and childhood developmental outcomes. However, the expression of both maladaptive and adaptive patterns of paternal behaviors and their associations with developmental outcomes may show variance across cultural settings. As individual, family, and community stressors increase across time periods, maladaptive paternal behaviors could potentially have the same extended effects on childhood development that generalize across cultural groups (see Masten & Cicchetti, 2010).

A good amount of work has been conducted with fathers in at risk families (see Chapter 6; Phares, Rojas, Thurston, & Hakinson, 2010). Studies in this domain have identified both risk (e.g., paternal depression, interpartner violence, destructive conflict behaviors) and protective factors (e.g., paternal warmth, social support, avoidance of destructive conflict behaviors) that may have an impact on paternal functioning at the individual, interpersonal, and the parenting and childhood outcome levels (Roopnarine & Dede Yildirim, 2017a, 2018). A goal has been to identify antecedent factors that influence the course of social and cognitive development in children. Empirical models have singled out personal and intrapersonal factors among men who face diverse challenges, such as socioeconomic disadvantage, poor neighborhood conditions, difficulties with intrapersonal and interpersonal functioning that may moderate and/or mediate the associations between maladaptive behaviors and childhood behavioral difficulties over time. Figure 2.2 above illustrates how protective factors can mediate the negative consequences of paternal functioning on childhood behavioral outcomes among at-risk fathers (Roopnarine & Dede Yildirim, 2018). Clearly, such attempts at determining paternal behavioral precursors to risks can strengthen our understanding of pathways of associations between maladaptive behaviors in men and developmental outcomes in children across cultural communities.

Masculinity and fathering

A number of prominent scholars (e.g., Pleck, 2010; Silverstein & Auerbach, 1999) in the psychological sciences have called for a de-gendered approach to conceptualizing parenting, questioned the emphasis on the "essential father," and have drawn attention to whether fathers contribute uniquely to children's development. Across cultural communities, men engage in fathering in gendered systems that promote inequalities in social roles inside and external to the family. Underneath the gendered systems, men possess internal scripts or schemas about what it means to be a man and a father that they acquired during their developmental histories (e.g., exposure to own father's scripts and behaviors, messages about fathering, models in the media and sports). These scripts form the basis of how men view fatherhood and structure male parenting (Marsiglio & Pleck, 2005; Sigel & McGillicuddy-De Lisi, 2002; Super & Harkness, 1997) and develop a personal identity with respect to their roles in the family and society (Stryker, 1968). The underlying processes of forming and maintaining fathering identity have been discussed elsewhere (Adamsons & Pasley, 2013). As will be seen in the next chapter, in the more traditional societies hegemonic masculinity has remained robust, whereas in developed societies men have made attempts to revise traditional internal scripts about masculinity toward more egalitarian views about roles within the family. Male–male parenting has also been examined in terms of non-binary conceptions of gender, challenging more conservative views of masculinity (Farr & Patterson, 2013).

There are extensive reviews of men, masculinity, and parenting (e.g., Marsiglio & Pleck, 2005; Pleck, 2010). Differences in parenting between mothers and fathers are given sufficient consideration in Chapter 4. It is our contention that gender, ethnic, and economic inequality worldwide influence how men parent children and that men themselves create unequal social and institutional structures for fathering. Rather than engaging in a discussion of the essential father and gender inequality, we present one model of the connections between masculinity and fathering that was developed by Pleck (2010). In brief, Pleck's model delineates associations between fatherhood and masculinity and childhood development and outcomes for fathers. Differentiations are made between fatherhood as parental status (e.g., biological father and as social father) and as fathering (parenting – expression of warmth and control). Masculinity is defined as male gender status (biological designation and social construction) and masculinity orientation (gendered dispositions, variations in beliefs or scripts about masculinity).

Pathways of associations are between parental status and parenting and between male gender status and parenting, where gender status may moderate the association between parenting status and male parenting. Because it is socially constructed, masculinity orientation is proposed to have reciprocal relations with parenting and parental status. This is a plausible proposition, given that having children may increase a man's awareness of masculine norms while entrenched beliefs about masculinity may predispose men toward behaviors that reinforce those beliefs (e.g., having more children, Pleck 2010). As in the process models discussed above, direct and indirect associations between parental status, male gender status, masculinity beliefs and childhood and paternal outcomes and moderating influences are also illustrated in this model (see Figure 2.3). Further, the model stipulates the reciprocal influences

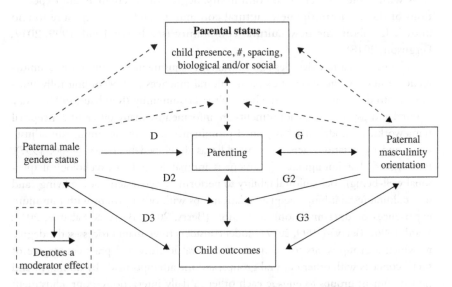

FIGURE 2.3 Model of masculinity and paternal parenting and childhood outcome

Source: Pleck, 2010.

between paternal male gender status, male parenting, and masculine beliefs and childhood outcomes and between these variables and parent and child outcomes (Pleck, 2010).

Frameworks for understanding immigrant and refugee fathers

In our constantly changing world community, families migrate from one community to the next for better economic and educational opportunities. Others flee different forms of religious, social, and political oppression for a better life elsewhere. Migrations occur within countries from rural to urban areas, within regions such as from Egypt to Saudi Arabia, and globally from the developing countries in the Caribbean and Africa to the developed countries of North America, Australia, and Europe. Population movements take many forms: some individuals live transnational lives, establishing residences in and moving freely between two or more cultural communities; some are refugees; some migrate for seasonal farm work and other types of employment, or schooling; and some leave their natal culture and settle permanently in a new cultural community (Sam & Berry, 2018). As might be expected, these different migration patterns involve different cultural and psychological adjustment strategies that are intertwined with a host of factors: linguistic competence, personal history of social, political, and economic instability, educational attainment, economic opportunities, personal coping mechanisms, ideological beliefs about gender and family roles, openness to beliefs and practices within the new cultural community, degree of acceptance and expectations of those within the new cultural community, and prior exposure to and knowledge about the new cultural community (see Berry, 1980, 1999, 2017; Ferguson, 2018).

Whereas just a few decades ago immigrant adjustment was viewed in a unidirectional light of shedding one's natal cultural practices and becoming fully integrated into the mainstream of the host cultural community (Rambaut, 1994), today cultural and psychological adjustments are informed by many different conceptual frameworks. A model that has gained prominence in studying immigrant adjustment and expectations across the world was developed by Berry (1980, 1997). It is argued that immigrant adjustment is intimately tied to psychological (personal well-being), sociocultural (ability to perform everyday activities in living), and intercultural (establishing adequate relationships with other groups with minimum experiences of discrimination) adaptation (Berry, 2017; Berry & Sabatier, 2011; Ward, 1996). Berry's (1999, 2017) model considers three main processes: the degree to which a group wants to maintain its cultural identity and practices, degree of social contacts with other cultural groups, and the attempts made by dominant and non-dominant groups to engage each other in daily interactions. Four adjustment patterns were delineated: separation (preference for natal culture practices), integration (combining elements of natal and new culture practices), marginalization (an orientation for neither natal nor new cultural practices), and assimilation (strong orientation to new culture).

It is proposed that individuals who adopt the integration approach will fare better in meeting the demands of life in their new cultural community than those who adopt any of the other three strategies. Parents who pursue the integration approach instigate better educational and mental health outcomes in children (Berry, Phinney, Sam, & Vedder, 2006; Chen, Benet-Martínez, & Bond, 2008; Coatsworth, Maldonado-Molina, Pantin, & Szapocznik, 2005; David, Okazaki, & Saw, 2009). Even though it makes intuitive sense that the integration approach may be more productive in adapting to a new cultural community than the others, this model has not been adequately tested with fathers in different immigrant or refugee groups. A study that examined the utility of this approach with Indian immigrants in the United States found that a more insular approach whereby parents strongly emphasize natal culture values had a positive impact on children's early academic performance (Sanghavi, 2010). An insular approach may serve immigrant and refugee families well in the short run, but it is highly unlikely that it will have the same effect on outcomes over time as fathers and children confront the demands of life in the new cultural community. More concretely, as they become more accustomed to life and interact with different health care, educational, legal, and social institutions in their new cultural community, immigrant and refugee fathers may adopt different adjustment strategies at any given point, vacillating between the need to integrate elements of the new cultural community and the need to maintain cultural practices that have been with them for some time.

Concluding remarks

Our attempt to discuss salient theories and models used to frame fathering studies did exclude some conceptual frameworks, such as generative fathering and fathers as resource providers, that have also contributed to our understanding of how men identify with the fathering role and about their investment in and involvement with children (see Hawkins & Dollahite, 1997). The diverse theories and models considered above postulate some major principles that are deemed central to our understanding of father–child relationships and childhood development across cultural communities. Attachment theory, the parenting styles typology framework, and interpersonal acceptance-rejection theory have broad appeal and their tenets have been tested in cultural communities across the world (see De Wolff & van IJzendoorn, 1997; Fox, Kimmerly, & Schafer, 1991; Khaleque & Rohner, 2012; Li & Lamb, 2015; Lucassen et al., 2011; Rohner, 2016). So too are the models that stipulate the adaptive strategies that parents utilize to rear children amidst social and economic challenges in different ecological niches. Establishing cultural pathways from male parenting to childhood development remains a major goal of fathering research and the field of child development overall.

Process models of fathering emphasize the range of intrapersonal and interpersonal factors that may have an influence on childhood development and the mediating and moderating variables that influence the relationships between father involvement and childhood development. In as much as fathering studies have overwhelmingly focused on normative patterns of development, developmental psychopathology provides a framework for examining the influence of both adaptive and maladaptive patterns of individual paternal behaviors and developmental outcomes within and across time periods. The utility of this framework has far-reaching implications for identifying risk and protective behaviors in fathers, their onset, course, and transformations as they influence childhood development at different periods in the life cycle.

As research moves toward greater emphasis on defining and assessing engaged fathering, it would be worthwhile for theories and frameworks to consider non-dyadic models of father–child relationships that view male parenting in the context of other caregivers – alloparenting and the concept of community fathering. As you may have gathered, across the world male parenting occurs within multiple vertical and horizontal relationships in the family and community. Anthropologists have documented different male caregiver involvement with children in some cultural communities (see Flinn, 1992; Marlowe, 2005). Much more theorizing is needed on how children shape the course of fathering, the biological basis of paternal care, and fathering in diverse family constellations.

3

THE MANY FACES OF FATHERING

Structural arrangements and internal working models

Men perform fathering roles within diverse living arrangements that include but are not limited to: visiting and common-law relationships (Anderson, 2007), full-time and part-time co-habiting relationships (Carlson & McLanahan, 2010), polygynous arrangements (Hewlett & Macfarlan, 2010; Hossain & Juhari, 2015), father–child or monocare households (Carvalho et al., 2015), stay-at-home father households (Kramer & Kramer, 2016), fathering in post-divorce arrangements (Amato, 1994; Fabricius, Braver, Diaz, & Velez, 2010), nonresident father living arrangements (Adamsons & Johnson, 2013), male–male families (Farr & Patterson, 2013; Golombok et al., 2014), and multiple caregiving and community fathering situations (Ball & Wahedi, 2010; Chaudhary, 2013; Flinn, 1992; Makusha & Richter, 2015). These marital and non-marital constellations for bearing and rearing children vary in terms of pair-bond stability, degree of trust and intimacy between couples/partners and the social alliances they form with other adult family members, residential patterns, ideological beliefs about what it means to be a man and father, the level of economic support and other resources fathers provide to family members, and the nature and quality of the relationship between fathers and children. Nor do the structures and functions within these relationships remain immutable; they change in response to social and economic conditions over time. Below, we begin by considering some of the more common family constellations in which men carry out fathering roles. Later in the chapter, we describe men's ethno-theories or beliefs about fatherhood, masculinity and manhood, and the division of household roles. An attempt is made to include children's perceptions of fathering.

Marriage

Approaches to marriage vary widely across cultures. Increasingly, same-sex relationships are recognized. Marriage among same-sex couples is permitted mostly in cultural communities in the developed world. In North America, Europe, and Australia marriage is based on love with or without the approval of parents. Economic independence and role sharing are valued. Couples weigh the cost-benefit of the relationship. If the costs outweigh the benefits, they can exercise the option of terminating the relationship. With greater equity in earning power and opportunities for equality outside of marriage, women are reluctant to accept micro-level disparities in the division of household labor (Greenstein, 2009). Post-marriage residence is often neolocal, and the two-generation household is common. Fathers are expected to provide economic support, have a common residence with their spouse and children, and be involved with their children emotionally and cognitively. Couples weigh the costs of having children (rational choice) (see Becker, 1981; Friedman, Hechter, & Kanazawa, 1994, for a discussion). The bet is that children will assist in sustaining commitment to a long-term union between couples.

That said, young adults in the developed world are also choosing to delay marriage, fertility rates have been declining, and out-of-marriage births are on the rise. To illustrate, as of 2016, about half of all adults were married in the United States (61% for Asian Americans, 54% of European Americans, 46% for Hispanic Americans, and 30% for African Americans), compared with 72% of adults in 1960. Today, the average age of marriage is 27.4 years for women and 29.5 years for men, compared with 20.3 years for women and 22.8 years for men in 1960 (PEW, 2017). Declines in marriage rates have been observed in Europe and Japan as well (see Eurostat, 2016; Statistical Handbook of Japan, 2018). A few underlying reasons for these shifts are economic conditions, level of material resources, and changing norms about marriage and intimate relationships.

Often independent of romantic love, most marriages in the developing world are usually arranged by family members on both sides. As women gain more economic power, traditional marriage practices are starting to change (e.g., India, Malaysia, Turkey; Metindogan, 2015; Roopnarine et al., 2013). Educational attainment and economic resources determine the choice of individual marriage partners and there are specific norms as to whom a person can marry. Marriage to individuals in the same caste is highly encouraged in India, and in some Islamic-based countries (e.g., Saudi Arabia) first-cousin marriage is permitted. In a few places, should the husband become deceased, the wife may marry the deceased's brother, and in other circumstances, a wife can marry the husband's brother because of disparity in gender ratio and scarcity of economic resources (Ember & Ember, 2002). Polyandrous living arrangements, where a woman has several husbands, are not that common but exist in places like India, Tibet, and Nepal. Polygyny, where a man has several wives, is practiced in Middle Eastern and African countries (Ahmed, 2005; Fouts, 2013) but exists in many societies across the world (Barber, 2008; Loue, 2006).

Agreements and exchanges of material resources are cemented prior to marriage in several cultural communities. Post-marriage residence is often patrilocal in developing countries, but in some where a bride price is required, matrilocal residence is practiced. Husband–wife roles are largely situated in a traditional gendered system of the division of household labor, and the existence of multigenerational familial living arrangements encourages strong social ties between family members and the distributive care of children (Chaudhary, 2013). The utilitarian function of children for long-term security in old age is valued (Kağıtçıbaşı, 2007). Figures 3.1 and 3.2 present the marriage rates in developed and developing countries.

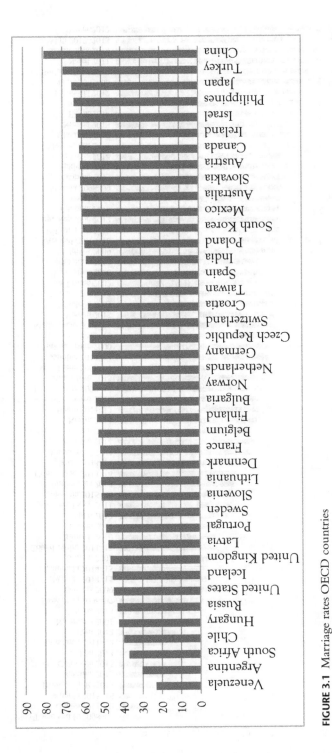

FIGURE 3.1 Marriage rates OECD countries

Source: Derived from OECD Family Database 2014, www.oecd.org/els/family/SF_3_1_Marriage_and_divorce_rates.pdf

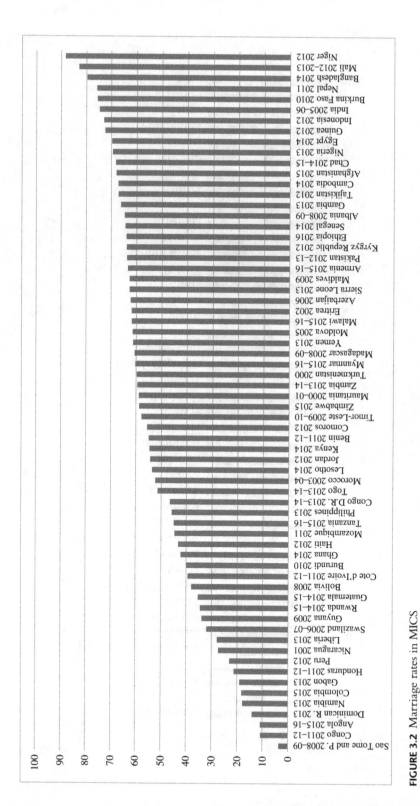

FIGURE 3.2 Marriage rates in MICS

Source: UNICEF MICS 2006–2016, *Demographic Health Surveys 2006–2016* (ICF, 2006–2016).

Visiting and common law relationships and multiple partner fertility

Men in several societies become fathers in visiting and common-law unions. As examples, in the Caribbean region, Brazil, and South Africa a number of children are born in non-marital residential and nonresidential unions. For men of African ancestry in the Caribbean and Brazil, non-marital relationship unions may have been adaptations to slavery, long stretches of colonization, and oppressive policies that disrupted the structure of families and contributed to family organization patterns that moved away from the marriage-based system. Early analysis (see Smith, 1996) of families in the Caribbean characterized nonmarital, nonresidential families as matrifocal, emphasizing conjugal ties that do not match the nuclear family ideal. Terms such as progressive mating and mate-shifting are used to describe the relationship unions of African Caribbean men (Anderson & Daley, 2015; Smith, 1996).

A significant number of Caribbean men and women have their first child in visiting unions. In this type of arrangement, the mating pair lives apart and economic support from the male partner is unpredictable. The male visits from time to time for sexual relations and to be with his offspring. After having children in visiting unions, men and women shift to common-law unions with other partners where they live together, share economic and other resources, and have more children within a largely traditional, gendered system of male–female roles. Marriage may occur as men age and acquire more economic resources (Anderson & Daley, 2015; Chevannes, 2001; Devonish & Anderson, 2017). A study of four communities in Jamaica showed that 20.5% of fathers below age 35 were married, but that figure increased to 44.8% for men over 35 years of age (Anderson, 2007).

Between 12% and 48% of unions were considered common-law in Jamaica (Anderson, 2007; Brown, Newland, Anderson, & Chevannes, 1997). The different relationship unions produce children from different mating partners. In Anderson's study, 53.9% of fathers had a child from one partner, 25.8% had children from two partners, and 10.6% had children from three partners (Anderson, 2007; Anderson & Daley, 2015). For Caribbean men who begin childbearing in marital relationships, having "outside children" is not unusual either. Father absence and family instability are major concerns in mate-shifting families. Jealousy, migration, and poor economic resources and reduced chances for stable employment alienate men from their children in visiting and common-law unions (Devonish & Anderson, 2017). Estimates from sociological studies indicate that most biological fathers had no or very limited contact with children from prior mating unions (Anderson, 2007).

Among Black households in South Africa, father absence is a serious problem. In 2009, fewer than 30% of Black South African fathers were present in the household with children under 15, whereas 53% of Colored, 83% of White, and 85% of families of Asian origin had fathers present in the household (Southern Africa

Labour and Development Research Unit, 2011, 2012, 2016; Statistics South Africa, 2011). As in the Caribbean, the marriage rate is low among Black South African men between 30 and 34 years of age (37%), and there is a tendency for these men to also bear children with different women before marriage (Richter, Chikovore, & Makusha, 2010). The brutal policies of apartheid had a significant effect on the livelihoods of Black men and their relationships with prior and subsequent wives/partners. Migration to seek employment is a key catalyst for father absence in South Africa (Makusha & Richter, 2015). Furthermore, the AIDS epidemic has orphaned a number of children in different African countries, and this has affected economic and care responsibilities toward children. About 28% of maternal orphans in South Africa live with their biological fathers (Woolard, Buthelezi, & Bertscher, 2012). In Tanzania, 35% of children live without a biological mother and 50% without a biological father. Nonmarital birth is the major cause of nonresidence among biological fathers in Tanzania (Gaydosh, 2017).

Multiple-partner fertility is also on the rise among low-income men in different cultural groups in the developed world (Cancian, Myer, & Cook, 2011). Using data from the National Longitudinal Study of Adolescent Health, Guzzo (2014) estimated that among parents with at least two children in the United States, the prevalence of multiple-partner fertility was 32.4% for fathers between 25 and 32 years of age. As indicated previously, multiple-partner fertility intensifies challenges associated with instability in living arrangements and ambiguities in how men negotiate and fulfill parenting roles and economic responsibilities to (ex-)partners and biological and nonbiological children (Fomby & Osborne, 2017). The percentage of fathers who had children with more than one woman across countries is presented in Figure 3.3.

Stay-at-home fathers

The stay-at-home father is not only counternormative, but it indicates a new trend in fathering where men are able to shed traditional role ideologies and engage in full-time caregiving (Chesley & Flood, 2017). Comparatively small in relation to other family forms, the stay-at-home father (not employed and living with children) is far more prominent in the developed than in the developing world. There were an estimated 2.2 million stay-at-home fathers in the United States in 2010 (PEW, 2014) and about 80,000 or roughly 4.6% in two-parent families in Australia in 2016 (Baxter, 2017). Due to variations in definition, far lower estimates have been obtained for stay-at-home fathers in the United States (US Census Bureau, 2015). The reasons fathers stay at home are diverse: unemployed or looking for work, disability, partner has better earning potential, and care for family and household (Chesley, 2011; Kramer & Kramer, 2016; PEW, 2014). Households in which fathers choose to stay at home tend to have higher incomes and more flexible gender roles compared with those in which men stay at home because they are unable to work or find employment (Kramer & Kramer, 2016).

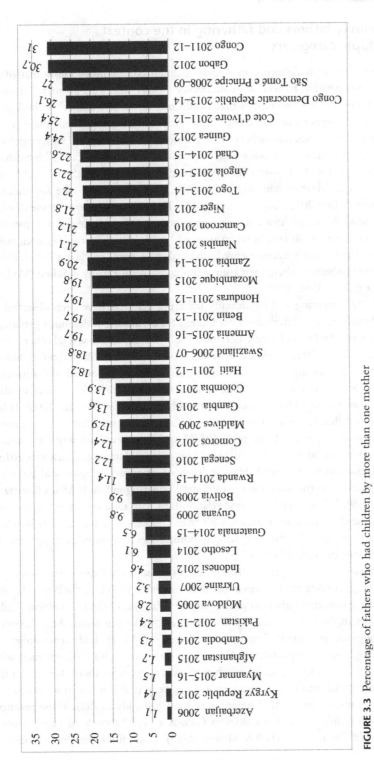

FIGURE 3.3 Percentage of fathers who had children by more than one mother

Source: Derived from *Demographic Health Surveys 2006–2016* (ICF; 2006–2016).

Community fathers and fathering in the context of multiple caregivers

Those familiar with fathering in African cultural communities know that other men act as surrogate fathers or "community fathers" and step up to fulfill some of the duties and responsibilities that would ordinarily be assumed by biological fathers. Under other circumstances, community fathers complement the paternal care offered by biological fathers. The construct of community fathering (performed by any male) is at odds with "the essential biological father" hypothesis (e.g., Pleck, 2010). In low-income communities in the United States and South Africa, men collaborate with kinship members to support and care for children (Madhavan & Roy, 2012; Roy & Smith, 2013). Three caregiving arrangements were distinguished in South Africa: active negotiations between maternal and paternal kinship members in situations when support for childrearing involves both sides; a pedifocal approach wherein many individuals take turns in caring for children; and flexible fathering where men assume multiple roles for many children (Madhavan & Roy, 2012; Roy, 2008).

Multiple caregiving and community fathering practices have been observed in Kenya, South Africa, Bangladesh, the United States, among Indigenous groups in Canada, in the Andaman Islands, in Trinidad and Tobago, and in several other countries (e.g., Flinn, 1992; Jayakody & Kalil, 2002; Pandya, 1992; Richter & Smith, 2006). Specific kinship terms are assigned to nonbiological social and surrogate fathers in South Africa where children refer to uncles (father's younger brother as *ubaba omncane*) or older brother (*ubaba omkhulu*) as father (Hunter 2006). It has been asserted that fatherhood can be a family affair in South Africa where kinship members help to pay the bride price (*lobola*) and damages (*isisu*) when the young father decides not to marry his child's mother (Clark, Cotton, & Marteleto, 2015). Paternal grandmothers extend different levels of emotional support and guidance to young fathers in the direction of committed fathering in South Africa (Swartz & Bhana, 2009). When men have good relationships with their own mother, they are more inclined to maintain contacts with their children (Clark et al., 2015). More often than not, the collective caregiving responsibilities of these other caregivers can surpass that of biological fathers.

Within other cultural groups, the concept of community fathering takes on special meaning. Among the Ongees of the little Andaman Islands in the Bay of Bengal all men are considered fathers to young children (Pandya, 1992). In a fashion similar to practices in African cultural communities (e.g., Xhosa in South Africa), young Ongee boys and girls view all men as fathers (*omoree*). Many children are presented with multiple social opportunities for social engagement with different men with the possibility of forming social bonds with one or more of them. Largely in the absence of social tensions between male caregivers, children are in a position to profit from interactions with different male models (Pandya, 1992). These practices are seen in indigenous communities in Canada where "a circle of care" involves extended family members (Ball & Moselle, 2015). Community fathering is obvious among Bangladeshi men where isolated fathering (parents migrate to work elsewhere), lone fathering (mothers leave their husbands behind to seek employment elsewhere), and sibling fathering (older brothers care for children) are practiced in rural and urban settings (Ball & Wahedi, 2010).

Nonresident fathers

Nonresidential fathering has been on the increase in the United States and is quite high in other parts of the world (e.g., South Africa). About 27% of children under 18 in the United States do not reside with their biological father (US Census Bureau, 2014) and 49.6% of indigenous children in Canada reside with both parents – biological or adoptive (Ball, 2015). Different estimates suggest that nonresident fathering is high in Jamaica, South Africa, and Tanzania (Anderson & Daley, 2015; Gaydosh, 2017; Statistics South Africa, 2011). Paternal nonresidence in the United States is connected to multiple factors: nonmarital birth, migration to find work, union status, multiple partner fertility, age of child at the time of separation, parents' age and education, payment of child support by fathers, gender of child, mother's entry into a new relationship, race/ethnicity, and geographical distance from children (see Adamsons & Johnson, 2013; Carlson, VanOrman, & Turner, 2017; Carlson & McLanahan, 2010; Cheadle, Amato, & King, 2010). Most of these factors are also associated with paternal nonresidence in the Caribbean, Latin America, and Africa (Anderson & Daley, 2015; Carvalho et al., 2015). Due to discrimination, indigenous groups in the United States and Canada have the added burden of being excluded from the educational and social service delivery systems that cater to the needs of their children (Ball & Moselle, 2015). This further distances fathers from children and increases the probability of nonresidential father–child living arrangements among Indigenous groups in North America.

It is understood that under favorable economic and social circumstances, children acquire several benefits from paternal coresidence: nutrition and survival, monitoring and guidance, immediate response to illness, access to health care and treatment, materials for schooling, and general protection. Thus, nonresidential fathering places children at greater risk of malnutrition and death, and poorer developmental outcomes (Adamsons & Johnson, 2013) with a greater likelihood that the impact of these risks will be more severe in the developing world (Anderson & Daley, 2015). Accepting that this may be so, contact between nonresident fathers and children does not necessarily show a linear decline over time, as has been previously purported. Using growth mixture models, Cheadle et al. (2010) determined four patterns of contact between nonresident fathers and children in the United States: 38% had high-stable contact with slight decreases over time, 32% had low-stable contact beginning early after separation, 23% had high levels of contact initially but showed a precipitous drop over time, and 8% started out with low levels of contact but showed significant increases over time. Because of extremely poor economic conditions, beliefs about progressive mating and biological fatherhood, it is speculated that the low-stable pattern may be the norm in communities in the Caribbean and South Africa regions (see Richter et al., 2010; Roopnarine & Jin, 2016).

Gay fathers

Parenting among gay fathers emerges from and occurs in different living arrangements. The primary ways in which gay fathers become parents are through adoption, surrogacy, joint parenting through divorce in a heterosexual marriage, or as single parents (Biblarz & Stacey, 2010; Brodzinsky & Pertman, 2011). Conservative estimates indicate that only a small percentage of male couples across cultural communities are parents. As of 2015, there was an estimated 435,862, male couples in the United States (83.8% European American and 5.5% African American). Among these families, 9.5% had children (US Census Bureau, 2016). A national survey of Australian gay, lesbian, bisexual, and transgender individuals indicated that 22.1% had children or step-children (Leonard et al., 2012), and in 2016 there were 23,700 male couples, with some estimates placing the number of male couples with children at 4.5% (Australian Bureau of Statistics, 2016). Male couples have far higher median incomes and educational attainment than heterosexual couples (Australian Bureau of Statistics, 2013). They not only express a desire for more egalitarian childcare roles, but gay and lesbian couples repeatedly report more equal involvement in childcare and seem to parent in a de-gendered division of labor system that is less characteristic of heterosexual couples (Farr & Patterson, 2013).

Polygamous arrangements

Polygamous arrangements exist in communities in Africa (e.g., Benin, Algeria, Chad, Congo, Egypt, Tanzania) and the Middle East (Saudi Arabia, Kuwait, Jordan, United Arab Emirates) and to a lesser degree in other parts of the world (e.g., Indigenous groups in Canada; Mormons in the United States) (Jankowiak, 2008; Loue, 2006 for a discussion of rates across countries). It is difficult to obtain accurate statistics on the prevalence of polygamous living arrangements across cultures. They are more common among agriculturists and pastoralists than in hunter-gatherer and industrialized societies (Hewlett & Macfarlan, 2010). Figures vary widely: from 15% among the Aka foragers to 40% among the Ngandu in central Africa (Fouts, 2013; Loue, 2006). Across 32 cultures, co-wives were present on average 24.9% of the time in married families (Barber, 2008). Some cultural groups (e.g., Egyptians) require men to inform their current wife or wives or a council about the acquisition of another wife (Ahmed, 2005).

Reasons offered for polygamous living arrangements include ego and satisfaction of men's sexual desire, religion and discrimination of women, pathogen stress, lower ratio of men to women, and defense of resources. A study that tested these propositions across 32 cultures found evidence for the resource defense, pathogen stress, and sex ratio hypotheses (Barber, 2008; Ember, Ember, & Low, 2007; Low, 1990). Research on polygamous families has mostly focused on the difficulties associated with living arrangements such as conflicts, dissatisfaction among women, and mental health outcomes in communities in Saudi Arabia, Kuwait, and Turkey (Al-Krenawi, 2013; Chaleby, 1985; Ozkan, Altindag, Oto, & Sentunali, 2006) with little emphasis on the distribution of care by fathers to offspring from different wives.

Ethnotheories about fatherhood and fathering

Belief systems or internal working models constitute the cultural scripts or schemas that shape and help to determine how fathers execute their roles and responsibilities within families in different ecological niches. Across cultural communities, men possess different "cultural scripts" about what it means to be a man and father. These scripts are shaped by religious beliefs and edicts, patriarchal traditions, and hegemony. Cultural belief systems or ethnotheories about fathering and childrearing may remain stable from generation to generation, or be revised within a single generation or across generations. They tend to vary by socioeconomic status (Goodnow & Collins, 1990; Sigel & McGillicuddy-De Lisi, 2002). It is to these internal scripts and their modifications over time that we turn to next.

Continuity and change in men's belief systems

Most would agree that conceptions of fatherhood and fathering are in a constant state of flux punctuated by transitions, changes, and continuities in traditional roles (see Bastos, Pontes, Brasileiro, & Serra, 2013). To be sure, significant changes in traditional conceptions of manhood and fathering are more evident in the developed than developing world. Relative to earlier estimates, today 57% of fathers (58% of mothers) in the United States say that parenting is important to their identity, and 54% of fathers (52% of mothers) find parenting rewarding all of the time (PEW, 2015). Moreover, fathers in same-sex relationships have more liberal views about gender roles than heterosexual couples in the United States (Farr & Patterson, 2013).

There is the suggestion that conceptions of the man as breadwinner and the woman as caregiver still define the parameters of fathering in most developing societies (see Georgas, Berry, van de Vijver, Kağıtçıbaşı, & Poortinga, 2006). That is, in cultural communities in the developing world, men place more importance on biological fatherhood and the provider role than on primary caregiving responsibilities. Traditional masculinity relegates women to situations in which they must routinely adjust work roles and economic activities to meet household and care responsibilities (see Roopnarine, 2015). By comparison, men privilege work over family roles in most cultural communities in the developing world, and in some, increased involvement in childrearing may precede changes in internal working models about masculinity and men's and women's roles in the family (Roopnarine, Krishnakumar, & Xu, 2009). Put differently, fathers in the developing world may be pressed into the service of caring for children out of necessity (e.g., wife working and lack of availability of alternative childcare) rather than to changes in ideological belief systems per se.

Now any appraisal of men's beliefs and attitudes about fatherhood and fathering would have to consider notions of continuity and change in traditional masculine ideologies and their implications for gender equity in family and work life, individual and inter-personal level functioning, and optimal childhood development. Fathering is a nonstatic entity evolving within the context of complex cultural systems and practices that affect a multitude of family processes. In this section, we examine what is changing in men's beliefs about fatherhood and fathering and what still has a firm grip on how men define their roles in the family across cultural communities. It is reasonable to assume that shifts in men's belief systems about their roles as fathers would be followed by decreases in traditional attitudes and behaviors with regard to family roles. As will be seen, some practices remain robust alongside changes in some aspects of men's belief systems about caregiving roles and responsibilities.

Europe and North America

Most men in Europe and North America have been revising their internal working models about what it means to be a man and father for some time now (Plantin, 2015). To this end, women's movements, policy initiatives, and equal opportunity laws among other factors have all helped to (re)shape men's and women's roles in the developed world. Egalitarian roles are emphasized but quasi-egalitarian roles are more evident among different ethnic groups in the European Union countries, Canada, Australia, and the United States. To shed light on how much men's and women's roles have changed in these developed countries, sociologists have utilized data from large scale surveys to determine convergence in time investment in household work and childcare across multiple European countries (e.g., Wall, 2015) and the United States (see Hofferth, Flood & Sobek, 2013; Hofferth & Lee, 2015, U.S. Bureau of Labor Statistics, 2014). As indicated above, an expectation is that there should be correspondence between changes in men's ideological beliefs systems about male–female roles and involvement in the more intense aspects of what have been traditionally considered women's responsibilities – childcare and housework. Cross-country surveys have also probed beliefs about whether men can rear children alone and be as competent as mothers are at achieving this feat.

From analyses of several surveys (e.g., the European Quality of Life Survey) conducted in Europe, indications are that most men and women across countries disagree with the traditional gender role model of the breadwinner father and the caregiving mother (Wall, 2015). Doubts remain, though, about the competence of men to care for children, as less than a third (30%) of individuals thought that fathers could rear a child alone (Wall, 2015). A pertinent question then is: How well do men's actual practices match the recorded changes in beliefs about and attitudes toward gender roles? In her analysis of data collected in 27 EU nations, Wall (2015) discovered that the gender gap between men's and women's participation in household work and childcare may have narrowed, but differences remain across all countries. Men in the 27 countries (e.g., Sweden, France, Finland, Luxemburg, Czech

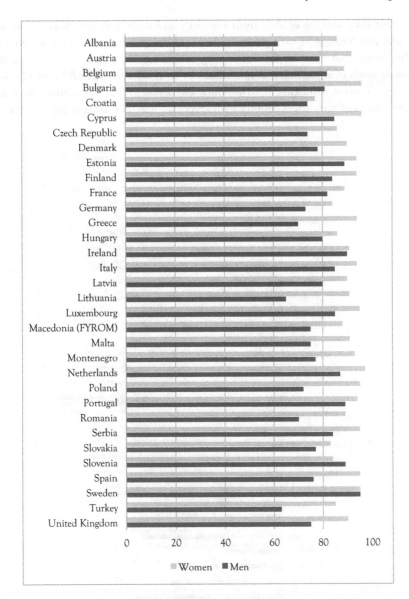

FIGURE 3.4 Paternal and maternal engagement in childcare daily

Source: Derived from European Quality of Life Survey, 2016.

Republic, Romania) spent far less time in household work and in caring for and educating children than women. Data from the United States paint a similar picture of gender discrepancies in household labor (US Bureau of Labor Statistics, 2015). Overall, better educational attainment and income were associated with men's level of participation in childcare across developed countries (see Wall, 2015).

Our own analysis of data from northern and eastern European countries on men's involvement in caring for children and doing housework lends support to the notion that men are far from being egalitarian. As Figure 3.5 indicates, the lowest levels of engagement in housework by men were found in Albania, Croatia, Greece, Kosovo, Montenegro, Macedonia, and Serbia. What was startling were the percentages of men across countries who reported that they never engaged in caring

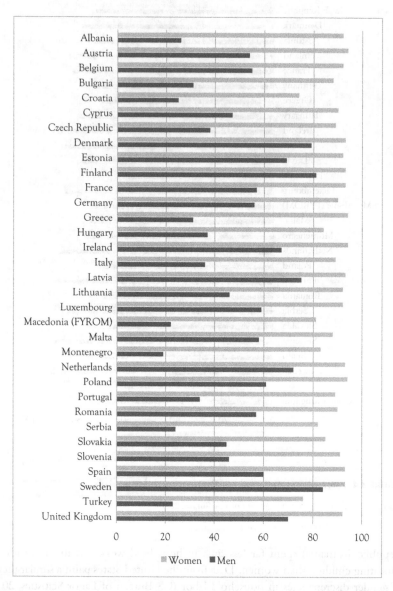

FIGURE 3.5 Paternal and maternal engagement in housework daily

Source: Derived from European Quality of Life Survey, 2016.

for children or grandchildren. If we rely on these and other data from the Eastern European countries (Kravchenko & Robila, 2015), it is safe to say that the gender gap and the move away from traditional masculinity and men's roles in the family are more visible in the Nordic countries and the United Kingdom than in Eastern Europe. For some men in Europe, fatherhood is a maturation process that leads to intrapersonal changes and to greater receptiveness to children's needs (Plantin, 2001, 2015). Considerations such as the latter may bring men to accept greater responsibility for caregiving within families.

The developing world

In several Asian (e.g., India, Pakistan, Bangladesh, Indonesia, Malaysia), Middle Eastern (Saudi, Arabia, Kuwait), Caribbean and Latin American (Jamaica, Guyana, Mexico), and African (Kenya, South Africa, Nigeria) countries, men's roles have been and continue to be shaped by religious beliefs and traditions. Biological fatherhood is emphasized across these regions as central to a man's identity and adds fulfillment to a man's life. Even in the face of diverse family structural arrangements and social and economic changes in the lives of women, traditional conceptions of masculinity prevail in the developing world (see Georgas et al., 2006). Men construct and interpret fathering roles predominantly through economic activities, male dominance, and gendered ideologies (see Anderson & Daley, 2015; Hossain & Juhari, 2015; Rohner et al., 2016). Let us take a closer look at men's conceptions of what it means to be a man and father in cultural communities in the Caribbean and Latin American, Asian, African, and Islamic-based societies.

The Caribbean region represents an ethnic (e.g., African Caribbean, Indigenous groups, mixed-ethnicity, East Indians, individuals of European ancestry), linguistic (e.g., Dutch, French, English, Spanish, Hindi), and religious diversity (e.g., Christianity, Orisha, Rastafarianism, Hinduism, Islam) rarely seen in other parts of the world. Histories of colonialism, slavery, and indentured servitude have all had an influence on current family structural arrangements and belief systems about roles and responsibilities to family members (Roopnarine & Jin, 2016). In the English-speaking Caribbean, Jamaican men strongly believe in biological fatherhood as measured by the number of offspring from different women, which is viewed as "God's Plan" (Brown et al., 1997; Roopnarine, 2013). To put it slightly differently, masculinity is demonstrated by having several children (virility) with different women, which signals sexual prowess and a man's status in the community. These perspectives are prevalent in Guyana and Dominica as well, and present a conflict between masculinity as the foundation of a man's identity and considerations of investment and involvement in children in order to add stability and happiness to their lives. It is unlikely that biological fatherhood invokes a greater sense of responsibility toward children and partner. The tension between being masculine and being a responsible father is palpable in Caribbean men as they attempt to (re) define their identity and care roles (Anderson & Daley, 2015).

Ethnographic and survey studies conducted in different ethnic groups across Caribbean countries indicate that men expressed very traditional views about family roles and their responsibility to act as the self-imposed "head" of the family, even when women are the chief and sometimes only breadwinners and shoulder many of the family's social and economic responsibilities (Anderson, 2007; Brown et al., 1997; Roopnarine et al., 1995; Roopnarine & Jin, 2016). Active socialization of hyper-masculine roles begins early in a man's life. By age 10, boys in Barbados, Dominica, and Jamaica postulated that they had to be tough and dominant, and by age 14, internal schemas about men as providers and traditional division of gender roles were firmly in place. Teenage boys advocated multiple partnerships and sexual dominance (Bailey et al., 1998). Although the dominant masculine role is prevalent among low-income males across Caribbean countries, ideas about responsible fathering without economic support are emerging among men in Jamaica (Anderson, 2007; Springer, 2009). Roughly 93.4% of middle-income fathers, 95.5% of working-class, and 94.5% of low-income inner-city fathers in Jamaica voiced support for such a possibility (Anderson, 2007; Anderson & Daley, 2015).

Beliefs about biological fatherhood carry significant social and cultural capital and are intrinsic to masculine identity and fatherhood in African cultural communities. For instance, in South Africa and other African countries, biological fatherhood accords a man status in the community and extends the family or clan name to the offspring that then enables identity development and social connections to the community, provides a bridge to resources, and offers children a sense of dignity and security (Eddy, Thomson-de Boer, & Mphaka, 2013; Hunter, 2006; Makusha & Richter, 2015). Not unlike in other patriarchal societies, men and fathers are the head of the household or the homestead and assume leadership roles in garnering resources and in protecting and guiding the family (Chikovore, Makusha, & Richter, 2013; Mwoma, 2015). Children bear costs in terms of social stigma and ridicule by community members if they cannot identify with a biological father (Eddy et al., 2013; Madhavan & Roy, 2012).

Fathers in several ethnic groups in Kenya too adhere to patriarchal traditions and long-held customs about men as the authority figures. Across the Abagussi, Lou, Gikuyu, Kamba, and Kalenjins in Kenya, men traditionally held superior positions to women. Men were viewed as economic providers and were expected to provide resources to immediate family and kinship members, while women were primarily responsible for household chores and caregiving. Fathers were the disciplinarians and served as advisors and mentors to boys; women served as mentors to girls (Mwoma, 2014, 2015). However, fathers' roles extended beyond provisioning and mentoring. Fathers were deeply involved in ceremonial functions such as circumcision and arranging the marriages of their children. Among the agropastoral Gusii, a major responsibility of fathers was to increase the family's material resources and to offer protection. Biological fatherhood was valued and offspring were considered as wealth (LeVine et al., 1996). A man's potency as shown by the number of his children, and the power a man acquires vis-à-vis the resources he possesses and reproductive viability are valued among the Luyia (Weisner, 1997); Kipsigis fathers also place a high value on the economic provider role (Harkness & Super, 1992). An argument has been made that Kenyan men are moving away from extreme patriarchal traditions (e.g., Mwoma, 2015), but to what extent these roles have changed has not been fully chronicled.

It is not uncharacteristic for fathers in the Latin American region to also express the view that "men are the head of the family." Throughout most of its history, males of European ancestry in Brazil were the ultimate patriarchs who wielded power over women and those they enslaved and oppressed. Patriarchy continued in Brazil through most of the last century. After 1988, the new civil code (Act 10,406 as of 2002) legally dismantled that power; both parents were given joint responsibility for children. How this legal prescription has affected views about the roles of fathers in Brazilian society is uncertain at this point. According to Bastos et al. (2013), traditional conceptions of masculinity and fathering co-exist with contemporary ideals of fathering in which men are engaged with children at various levels from the birth process to early caregiving and schooling. Supposedly, in the new fathering men engage in introspection, examining the fathering they received and vowing to supplant it with a model of responsive and sensitive caregiving. Fathering in Mexico has undergone similar transformations, wherein some men have moved from the patriarchal (hierarchical, authoritarian) to a relational, more democratic model of investment in the family (Velázquez, 2015). Descriptive accounts from small-sample qualitative and larger demographic studies support the birth of the new fatherhood in some segments of Brazilian and Mexican cultural communities (see Bastos et al., 2013; Carvalho et al., 2015; Velázquez, 2015 for reviews).

For Brazilian and Mexican men with more traditional ideas about fathering, confusion about the breadwinner, authoritarian father and the contemporary demands of the new fatherhood are obvious (Carvalho et al., 2015; Velázquez, 2015). Changes in men's ethnotheories about fathering are often propelled by changes in women's roles and the insistence by women and children that men become more fully integrated into family life. More to the point, the incipient changes in men's involvement in the family are the result of a steady process of negotiations and renegotiations of role responsibilities and of time management between men and women (Velázquez, 2015). With the diverse histories and cultural practices of ethnic groups in Brazil and Mexico, different family models are manifested where paternal engagement with children varies amidst endorsement of the male provider and protector roles (Barker et al., 2011; Wagner et al., 2005).

In India, husband–wife roles and fathering responsibilities, situated within the concept of *palanposhan* (protecting and nurturing), remain largely traditional. *Manusmriti* (200 BCE) or the "Laws of Manu" extoll traditional ways of living. Manu's edicts enjoin an androcentric view of roles in the family; men generally have an upper hand in controlling financial resources and in decision-making. Women are expected to display loyalty and devotion (*pativrata*) to their husbands (Chekki, 1988; Dhruvarajan, 1990; Shukla, 1987). Assessments conducted two decades apart on the ideological beliefs about childcare, filial, financial, and household responsibilities in middle-class husband–wife pairs in single-earner and dual-earner,

TABLE 3.1 Beliefs about manhood, fatherhood, and roles in different geographic locations

Cultural setting	Concept	Family structure and socialization goals	Traditional beliefs in men's roles	Contemporary beliefs about caregiving roles	Male–female roles
India	Laws of Manu; asli mard (real man)	Hierarchical; son preference; collectivistic focusing on interdependence, obedience and loyalty to parents	Superiority of men, subordination of women (pativrata); austere father; manages children's lives	Changing slightly; still largely hierarchical and traditional	Markedly unequal
Malaysia (Kadazan)	Adat	Hierarchical; submission of women to men, collectivistic, loyalty to parents	Superiority of men, subordination of women; strict father	Changing slightly; still largely hierarchical and traditional	Unequal
Caribbean (Jamaica, Guyana, Dominica)	God's plan; sexual prowess; virility	Hierarchical; emotional extendedness, extreme control, obedience and respect for parents	Men as head of household; economic provider; strict and controlling	Largely hierarchical and traditional; roles largely bifurcated	Markedly unequal
Japan	Ie	Hierarchical; female emotional matriarchy	Men as head of household	Changing, but still traditional	Changing but unequal
China	Confucianism	Hierarchical; son preference; collectivistic; guan (governing children's lives)	Strict father, kind mother; father as moral teacher	Convergence of roles between mothers and fathers	More egalitarian; increased role sharing
South Africa (Blacks)	Household head; biological fatherhood	Hierarchical; men associated with economic provider role, women caregiving	Man head of household or homestead; confers status to children	Largely hierarchical and unequal	Markedly unequal
Brazil	Rua, casa	Hierarchical; men viewed as liaison to outside world; women associated with domestic sphere and childrearing	Men head of household; control of women; father as provider, worker, protector	Changing in urban areas but still largely hierarchical	Unequal

Source: Created from information in Anderson & Daley, 2015; Hossain & Juhari, 2015; Mwoma, 2015; Li & Lamb, 2015; Naito & Gielen, 2005; Rebhun, 2005; Roopnarine et al., 2013.

extended and nuclear families in urban areas of India indicated that not much has changed (Tuli & Chaudhary, 2010). Traditional beliefs about structural-functional roles remain strong and there was consistency in beliefs about women assuming primary responsibility for caregiving in the home over time (Kapoor, 2006; Saraff & Srivastava, 2008; Sriram, Dave, Khasgiwala, & Joshi, 2006; Suppal & Roopnarine, 1999; Suppal, Roopnarine, Buesig, & Bennett, 1996). There was a strong tendency for young men in India to endorse traditional views of what it means to be masculine or a "real man" (*asli mard*) (Dutta, 2000; Verma et al., 2006), and they had a greater proclivity to endorse men being tough (86%) compared to men in Brazil (44%), Chile (38%), and Rwanda (19%) (Barker et al., 2011).

Even though studies suggest that women's employment outside of the home influences the selection of marital partners and has altered the gender imbalance in decision making within the family in some regions of India, a "muted silence" exists about role changes (Dutta, 2000; Singh & Ram, 2009). In urban settings (Mumbai, Baroda, and Jaipur), the ideal father is still expected to provide guidance, teach, offer friendship and assist in fostering health and security in children (Saraff & Srivastava, 2008; Sriram & Sandhu, 2013). Across six studies, most men and women define the "ideal father" as one who provides for the child's present and future needs (Sriram & Navalkar, 2012). These views were also underscored by Bangladeshi Muslim, Pakistani Muslim, Gujarati Hindus, and Punjabi Sikh immigrant men in Great Britain (Salway, Chowbey, & Clarke, 2009). Among families in India and Indian immigrant families in the developed world, financial provision may precede the importance of managerial functions that fathers assume in their children's lives.

Arguably, more so than in other regions of the world, hegemonic models of masculinity and religious beliefs are woven into men's roles as fathers and providers in Islamic-based societies in the Middle East (e.g., Saudi Aribia, Kuwait, Lebanon, Palestine), North Africa (Egypt, Morocco), and in Asia (e.g., Bangladesh, Indonesia, and Malaysia). Whether these are situated in principles outlined in the Qur'an, the holy book of Muslims, and Sunnah (teachings of Muhammad) has been a point of contention. It is usually voiced that Muhammad advocated equality between men and women and the equitable treatment and nurturance of sons and daughters (Hossain & Juhari, 2015). Be this as it may, fathers in Islamic-based societies are largely identified as patriarchs; women should be submissive and docile (Ahmed, 2013; Hossain & Juhari, 2015; Noor, 1999). Different forms of female seclusion, veiling, and male guarding are seen across Islamic-based societies (Hossian, 2013). For these reasons, most Islamic-based societies are viewed as collectivistic and authoritarian (see El Feki, Heilman, & Barker, 2017).

Two concepts shed light on men's roles in Islamic-based societies: *Sharia* and *Adat*. Principles within these two concepts instantiate the father as the provider of the family, as offering protection and guidance to his children, inculcating the religious teachings of Muhammed in them, and giving the daughter's hand away in marriage (Hossain & Juhari, 2015; Juhari, Yaacob, & Talib, 2013). Leading scholars (Ahmed, 2013; Hossain & Juhari, 2015) on fathering in Islamic-based Arab and non-Arab societies submit that these traditional views about men's roles are slowly changing in urban areas and that there is more room to entertain and mobilize these changes in the Islamic-based societies of Asia such as Bangladesh and Malaysia than in the Arab countries of the Middle East. Changes in gender roles are also intimated for families in urban areas of Egypt (Ahmed, 2013) and for Palestinians in Israel (Strier, 2014, 2015).

Societies in changing political and economic systems

The former Soviet Bloc countries of Eastern Europe present a unique opportunity to explore beliefs about fathering in changing economic and political systems. Across Bulgaria, Croatia, the Czech Republic, Hungary, Poland, the Russian Federation, Slovakia, and Slovenia, 40–60% of the respondents believed that "A man's job is to earn money; a woman's job is to look after the home and family" (World Health Organization, 2007). On statements such as "A man has to have children in order to be fulfilled," "A child needs a home with a mother and father to be happy," and "Children often suffer because fathers concentrate too much on work," men and women in Georgia had stronger attitudes about the notion that a man needs to have children in order be fulfilled than in Lithuania where such attitudes were weakest. Not as low as in Lithuania, attitudes were less positive in terms of the connection between having children and fulfillment in Bulgaria compared with the Russian Federation and Romania. Furthermore, there was strong endorsement across countries that two parents are necessary to successfully rear children. Among families across these countries, work was perceived as an obstacle to being a good father. As such, separating the work – fathering conundrum appears complicated because being a good provider may aid the process of being a good father (Kravchenko & Robila, 2015).

Another country that has experienced drastic social and economic changes is China. With over 1.4 billion people, China is a recently developed country with the second largest economy in the world. Influenced by Confucianism, Buddhism, and Daoism, and embedded within a collectivist orientation of interdependence and interpersonal harmony in family relationships and childrearing, in the past Chinese mother–father roles were mainly characterized by the "strict father, kind mother" concept. Throughout recent history, mother–father roles in Chinese society were divided along gender lines (see Li & Lamb, 2015). As in India, Korea, Japan and elsewhere, gender and age held center stage in the hierarchal nature of human relationships in China (Hyun, Nakazawa, Shwalb, & Shwalb, 2016). Chinese men were the head of the family and responsible for decisions pertaining to family affairs; they were the disciplinarians and ensured that family honor was maintained. Fathers were expected to be filial to ancestors, and through men the family lineage was extended. The father–son relationship held an esteemed position within the family and society. Sons were privileged over daughters. They usually received more resources than did daughters. Unlike some cultural communities considered in this chapter, Chinese fathers and mothers worked in a more complementary manner to implement childrearing goals and expectations (Hyun et al., 2016).

The integration of women into the domain of work during the Communist Revolution may have been a precursor to more substantial changes in family roles that are witnessed in present day China. Recent geographic, social, and economic mobility coupled with legal reforms during the Revolution has quickened the pace of changes in contemporary childrearing patterns in China. In contrast to Japan and Korea, China has been able to narrow the gender gap in employment considerably (Qian & Sayer, 2016). Nevertheless, the degree to which men's roles have changed in terms of caregiving is ambiguous. It has been argued that increased employment opportunities for women, family planning, reduction in family size, spatial distance from grandparents, and the gradual inculcation of childrearing practices that value independence and creativity in children have drawn men away from traditional conceptions of masculinity (Li & Lamb, 2013, 2015). There is some evidence that Chinese men have a more positive attitude toward their responsibility for infant care than their predecessors (Liu, 1995). However, a comparative sociological analysis of gender ideology in South Korea, Japan, China, and Taiwan showed that Chinese and Taiwanese couples had less egalitarian gender ideology than those in South Korea and Japan (Qian & Sayer, 2016). Other studies show that Chinese men still lag behind women in assuming caregiving roles (Xu & Zhang, 2007), are far more controlling of sons than daughters (Chen et al., 2000; Yang & Zhou, 2008), and indicate a preference for traditional socialization goals for children compared with mothers (Anderson, Qiu, & Wheeler, 2017). Within the changing dynamics of family relationships, there is waning preference for sons over daughters in China and Korea.

Children's narratives of the role of fathers

In keeping with principles outlined in the United Nations Convention on the Rights of the Child, soliciting and listening to children's voices about fathering would certainly add to our understanding of how to meet their developmental needs and enumerate how to better protect their rights. It is rather obvious that children's input on fathering roles and responsibilities can inform policy initiatives in several domains: developmental needs of children, health and nutrition, gender inequality, and child maltreatment. While the case of Malala Yousafzai, the Nobel Laureate, is exemplary in advocating for the rights of young girls, regrettably, the voices of children have rarely been included in developmental theories or policy formulations on fathering. A handful of studies have solicited children's overall perceptions of parenting but less so their perceptions of what fathering means to them. The prevailing practice has been to ask children to assess the nature of their relationships with their fathers. For instance, dimensions of paternal warmth and control as a construct have been the subject of psychological studies across numerous cultural communities (see Khaleque & Rohner, 2013; Sorkhabi, 2005; Roopnarine et al., 2013), but rarely have children's conceptions of fathering and how these conceptions change over time been the subject of scientific inquiry. Hence, only the bare outlines of children's perceptions of fathering across cultural settings are presented in this chapter.

It is not unexpected that in societies with progressive family policies, namely those in the Nordic countries, children would have more positive views about their fathers compared with those in other cultural communities that lack such policies. For decades, Sweden has actively engaged in a process of the democratization of childhood by implementing laws that protect children (e.g., the Aga Law on physical punishment), providing high quality childcare, and offering liberal paternal leave relative to many other societies around the world (see Plantin, 2015). Different surveys of Swedish children suggested that fathers were emotionally connected to their children and involved in their daily lives (Hyvönen, 1993). Of children between 10 and 12 years of age, 86% of boys and 80% of girls specified that their fathers were often available to spend time with them (SCB, 2011).

In tradition-based cultural communities, children's views of fathers tend to reflect spatial and social distance in patterns of availability. A study of Turkish families (Ozgün, Çiftçi, & Erden, 2013) suggests that while preschoolers and their fathers perceived the primary role of the father to be that of a provider, which was followed by play partner, and disciplinarian, children differed from fathers regarding their interpretations of disciplinary practices and how they were enforced. Across the board, fathers were perceived as harsh disciplinarians, who scolded and yelled at children when they behaved inappropriately. Half of the fathers did admit that they used harsh, controlling methods while disciplining children; the other half reported using more democratic approaches that involved reasoning and reinforcement. Discrepancies were also identified in children's and father's perceptions of fulfilling the emotive component of the father's role. Fathers reported meeting children's emotional needs through the display of love and affection; children disagreed and viewed fathers as unavailable and somewhat distant in this regard (Ozgun et al., 2013).

Divergent perspectives on the father's role were also evident between men and their offspring in Korean families. Fathers perceived their roles as playmates (35.8%), counselors (31.5%), providing emotional support (18.9%), financial provider (4.6%), and disciplinarians (4.3%) (Kim, 2011). Wives generally agreed with men's accounts of their roles. However, Korean elementary school-aged children saw fathers' roles quite differently. The most common portrayals of fathers were as economic provider, as exhausted from work, and as a friend (Cho, 2010, 2011). Older children described their father in terms of economic provider, mature personality, and as a counselor to them. Girls painted their father as loving and gentle whereas boys saw them as being tired from work and inaccessible (Choi & Cho, 2005). Here too, fathers saw themselves as more available, but children's perceptions failed to confirm that kind of self-assessment.

As in other patriarchal societies where obedience and unilateral respect toward parents are expected of children, it would not be far-fetched to imagine that children in Islamic-based societies would have more traditional perceptions of fathers' roles within the family. Among a sample of Kuwaiti 10–11 year-olds, 60% of boys thought that fathers were more powerful in the family, whereas 52% of girls saw their mothers as the more powerful figure in the family. More boys (61%) and girls (53%) indicated that their father was more prestigious than their mother

(Ibrahim, 2010). It is tempting to think that the perceptions of these Kuwaiti children may signal that girls in Arab societies are leaning more toward egalitarian views about mothers' and fathers' power in the family, but Egyptian and Saudi children saw fathers in a less positive light. Particularly disturbing was that Egyptian children perceived their fathers to be negligent and abusive more so to daughters than to sons (Hashem, 2001). More favorable views about fathers as loving and caring were expressed by children in India (Kaur, 2018), revealing a degree of variability in children's perceptions of fathers in traditional, patriarchal societies that has hitherto been unacknowledged.

Auxiliary information on children's perceptions of fathering roles can be gleaned from studies of what it means to be the ideal and real father (Goetz & Vieira, 2009). In a sample of 10- and 11-year-old middle-income children in southern Brazil, there were stark differences in children's perceptions of the "ideal father" and a "real father." To accomplish the requirements of an ideal father, men would have to be more involved in tasks that approach engaged fathering: monitoring hygiene, feeding, helping with schoolwork, providing medicine and materials for school, offering behavioral guidance, engaging in play, providing leisure activities, and displaying affection. "Real fathers" fell short in all of these activities. A related study asked 5–11 year-old children in three different regions of Brazil about "What is it to be a father/a mother" (Carvalho et al., 2010). The top four responses were: plays with, provides for, is affectionate and loving to his children, and provides general care for his children. Offering general care was the most prevalent attribute assigned to mothers.

How do conceptions of fathering roles change as boys make the transition to young adulthood? An ethnographic study in South Africa (Spjeldnaes, Moland, Harris, & Sam, 2011) outlines the painful journey of growing up without fathers – men who were characterized as irresponsible and disrespectful by not meeting the economic and emotional needs of their families ("Not man enough"). Due to inadequate access to resources, the boys underlined the economic provider role as key to any future relationship they may encounter with a wife or partner, but also stated that emotional investment was equally important. Providing for the family was an essential component of fatherhood, but this should not preclude fathers from being present in the home. What these perceptions suggest is that responsible fatherhood lies in both economic provision and care and guidance of children. Clearly, there is movement toward embracing conceptions of the new fatherhood, but economic challenges in South Africa remain a formidable obstacle to responsible fathering in these young persons' minds.

From these brief narratives, children seem to have a good working understanding of how fathers behave in families and of what it means to be a responsible father. When articulated within the family and in the public arena, children's knowledge systems of what it means to be a father may assist in precipitating changes in paternal investment and involvement with children across the world. How children view the nature and quality of the parenting they receive from fathers is quite important for the development of inclusive policies toward responsible fathering.

A few final comments

For too long we have ignored the diverse structural constellations within which men become fathers and execute caregiving roles across cultural communities. This has hampered attempts to construct a more inclusive contour of fathering that represents the diverse social-structural living arrangements of men and the pathways through which fathers influence the overall development and well-being of children. A constant difficulty is that we have used the structural attributes of the married, two-parent norm as essential for gauging fathering in other family social and cultural living arrangements. Far less is known about the social alliances that men establish in different social and structural configurations to rear children, and about the inherent rewards and challenges men encounter in caring for children across the world.

Based on the information gathered in studies from Europe and North America, it appears that fathers are on a journey toward developing egalitarian roles in the two-parent, nuclear model. Appreciable shifts are observed in men's beliefs about what it means to be a father in the developed world, but men's and women's roles are far from egalitarian. Visible changes are occurring in men's beliefs about what it means to be a man and a father in the developing world as well, but this is occurring at a more measured pace. Biological fatherhood and traditional masculinity continue to define and shape men's roles in families throughout the developing world. By their very underlying premise, these traditional beliefs may thwart engagement in the gender equality project (Plantin, 2015). A psychological portrait of families in 30 nations in developed (e.g., Canada, France, Germany, the Netherlands, the UK, the USA) and developing countries (e.g., Algeria, Ghana, India, Indonesia, Mexico, Pakistan) revealed that patriarchal traditions exert a durable influence on men's roles in the family in many developing countries (Georgas et al., 2006).

4

LEVELS AND QUALITY OF PATERNAL INVOLVEMENT

Our postmodern world is driven by increasing political, economic, social, and technological transformations. In the Asian region, China and India have witnessed tremendous economic growth over the last two decades. Political changes in Russia and the former Soviet Bloc countries of Eastern Europe (e.g., Estonia, Romania, and Bulgaria) have resulted in new capitalist market systems that have moved away from the communist system of governance and modes of production. Political conflict, poverty, and oppression have contributed to increased international migration from the developing to the developed world. All of this is happening as countries in the developing world are working toward sustainable development goals that would ideally further reduce poverty and its associated ills, provide greater access to adequate health care, and high quality early childhood education for children (see demographic characteristics of children in Table 4.1; UNICEF, 2016). Aware of these issues, researchers in developmental psychology, anthropology, human development, sociology and the health sciences have taken great care to explore paternal involvement amidst these dynamic social and economic changes in the twenty-first century.

Banking on a literature that is disproportionately located in the developed countries (e.g., United States, Canada, Australia, Sweden, Great Britain, and Japan), we want to emphasize that what men articulate they should accomplish "in principle" and their actual involvement in childcare can be discordant, even in countries with progressive family policies (Wall, 2015). Remember also that there are discrepancies in maternal and paternal reports of father involvement in caring for children (Mikelson, 2008). Mostly, studies indicate that the gap between paternal and maternal involvement in the basic care of children has decreased in the developed world (see volumes by Cabrera & Tamis-LeMonda, 2013; Lamb, 2010). From a modernity perspective, it would be reasonable to assume that gender disparities in childcare roles and childrearing responsibilities might be shrinking in developing societies too.

TABLE 4.1 Mortality and nutritional status of children in different regions of the world

Region	Under 5 mortality (2015)	Under-weight (%)	Stunting-moderate-severe (%) (2010–2015)	Orphaned by HIV/AIDS (2014, estimates)**	Birth registration (2015)	Fertility rates (2015)
Sub-Sahara	83	19	36	11,000	46	4.9
Eastern and Southern Africa	67	16	36	7,600	45	4.5
West and Central Africa	99	22	35	3,400	45	5.4
Middle-East and North Africa	29	7	18	71	89	2.9
South Asia	53	30	37	580	62	2.5
East Asia and Pacific	18	5	11	770	80*	1.8
Latin America and the Caribbean	18	3	-10	500	94	2.1

Notes: *Under 5 mortality*: The probability of dying between birth and age 5 per 1000. *Stunting*: Children 0–59 months who are below minus two standard deviations from median height-for-age of the WHO Child Growth Standards. *Birth Registration*: Percentage of children under 5 years who were registered at time survey. *Fertility*: Number of children born per women if she lived to end of childbearing years

* Excludes China
** UNAIDS 2014 HIV and AIDS estimates, based on 2015 Spectrum modelling, July 2015

Source: From UNICEF, *The State of the World's Children*, 2016.

Unfortunately, this is not entirely true. A wide gap exists between mothers' and father's participation in basic childrearing activities in developing societies. The bottom line is that regardless of the level of economic development within countries, women spend more time in "care work" than men do. Women also receive less recognition and compensation for care work than men do in almost all societies (Levtov et al., 2015).

To elaborate on paternal care, we rely on constructs delineated in Pleck's (2010) newer conceptualization of father involvement and engagement and on propositions in the parenting frameworks and theories discussed in Chapter 2. An attempt is made to piece together a disparate and unwieldly literature on the level and quality of father involvement with children across different regions of the world. On a more general level, the care of children is composed of multiple components such as physical care, cognitive engagement, meeting social and emotional needs, transportation to diverse activities, leisure activities, attending to health care needs, and providing resources (financial resources, in kind support, and child support payments). From a psychological standpoint, caring for children is often measured in time spent, the frequency and quality of involvement, satisfaction with the parenting role, and the emotional and economic costs to men and women (Amato, 1998;

Pleck, 2010). Mindful of this, researchers have assessed both direct (e.g., holding, social interactions) and indirect care (e.g., provisioning, protection) in cultural groups with diverse modes of economic production (see Gray & Anderson, 2010; Hewlett & Macfarlan, 2010; Pleck, 2010).

The intention here is to bring to the fore the variability that exists on key measures of fathers' basic care and in their cognitive and socio-emotional engagement with children in different regions of the world. Findings from both quantitative and qualitative studies are integrated in this chapter. A deliberate attempt is made to highlight the unique features of fathering in developing societies. We begin with a look at fathers' involvement in prenatal care, pregnancy, and the birthing process across cultural communities.

Paternal involvement during pregnancy and childbirth

Having a child can be a moving and rewarding experience for most parents. The joy and excitement of having a child can be accompanied by concerns about becoming pregnant, the progression of the pregnancy, the termination of the pregnancy, and the birth outcome. New fathers show a greater likelihood of becoming depressed than males of the same age and this becomes exacerbated among men in difficult circumstances (e.g., poverty, incarceration, nonresidential living arrangements) (Garfield et al., 2014; Ramchandani, Stein, Evans, & O'Connor, 2005). Men may also experience fear, anxiety, and stress due to limited involvement in prenatal care, lack of information about pregnancy, poor access to medical care, a negative birth process and outcome (e.g., a premature infant or an infant with disability), and inadequate preparation for parenthood and parenting (Boyce et al., 2007; Finnbogadóttir, Svalenius, & Persson, 2003; Howe, Sheu, Wang, & Hsu, 2014; Redshaw & Henderson, 2013; Smith & Howard, 2008; Widarsson, Engström, Tydén, Lundberg, & Hammar, 2015; Yu et al., 2012) or to difficulties in adopting a child among heterosexual and same-sex couples (Goldberg, 2010).

As stressful as having a child can be sometimes, there are benefits to paternal involvement in the pregnancy and birth process for both men and women. Father/ partner involvement in and the physical and the psychological support offered during pregnancy and birth can ease some of the stress and anxiety that couples experience during the transition to parenthood in developed and developing societies. Women value the emotional support (e.g., care, empathy) offered by fathers, which was associated with less anxiety, less perceived pain and fatigue, and greater satisfaction with the birth experience (Dellman, 2004; Malik et al., 2007; Plantin et al., 2011; Redshaw & Henderson, 2013; Smith & Howard, 2008). Higher levels of paternal involvement are also linked to better health and mental health outcomes in women one-month postpartum and to breast-feeding during the first few days and at three months postpartum in developed societies (Redshaw & Henderson, 2013). For men in the United States, involvement in pregnancy and the birth process was associated with greater satisfaction with the fathering role, a stronger commitment to the father–mother relationship, greater devotion to co-parenting, increased sense of self-worth, and higher levels of paternal involvement in caring for infants during the post-birth period (Cabrera, Fagan, & Farrie, 2008; Fagan, 2014). Among non-resident, unmarried fathers, witnessing the birth of the child and having the father's name on the birth certificate improved the chances of the father staying in contact with the mother and the child among families in the United States (Kiernan, 2006). When fathers were dissatisfied with the birth process it was associated with higher levels of depressive symptomology at 4–6 weeks post-birth (Gawlik et al., 2014).

Early prenatal contact with health professionals and a planned, happy pregnancy were associated with greater paternal involvement, and women whose partners were more involved prenatally and during labor were more likely to breastfeed for longer periods (Redshaw & Henderson, 2013). There is sufficient evidence to suggest that most fathers accompany their wives or partners to prenatal visits and are present at the birth of their child in the United States and Europe. Men in these and other developed countries (e.g., Australia, New Zealand) report high levels of satisfaction with the outlook of having a child (e.g., Maridaki-Kassotaki, 2000) and the childbirth experience (Howarth, Scott, & Swain, 2017; Yogman & Garfield, the Committee on the Psychological Aspects of Child and Family Health, 2016). Enrollments in prenatal preparation classes are also high in developed countries (90% in Sweden and 80% in Denmark) but vary a bit. Results from a national study of a multi-ethnic sample of primiparous and multiparous mothers from different socioeconomic backgrounds in England conducted three months post-birth (Redshaw & Henderson, 2013) showed that fathers were sufficiently involved in the pregnancy: 62% of fathers were present at the pregnancy test, and 63% were present for at least one prenatal visit, and 89% were present for one ultrasound. Most men in Spain attended medical check-ups, with a smaller percentage attending prenatal classes (Marotto-Navarro et al., 2013). It was quite the opposite in Singapore, where few fathers attended prenatal education classes (Poh, Koh, Seow, & He, 2014). Among different ethnic groups in the United States, African American and Hispanic American men may not attend prenatal classes frequently, but in excess of 88% discussed the pregnancy with their partners (Tamis-LeMonda, Kahana-Kalman, & Yoshikawa, 2009), and about half of African American mothers had the infant's father present during a doula visit in a medical setting (Thullen et al., 2014).

There is an encouraging trend toward greater paternal involvement in prenatal visits and presence at the birth of children in the developing world. Precisely what this "greater involvement" means, though, is more accurately interpreted within the context of cultural beliefs about men's roles in the family, cramped hospital facilities, and delivery practices that may exclude men. Therefore, greater participation can entail providing transportation for the mother to visit the clinic but not necessarily attending any of the sessions, ensuring proper nutrition, taking care of children, and paying medical bills (Olayemi, Bello, Aimakhu, Obajimi, & Adekunle, 2009; Singh, Lample, & Earnest, 2014). Across 36 low- and middle-income countries in Asia, Africa, and Latin America and the Caribbean, men's involvement in prenatal care ranged from 96% in the Maldives to 18% in Burundi. In 18 countries it was below 40% (e.g., Honduras, Sierra Leone,

Zimbabwe, and Pakistan) (Levtov et al., 2015). Another survey (Barker et al., 2011) conducted on families in India, Bosnia, Chile, Brazil, Mexico, Rwanda, and Croatia indicated that on average 84% of men reported making at least one pre-natal visit (78% in Brazil to 92% in Mexico) which is slightly higher than visits made by men in Palestine, Morocco, Egypt, and Lebanon (El Feki et al., 2017). About 53.3% of men in the African nation of Mali accompanied their wives on prenatal visits (Sleigh et al., 2013), less than half did in Nigeria (Olayemi et al., 2009; Iliyasu et al., 2010), and in Kibibi, Uganda few men attended or were aware of the benefits of their attendance at prenatal visits (Singh, Lample, & Earnest, 2014).

The transition to parenthood has received quite a bit of attention in recent years. As indicated already, depending on material resources, access to health care, edu-cational attainment, partner relationship, and support, the transition to parenthood can be a rewarding experience for most couples, but for others challenges can range from anxiety and depression to uncertainty about becoming a father (Boyce et al., 2007; Howe et al., 2014). In what has been described as couvade (brooding, hatch-ing), primiparous fathers in particular seem to experience psychological changes that by some accounts resemble those that women exhibit during pregnancy. Men in cultural communities in different parts of the world (35% in Russia, 25–52% in the United States, 68% in China, 68% of Turkish immigrant men in the United States) reported symptoms such as weight loss, nausea, anxiety, being emotionally vul-nerable, back pain, and sleeping problems during pregnancy (see Brennan, Marshall-Lucette, Ayers, & Ahmed, 2007; Finnbogadóttir, Svalenius, & Persson, 2003; Khanobdee, Sukratanachaiyakul, & Gay, 1993; Kutahyalioglu, 2017; Tsai & Chen, 1997).

Of course, there are other changes that men experience during the transition to parenthood. Men experience reduced libido and changes in sexual activity, and South American men tended to withdraw from subsistence activities prior to and after the birth of the child, and changed diets (Paige & Paige, 1981). Ugandan men felt emotionally connected to the pregnant woman regardless of union status (Kaye et al., 2014). Whether the physical and psychological symptoms men express dur-ing pregnancy are avenues through which they show empathy and concern for the welfare of the expectant mother or not, it can draw the father into emotional invest-ment in the pregnancy and birth process. This may favor greater involvement with the child, the establishment of paternity within the cultural context, and strengthen the pair bond between partners (Gray & Anderson, 2010; Paige & Paige, 1981). A reasonable question is whether the physical and psychological symptoms men express during the different trimesters of pregnancy predate the pregnancy itself or are related to anticipatory anxiety and lack of preparedness for becoming a parent.

When it comes to birth, presence in the delivery room is quite common in Scandinavian countries (Johansson, Rubertsson, Rådestad, & Hildingsson, 2012) and men view pregnancy and birth as shared and complementary experiences (Fen-wick, Bayes, & Johansson, 2012). Ninety percent of British men (81% for Black or Minority Ethnic origin fathers to 93% for White British fathers), 90% of Polish fathers in some hospitals in Warsaw (Wielgos et al., 2007), and 83% of men in Berlin,

Germany were in the maternity ward (David et al., 2009). Lower numbers were observed for men in Spain (67.3%), Greece (54.3%), and Georgia (40%) (Marotto-Navarro et al., 2013; Pestvenidze & Bohrer, 2007; Sapountzi-Krepia et al., 2010). Discrepancies in paternal presence at birth across countries may be attributed to variations in family leave and other policies in different European countries, educational attainment, and employment patterns and constraints (Fägerskjöld, 2008).

Men in developing countries may not necessarily be involved in labor but are present at the hospital, within the building, or nearby. Using the Standard Cross-Cultural Sample (SCCS) data, Lozoff (1983) determined that men were present at birth in 27% of the 120 societies examined. If present, fathers were observers much of the time, which meant that midwives and other relatives were more involved with the delivery than were fathers. Around this time, fathers spent more energy in providing material than emotional support to mothers (Huber & Breedlove, 2007). A later survey showed that since Lozoff's (1983) study things have not changed that much for men in the developing world despite the introduction of programs designed to encourage them to become more involved in prenatal classes, pregnancy, and childbirth (see Chapter 6). Across five countries, Chile had the highest percentage of men (50%) present in the delivery room whereas India (2%) and Brazil (7%) had the least number of men present at the birth of their last child (Barker et al., 2011). Men were also conspicuously absent during childbirth in Arab countries (El-Feki et al., 2017). Traditional beliefs about men's roles and hospital practices may contribute to the lackluster involvement of men in delivery in some developing countries (see Deave & Johnson, 2008; Sansiriphun et al., 2010). A paradox is that women prefer their partners/husbands to other women in the delivery room (Levtov et al., 2015).

Because most maternal and child deaths occur in the developing world (UNICEF, 2018), men have an important role to play in ensuring that women have adequate health care during pregnancy and subsequently that children do too. As has been mentioned, paternal involvement during pregnancy and childbirth has positive associations with women's health and mental health in developed countries (e.g., Redshaw & Henderson, 2013). A meta-analysis of 14 studies from developing societies (e.g., Nigeria, Bangladesh, India, Lebanon, Nepal, and Turkey) provides further insights into this issue (Yargawa & Leonardi-Bee, 2015). Male involvement in supporting the health of women (15–49 years) decreased the odds of postpartum depression and it appears to have greater benefits during the pregnancy and postpartum periods than during the delivery itself. This may imply that paternal support during pregnancy and the postpartum period may be essential to warding off health challenges that women may face during the transition to parenthood. This said, in some of the developing world paternal involvement in pregnancy and childbirth can be both beneficial and undermining. Men with more traditional ideologies can dominate decision-making by preventing women from seeking prenatal care and may also blame women for a difficult pregnancy and an unanticipated birth outcome, thereby creating heightened anxiety during pregnancy and the post-birth period (Levtov et al., 2015).

Across the pregnancy, birth, and postnatal periods, the couple/partner relationship remains an essential factor in the level and quality of father involvement and the support offered to the partner. Commitment to a loving relationship, adequate communication, and being aware of relationship difficulties that may be induced by a difficult pregnancy and an unexpected birth outcome can all strengthen paternal involvement during the transition to parenthood and through the early childhood period, across cultural communities. For nonresident fathers, contact with the partner during the birth and post-birth period may mean sustained involvement with young children over time.

Modes of paternal care

Basic caregiving

As hinted above, time-use, observational, and questionnaire data suggest that paternal and maternal responsibility for a broad range of basic caregiving activities are far from equal in heterosexual, two-parent families in different ethnic and cultural groups across the world. Various studies indicate that the discrepancies are less blatant in the European countries (e.g., Sweden, Denmark, and Finland) with more progressive leave policies and with well-developed early childhood care and education systems (e.g., Reggio Emalia in Italy, Edwards & Gandini, 2018) than in the developing societies where families struggle daily to meet children's care, education, and health needs. Whether the care patterns of fathers are directly linked to employment factors and family leave policies in the European countries has been actively debated (see Plantin, 2015; see also Chapter 7). Of interest here is how much direct and indirect care responsibility men assume in different family constellations and contrasting economic systems in developed and developing societies. We should warn that research on paternal involvement with children with disabilities across cultural communities is sparse (see Macdonald & Hastings, 2010 for a review of fathers and children with disabilities).

During the immediate post-birth period, more than three-quarters of fathers in an English sample engaged in changing diaper, giving a bath, helping with feeding, and participating in other aspects of care offered to infants (Redshaw & Henderson, 2013). Lower rates of participation were obtained for Greek fathers living in urban areas (26.2% fed the infant occasionally, 28.7% changed diaper, and 43.8% bathed the infant) (Maridaki-Kassotaki, 2000; see also Fuertes, Faria, Beeghly, & Lopes-dos-Santos, 2016, for data on Portugal). This level of variability in paternal involvement patterns is also apparent in families with children with disabilities, who are more prone to parenting stress and more susceptible to mental health difficulties than are other parents (Oelofsen & Richardson, 2006; Olsson & Hwang, 2006). Some fathers with children with an intellectual/developmental disability were less likely to embrace childcare than mothers were, and traditional role responsibilities became pronounced in these families (Dyer, McBride, Santos, & Jeans, 2009; Gray 2003), but other fathers seemed more willing to become involved in their children's lives

(Carpenter & Towers, 2008). Among highly educated men there were no significant differences on measures of childcare involvement, child socialization, decision-making, and social activities between fathers of children with and fathers of children without intellectual disabilities in the United States (Young & Roopnarine, 1994). Additionally, fathers with children with disabilities in the United States were also reasonably involved in feeding, dressing, teaching/therapy, and driving children to appointments (Simmerman, Blacher, & Baker, 2001) and those in the United Kingdom were very engaged with their children with autism (Potter, 2016).

An analysis of time-use data (Craig & Mullan, 2011) on maternal and paternal engagement in talk-based care (e.g., talking, listening, teaching) and physical care that involved routine activities (e.g., feeding, bathing, dressing, putting children to sleep, carrying, holding, cuddling, hugging, soothing, transporting children) in Australia, Denmark, Italy, and France showed that mothers' overall time in childcare with at least one child between 0 and 12 years of age exceeded that of fathers in all four countries, with fathers' average care time being 35% in Denmark, 30% in Australia and Italy, and 25% in France. Fathers in Australia spent the most time in childcare. Regardless of household type (male breadwinner, dual full time, 1.5 earner, and father not employed full time), fathers across the four countries spent about 50 minutes per day in total childcare. Father care was highest in male breadwinner mother-at-home families and lowest in dual full-time earner families (see also Huerta et al., 2014 for similar estimates on families in 18 OECD countries). Fathers in Spain spent on average 38.59 minutes per day in physical care and 19.62 minutes in interactive care with children 0–11 (Gracia, 2014) and it was 2.14 hours per day (15 hours per week) in Portugal (Wall, 2015). Father involvement in a mixed-ethnic sample of multiple-fertility fathers in the United States was moderate (Bronte-Tinkew, Horowitz, & Scott, 2009) but high among Samoan and Tongan fathers in New Zealand (Tautolo, Schluter, & Paterson, 2015). By comparison, gay couples in the United States not only supported the ideals of sharing childcare equitably, they actually did.

In the East Asian countries, Japanese fathers spent 39 minutes daily in childrearing (Cabinet Office, 2013), Taiwanese fathers spent less than one minute during a one-hour period feeding infants (Sun & Roopnarine, 1996), 30.6% of Chinese fathers with preschoolers and 31.2% with school-aged children reported spending no time or less than 1 hour per day with children (Liu & Zhao, 2006), and Korean fathers spent roughly 44 minutes per day (166 minutes on weekends) playing with or taking care of children (Ahn et al., 2013). About half of Korean fathers gave the child a bath (54.8%), 67.7% soothed the child, 58.9% put the child to sleep, 54.7% changed diaper, and 19.25% cooked for the child (Hyun, 2013). Involvement in changing diaper and feeding infants was comparatively low among Indian and Malaysian fathers (Roopnarine, Lu, & Ahmeduzzaman, 1989; Roopnarine et al., 2013).

A cross-national comparison (Barker et al., 2011) of men caring for children below 4 years of age in Bosnia, Brazil, Chile, Croatia, India, Mexico, Rwanda, and South Africa provides further support for the gendered pattern of care observed worldwide. Across countries, 44.2% of fathers participated in daily care of children (from 63% in Croatia to 36% in Chile), 39.4% changed the child's diaper/clothes (from 52% in Brazil and Croatia to 19% in India), and 32.8% cooked/fixed food for the child (from 46% in Brazil to 18% in India) several times a week or more. For men in Palestine (12% changed diapers, 14% bathed the child), Lebanon (24% changed diapers, 25% bathed the child), and Morocco (15% changed diapers, 17% bathed the child), early investment in care of children was also low (El Feki et al., 2017). Father–child contact was extremely poor among nonresident men in Mali (Sleigh et al., 2013) and South Africa (NIDS, 2010–2011) and Kipsigis fathers in Kenya rarely bathed, fed or took infants outside of the home (Harkness & Super, 1992). Father care was minimal in Turkey, prompting researchers to label men as "helpers" rather than caregivers (Metindogan, 2015).

The preceding is not meant to imply that fathers across the developing world uniformly demonstrate low levels of care involvement with children. In a few societies, father care was comparable to levels in the developed world. For instance, Jamaican fathers in common-law relationships spent 0.75 of an hour cleaning and 1.08 hours feeding one-year-old infants per day (Roopnarine et al., 1995), Kadazan fathers in Malaysia spent an hour or less in feeding and cleaning infants per day (Hossain et al., 2007), and care was shared between mothers and fathers in some communities in Brazil (Carvalho et al., 2015). To clarify, the extreme variability in fathers' involvement in care in communities in developing countries may be a reflection of the disequilibrated state that men find themselves in when trying to straddle traditional gender ideologies about what it means to be a man and father and their caregiving responsibilities to children in difficult economic situations. Undeniably, in cultural communities where gendered ideologies about men's roles in the family are still fully entrenched in patriarchy, fathers had the lowest levels of participation in basic caregiving activities.

Paternal care in the context of other family members

A majority of the care young children receive in the developed countries occurs in co-parenting, nuclear or single-parent family settings in collaboration with additional caregivers in home-based or center-based care facilities. However, care patterns are culturally mediated; intensity and number of caregivers are dictated by available resources, beliefs about childrearing, and family structural arrangements. Thus, paternal care transpires in the context of other family members or paid help. The presence of other caregivers can alter the level of care offered to children by fathers.

While in the developed world grandparent/relative care was low in countries that had good childcare systems for families (it ranged from 55–56% in Greece and the Netherlands to below 10% in the Nordic countries for 0–2 year-olds; OECD Family Database, 2016), multiple caregivers or extended kinship members offer appreciable amounts of care and support to children in a number of cultural communities across the world. Extensive observations of low-income European American and African American families revealed that relatives interacted with infants twice as much as fathers did (Fouts, Roopnarine, & Lamb, 2007), 64.5% of working parents in Korea had support from grandparents (Jung & Kim, 2012) and in Japan, a little over half of families had support with childrearing from grandparents (National Institute of Population and Social Security Research, 2010). Alloparenting is quite common in South Africa, and other African countries (see Fouts, 2013; Hewlett & Macfarlan, 2010; Marlowe, 2005) and in India grandparent care is widespread (Roopnarine et al., 2013).

A look at routine forms of care in post-communist Russia Federation, Bulgaria, Lithuania, Georgia, and Romania illustrates the complexity of paternal care responsibility in the context of other individuals in the household (Kravchenko & Robila, 2015). Paternal and maternal reports of father involvement with children alone, jointly with mother, and in the context of care by others indicate that father care alone was relatively low in the areas of putting the child to bed, dressing the child, caring for the child during illness, doing homework, engaging in leisure activities, and transporting children in all five countries. Most of fathers' basic care involvement with children occurred jointly with mothers, and in all five countries, other individuals in the household assumed more care responsibility for children than did fathers (Kravchenko & Robila, 2015). It appears that in these countries fathers may rely on others to fulfill routine care responsibilities, thereby slackening their level of involvement with children.

Multiple forms of care in Caribbean countries have already been touched upon in Chapter 3. Overall, father care interactions (10.3%) were lower than that of siblings (16.3%) and grandparents (17.6%) toward children in Trinidad and Tobago (Flinn, 1992; Roopnarine & Jin, 2016). Among the Hadza of Tanzania, mothers interacted with children younger than one year of age 78.4% of the time, fathers 17.8% of the time, older sister 18.3% of the time, maternal grandmother 9.4% of the time, and others 30% of the time observed (Marlowe, 2005). Father care in Cape Town, South Africa (Clark et al., 2015) and in Indigenous groups in Canada (Ball & Moselle, 2015) is also braided with those offered by kinship and nonkinship members. Young Black fathers in South Africa seem to form strong social alliances with their mothers to raise children, and in some instances paternal grandmothers may act as co-parents. In a similar vein, indigenous fathers in Canada rear children in complex families with permeable boundaries that consist of children from previous relationships and new partners, and with support from other members in their community.

It has been asserted that fathers' childcare involvement peaks in the preschool years and shows a steady decline thereafter (Baxter & Smart, 2011; Yeung, Sandberg, Davis-Kean, & Hofferth, 2001). Note that paternal care relative to that provided by different household members is not static either. Involvement in caregiving fluctuates among different caregivers as the child ages. In a study conducted in Shanti Nagar outside of New Delhi, multiple caregiving increased after 7 months of age from 38% to 61% whereas mother care dropped sharply from 56% to 32% when infants reached 18 months of age (Sharma, 2000). Fluctuations were observed for other adults as well: grandmother care peaked between 7 and

11 months (15% to 24%) and again at 24 months (14% to 17%), caregiving by aunts (8% to 24%), siblings (5% to 14%), and fathers (5% to 16%) peaked between the second and third year of life, and for uncles a decline was observed at 11 months (14% to 10%) (Sharma, 2000). It is perhaps not difficult to see that diverse caregivers in extended family systems in developing societies do influence levels and patterns of fathers' contributions to childrearing.

Paternal closeness and emotional investment in children

Warmth and control

Parental warmth and affection are the sine qua non of sensitive caregiving, and are displayed through such behaviors as kissing, hugging, caressing the child, and saying positive things to the child (e.g., praising, complimenting). Attachment theory (Ainsworth et al., 1978; Bowlby, 1969), interpersonal acceptance-rejection theory (Rohner, 1986, Rohner & Khaleque, 2005, 2013), and the parenting styles framework (Baumrind, 1967, 1996) discussed in Chapter 2, all emphasize the importance of parental warmth for the development of trust, social competence, and social adjustment in children. What also comes through clearly from these frameworks and related research is that different dimensions of parental control are linked to negative social and cognitive outcomes in children across cultural communities (MacKenzie et al., 2013; Rohner & Khaleque, 2013; Dede Yildirim & Roopnarine, 2017a).

For a long time, a general claim has been that fathers in some Asian cultural communities, such as in India and China, maintain a good deal of affectional distance from children. These societies embrace collectivistic childrearing tendencies (interdependence, respect for elders, interpersonal harmony), value proper demeanor, and in some such as Thailand, orderliness, politeness, compassion, gentleness, and quietness are encouraged. As you may remember from Chapter 3, because of cultural belief systems related to vertical and horizontal relationships in Indian society, fathers were not seen as essential to early caregiving (Kakar, 1992), and in Chinese families the father was viewed with reverential awe (Li & Lamb, 2015). An observational study conducted in the home environment in New Delhi, India showed that fathers and mothers did not differ in affection extended to one-year-olds (Roopnarine et al., 1990). Other observational studies conducted in Taiwan with one-year-olds (Sun & Roopnarine, 1996) and in Chaing Mai province in northern Thailand with preschool-aged children in home settings (Tulananda & Roopnarine, 2001) also failed to show differences in the display of affection between mothers and fathers toward boys and girls. Similarly, children's reports suggested that Chinese mothers and fathers displayed equal levels of warmth to them (Chen et al., 2000). This may signal that fathers in some Asian cultural communities are aware of the emotional needs of children as the ethos of family social organization patterns and childrearing practices continues to change in the context of economic and technological growth (Li & Lamb, 2015).

Levels of paternal nurturance vary widely across cultural communities. In the United States 73% of fathers hugged 0–2 year-old children every day (87% of mothers did)

(Child Trends, 2002), 100% of low-income resident fathers showed affection toward their children several times a week (Astone, Karas, & Stolte, 2016), and African American fathers were more affectionate to their 3–4 month-old infants than were mothers (Roopnarine et al., 2005), as were Aka foragers in the Central African Republic (Hewlett, 1987; Hewlett & Macfarlan, 2010). Among Brazilian fathers, affection was high in the hierarchy of care offered to 4–6 year-old children (Bossardi, Gomes, Vieira, & Crepaldi, 2013). By comparison, the display of affection can be low in Caribbean countries. Only 28% of Trinidadian boys reported being hugged and 38% received affection through touching and patting on the head (Awong-Persaud, 2003), and in Jamaica, paternal affection shown toward children was sporadic (Leo-Rhynie & Brown, 2013).

It was estimated that in most of the world's cultures parents are quite accepting and extend appropriate levels of warmth to children (Rohner, 2016). A study of parenting and childhood outcomes among gay adoptive parents, lesbian adoptive parents, and heterosexual adoptive parents, indicated that gay parents displayed more warmth toward children, were more responsive during parent–child interactions, and showed less disciplinary aggression than heterosexual couples (Golombok et al., 2014). Analysis of warmth and control directed by fathers in heterosexual families toward 9–10 year-olds across 10 communities in nine countries (China, Colombia, Italy, Jordan, Kenya, Thailand, the Philippines, Sweden, and the United States) revealed high levels of paternal and maternal warmth and low levels of hostility/ rejection/neglect across developing and developed countries (Putnick et al., 2012). What was unexpected were the high levels of paternal warmth and low levels of rejection in the developing countries of Jordan, Philippines, and Colombia, where men's roles are decidedly more traditional and in which fathers exercise more control over children. In Jordan, a traditional Muslim country, father warmth was comparable to that in the developed countries, and in Kenya, another country where paternal involvement with children is generally low, fathers reported higher levels of warmth toward children than did mothers. Paternal and maternal warmth were significantly correlated in Italy, Jordan, Philippines, and the United States, and paternal and maternal hostility/rejection/neglect were significantly correlated in China, Colombia, Italy, Jordan, Thailand and the United States. Related work on fathers in Trinidad and Tobago supports a more nuanced view of paternal warmth and rejection in the developing world (Roopnarine et al., 2013).

It is probably true that fathers across the world aspire to or are becoming more sensitively attuned to children's emotional needs, but in some cultural settings mothers and fathers use combinations of high warmth and high control during parenting (Roopnarine et al., 2013). For example, Indian parents manage (Saraswathi & Dutta, 2010) and Chinese and Chinese immigrant parents in the United States engage in an active process of governing children's lives (e.g., *guan*) (Chao, 1994; Li & Lamb, 2013, 2015). Seemingly, both approaches to childrearing appear controlling, if not, authoritarian. Findings from a study carried out in Trinidad and Tobago exemplify this mode of parenting. Paternal and maternal warmth assessed in families with preschool-aged children indicated two clusters of fathers: one group reported high levels of warmth and low levels of control that are similar to those in other settings in the developed world (e.g., Putnick et al., 2012); the other group reported high levels of warmth and high levels of control. Discussing these clusters, Roopnarine et al. (2013) pointed to the complexity of paternal engagement with children in harsh ecological niches where citizen insecurity may be high and neighborhood infrastructure and collective efficacy weak. Alternatively, it could be that in some cultural communities paternal warmth is not inimical to exercising control when families engage in a systematic process of child training. The paternal practices in the Caribbean region deviate from the tenets of Baumrind's parenting typologies of authoritative, authoritarian, and permissive parenting styles and the premises in Rohner's interpersonal acceptance-rejection theory. According to these perspectives, during optimal parenting, high levels of warmth are normally expressed in the context of low levels of harshness.

Paternal parenting styles have been assessed across cultural settings (see Sorkhabi, 2005). For example, Lee, Keown, and Brown (2016) examined maternal and paternal parenting styles in Korean immigrant fathers and mothers of 6–10 year-old children in New Zealand. There was quite a bit of overlap between fathers' and mothers' endorsement of culture-specific Korean childrearing values such as use of shaming/love withdrawal, directiveness (correcting child's behavior), protection (monitoring), devotion, and involvement, and the levels of authoritative (warmth/ acceptance, reasoning, and democratic participation) and authoritarian parenting styles (physical punishment, verbal hostility, and punitive/non-reasoning parenting strategies). Fathers and mothers were more likely to endorse high levels of involvement and moderate levels of shaming/withdrawal. Among Caribbean immigrant parents with preschool-aged children living in the United States, there were no significant differences between mothers' and fathers' reports of authoritative, authoritarian, and permissive parenting styles. Assessments of the prevalence of parenting styles in Italian families showed that 23.9% of fathers were judged by their children to be authoritative, 14.1% authoritarian, 28.2% neglectful, and 33.8% were indulgent based on acceptance/involvement and strictness/supervision parenting scores (Di Maggio & Zappulla, 2014). Far higher numbers of Jamaican fathers were judged authoritative by their children (Ramkissoon, 2002).

Recently, researchers have shifted focus from observing parenting styles to examining the nature and quality of interactions between fathers and children. Tamis-LeMonda, Shannon, Cabrera, and Lamb (2004) observed mother–child and father–child modes of social engagement (e.g., cognitive stimulation, intrusiveness, positive regard, and detachment) during in-home, semi-structured free play in a racially diverse sample selected from the Early Head Start Program in the United States. There were few differences between mothers and fathers in modes of social engagement when children were 24 and 36 months old. Mothers' and fathers' scores on sensitivity, positive regard, cognitive stimulation, detachment, intrusiveness, and negative regard were significantly related at both assessment points. Fathers' positive regard, sensitivity, and cognitive stimulation at 24 months were predictive of maternal cognitive stimulation, sensitivity, and intrusiveness at 36 months, a sign that paternal behaviors influenced how mothers interacted with children over time.

Fathers were equally as sensitive during interactions with young children, as were mothers, and both showed low levels of intrusiveness (Cabrera, Shannon, & Tamis-LeMonda, 2007), and in another investigation low-income mothers and fathers in the United States did not differ in their playfulness, defined as the degree to which parents use creativity and curiosity with children during play (Cabrera et al., 2017). However, in a Dutch sample mothers were more sensitive to children than were fathers (Hallers-Haalboom et al., 2014, 2017).

A general misunderstanding is that fathers across cultural communities are less emotionally sensitive and affectionate toward young children. It is clear that fathers display levels of warmth that are comparable to those of mothers in some societies, and in at least two ethnic/cultural groups fathers were more affectionate to infants than were mothers. Commonalities were also observed in maternal and paternal parenting styles. Nonetheless, it is reasonable to conclude that differences remain between mothers and fathers in their nurturance and sensitivity displayed toward children during everyday socialization.

Proximity and holding

A vast parent–child attachment literature underscores the importance of parental sensitivity for effective childrearing and positive childhood development (Ainsworth, 1989; Lamb, 2013; Lamb & Lewis, 2010). To reiterate, across cultural communities, fathers and mothers who use sensitively attuned caregiving practices facilitate the development of secure bonds between children and parents (Bretherton, 2010; Lamb, 2013). Earlier it was specified that the percentages of children who develop secure attachments with fathers were similar to those obtained for mothers at least in the developed world (Brown et al., 2012; van IJzendoorn et al., 1992).

Two behaviors, father–child holding and being in close proximity to children, are important for the development of attachment bonds (Ainsworth et al., 1978; Bowlby, 1969). Furthermore, the continuous contact and care and pediatric care models emphasize the adaptive value of close parent–child contact for meeting children's physiological and psychological needs (LeVine, 1974; Henry, Morelli, & Tronick, 2005). Ethnographic accounts of foraging groups indicate that Aka fathers in the Central African Republic held their infants (1–4 months of age) about 22% of the time compared with 1.9% of the time among Bofi foragers (18–35 months of age), 2.6% of the time among the Efe (1–4 months of age) of the Ituri rain forest in the Democratic Republic of Congo (formerly Zaïre), and 2.5% of the time among the Hadza (0–9 months of age) of Tanzania (Fouts, 2013). Holding was exceedingly low among Gusii and Kipsigis fathers in Kenya and these fathers did not carry children much either (Harkness & Super, 1992; Mwoma, 2015). Using the level of Aka paternal intimacy with children as a barometer, Indian fathers held infants about 2% (mothers 8%) of the time (Roopnarine et al., 1990) and Taiwanese fathers held infants 1% of the time (mothers 7%) during in home observations of both groups (Sun & Roopnarine, 1996). Amounts of holding by fathers in most regions of the world are below those of the Aka foragers.

Not only do Aka fathers hold their infants more than other fathers around the world, they also are in close proximity to children for most of the day than are other men (more than 50% of daylight hours). Efe fathers were also close to infants (within 3 meters) for 40% of the time observed. This is in contrast to only 15% of the time that Lese fathers were around infants (Fouts, 2013). Gusii fathers were around children but interactions with them were low (Harkness & Super, 1992). Fouts (2013) and Hewlett (1991) proposed that the higher levels of engagement in holding and being around children by Aka forager fathers, relative to fathers in other parts of Africa, might be attributed to egalitarianism. Resources provided by kinship members and monogamy also have an influence on paternal involvement among forager fathers (Fouts, 2013; Hewlett, 1991).

Disciplinary practices

Whereas parental warmth and sensitivity facilitate social development and adjustment, harsh and controlling behaviors invariably undermine optimal childhood development (Khaleque & Rohner, 2013). Two reports on the State of the World's Fathers (Heilman et al., 2017; Levtov et al., 2015) identify trauma (e.g., abuse and neglect) inflicted on children as a serious problem across societies. By most accounts, physical punishment is a contributing factor to abuse and neglect. A meta-analysis of 88 studies suggests strong associations between physical punishment and aggression, antisocial behaviors, among other social difficulties in children (Gershoff, 2002; see also Gershoff, Goodman, Miller-Perrin, Holden, Jackson, & Kadzen, 2018). In view of the deleterious effects of physical punishment on childhood development, we consider the disciplinary practices that fathers employ to address children's behavioral transgressions across some cultural settings.

Contrary to the long held impression about fathers as disciplinarians, mothers and fathers appear equally as likely to physically punish children and there is also little disparity between them in how often they do this. A study (Nobes & Smith, 1997; Nobes, Smith, Upton, & Heverin, 1999) of mothers and fathers in England showed that most parents smacked their children with an open hand (slapping, beating, and pushing). There was no significant difference in aggregate scores of different modes of punishment between fathers and mothers, but fathers were more likely to use physical restraint (forceful holding and pushing) than did mothers. No gender-of-parent differences were recorded in the use of ingestion (washing child's mouth with soap and water, forced feeding) or punishment by example (pinching, hair pulling, squeezing to demonstrate consequences of child's behaviors). Fathers punished boys more severely than they did girls. With vocal advocacy for child-centered approaches in childrearing across Europe, it is likely that the use of physical punishment has changed in England since the 1990s.

Lansford and her colleagues (Lansford et al., 2010) examined rates of mild and severe forms of physical punishment in China, Colombia, Italy, Jordan, Kenya, the Philippines, Sweden, Thailand, and the United States. Between 44% (Kenya) and 0% (Sweden) of mothers of girls, and 56% (Kenya) and 0% (Sweden) of mothers of boys believed that physical punishment was necessary to rear children. Almost identical rates were found for fathers: between 48% (Kenya) and 0% (Sweden) of fathers of girls and 54% (Kenya) and 0% (Sweden) of fathers of boys believed that physical punishment was necessary to rear children. Across countries, 54% of girls and 58% of boys received mild physical punishment and 13% of girls and 14% of boys received severe physical punishment from parents or someone in the household. Fathers used less corporal punishment than did mothers, and boys received more corporal punishment than did girls. With the exception of Sweden and Thailand, mothers exceeded fathers in spanking, hitting, or slapping the child, and in Kenya and Italy, mothers grabbed/shook the child more often than did fathers. Swedish fathers grabbed/shook children more than mothers did. It should come as no surprise that no Swedish father or mother endorsed the use of physical punishment, and that the frequency of physical punishment was lowest in Sweden in comparison to the other eight countries. Sweden has long advocated for the democratic rights of children, and decades ago actually implemented laws that prohibit the physical punishment of children (Ministry of Health and Social Affairs and Save the Children, Sweden, 2009).

It is not a truism that beliefs in and use of physical punishment are far higher in the developing than the developed world. While in some regions of the developed world (e.g., the Nordic countries) physical punishment and the public humiliation of children are banned, in the developing world the endorsement and use of different forms of physical punishment are considered normative and both mothers and fathers use physical punishment at unacceptably high rates. Surveys conducted on parents in 34 countries in Latin America and the Caribbean, Africa, and Asia indicate that the endorsement of the use of physical punishment ranged from 6% in Montenegro to 92% in the Syrian Arab Republic (Cappa & Khan, 2011). Favorable attitudes to physical punishment, and the use of physical punishment, were high in African and Caribbean countries. Unfortunately, in this report no data were furnished on fathers' use of physical punishment.

A small-scale study of Indo-Guyanese families suggested that mothers used physical punishment more than did fathers (71.7% versus 64.2%; Roopnarine, Evans, & Pant, 2011) and in a mixed ethnic-sample of families in Trinidad and Tobago, 75.2% of fathers and 77.7% of mothers spanked, and 37.3% of fathers and 40.1% of mothers whipped children (Primus, 2018). In both settings, hitting children was accompanied by other forms of physical punishment such as pushing, hair pulling and twisting the child's ear (Roopnarine et al., 2013). Rates of physical punishment were also high in African and Middle Eastern countries. Across Lebanon (33% of fathers and 40% of mothers), Palestine (40% of fathers and 71% of mothers), Egypt (41% of fathers and 79% of mothers), and Morocco (29% of fathers and 72% of mothers), mothers spanked children more than did fathers (El Feki et al., 2017).

Father engagement in social and cognitive activities

A thesis that has been advanced by researchers is that fathers avail themselves as playmates to children rather than caregivers (Lamb, 1977; Paquette, 2004). While fathers are more likely to engage in non-routine forms of care such as playing with and reading to children than routine forms of physical care, as will become apparent, mothers are more likely to play with children than are fathers in several cultural communities across the world (Roopnarine, 2011). Let us take a closer look at father engagement in cognitive and social activities with children across developed and developing societies: playing with, reading to, and telling stories to children.

Playing with, reading to, and telling stories to children represent three core aspects of paternal engagement that are associated with cognitive and social developmental outcomes in children (Christie & Roskos, 2015; Mol & Bus, 2011; Neumann, Hood, & Neumann, 2009; Raikes et al., 2005; Roopnarine, 2011). For example, reading and telling stories are related to the development of language skills (Tamis-LeMonda et al., 2004) and agency in children (Baumrind, 1996). Given their implications for childhood development, mothers and fathers across societies are encouraged to engage in these activities from the time of children's birth onward. Advice from pediatricians and parenting experts about engagement in these activities abounds in the developed countries, but such information is often out of reach for most parents in the developing countries – though fathers can access parenting information online. The degree to which fathers engage in playing with, reading to, and telling stories to children in developing societies is a cause for concern.

Father–child play

In the northern European countries, the United States, and Canada, play is an integral part of child-centered, neo-constructivist approaches to childrearing. Parent–child play is embraced as part of contemporary childrearing and as beneficial to early childhood development. Quite the opposite is the case in several developing countries where play is seen as frivolous, something children engage in naturally. There are doubts about its value for childhood development (Roopnarine, 2011; Roopnarine, Dede Yildirim, & Davidson, 2019). To complicate matters further, some view parent–child play as a modern invention of middle-class parents in the technologically developed societies as a "window to jump-start academic preparedness" (Lancy, 2007, p. 279). As the following discussion reveals, play and playful activities constitute a major source of social commerce between fathers and children in most cultural communities.

Fathers' engagement in play with children has been assessed cross-nationally by UNICEF in its Multiple Indicator Cluster Surveys (MICS) (UNICEF, 2015) and by the IMAGES Project (Barker et al., 2011). We used data from the UNICEF surveys to calculate the percentages of men who played with preschool-aged children in countries primarily from the developing world. Figures 4.1 and 4.2 present the percentages of men who engaged in playing with preschool-aged children in the past three days across two regions. As can be seen, in both the Caribbean and Central American and African regions, fathers in almost all countries were far less likely to engage in playing with children than were mothers. The lowest levels of play occurred in the African countries of Mali, Chad, Guinea Bissau, and in the

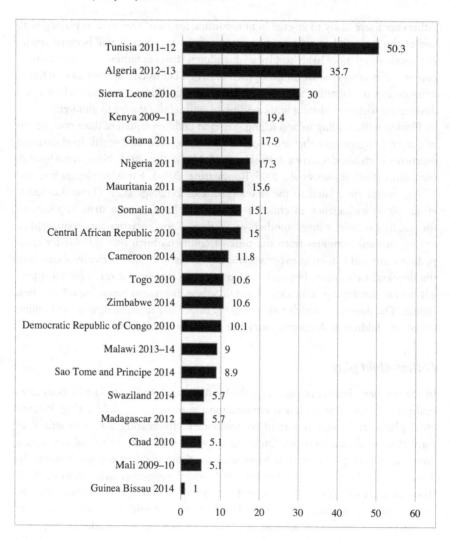

FIGURE 4.1 Percentage of men who engaged in playing with preschool-aged children in African countries

Source: Derived from UNICEF MICS, 2009–2016.

Caribbean and Latin American countries of Panama, the Dominican Republic, and Suriname. Among foraging groups in central Africa, AKA fathers' relative time investment in play with infants was 23% and mothers' was 13% compared with their involvement in caregiving and other activities (Hewlett, 1987). In other communities in Central Africa, Lese fathers spent more time in play (18%) than Efe fathers (7%) (Fouts, 2013). Another study (Barker et al., 2011) reported higher rates of paternal engagement in play with children in India (46%), Brazil (83%), Chile (70%), Croatia (76%), and Mexico (64%).

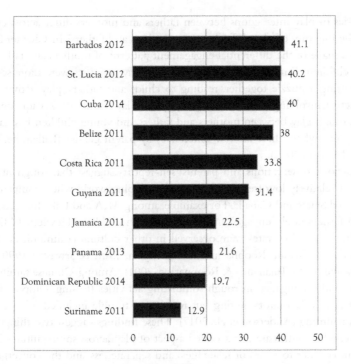

FIGURE 4.2 Percentage of men who engaged in playing with preschool-aged children in the Caribbean and Central America

Source: Derived from UNICEF MICS, 2009–2016.

Assessments of the actual time fathers spend in play with children also suggest that mothers either play longer with children or were comparable to fathers in time invested in play. Jamaican mothers spent significantly more time in playing with infants than did fathers (Roopnarine et al., 1995), and this was also true for traditional families with infants in rural Malaysia – probably an artifact of the greater responsibility mothers assume in the basic care and nurturance of children during the infancy and preschool years (Hossain et al., 2005). Likewise, mothers in Estonia, Finland, the Russian Federation, Brazil, the United States (African Americans), and a setting in South Korea (Tudge, 2008) engaged in more play with young children than did fathers, and mothers in Portugal did the same (Fuertes, Faria, Beeghly, & Lopes-dos-Santos, 2016). By comparison, there were no mother–father differences in overall levels of play in Kadazan families in Malaysia (Hossain et al., 2008), among families with older children in southern Brazil (Benetti & Roopnarine, 2006), and in families in the United States (Yeung, Sandberg, Davis-Kean, & Hofferth, 2001). This may encourage a conceptual shift in propositions about fathers as "playmates" to children.

Up to now, the focus has largely been on rates of father engagement in play. What types of play are fathers likely to participate in with young children, and do modes of play interactions between fathers and mothers differ across cultures? Does the intensity of play differ between mothers and fathers? In Chapter 3, mention was made of the differential engagement patterns of mothers and fathers with young children. European American mothers' play activities were more sedentary (e.g. putting a puzzle together, reading to child) and fathers' play activities were more active, involving minor and major physical play (Lamb, 1977; Paquette, 2004). Active, rough play between mothers and fathers and young children has narrowed to the point where there are few differences by parent gender (Laflamme, Pomerleau, & Malcuit, 2002).

Behavioral observations and parents' self-reports suggest that rough play itself occurs at relatively low frequencies in the developing world when compared with the United States and Canada. For example, among AKA and Baka foragers, mothers and fathers rarely engaged in rough play with children (Hewlett, 1987; Hirasawa, 2005), and low rates were observed in other cultural communities in India, Thailand, and Taiwan (Roopnarine, Talukder, Jain, Joshi, & Srivastav, 1990; Sun & Roopnarine, 1996; Tulananda & Roopnarine, 2001). Among Chinese families with toddlers, fathers engaged in rough stimulating activities (tossing, jump and attack, dumping) in a laboratory setting but rough and tumble included other activities such as counting (Anderson et al., 2017). These findings suggest two things: rough father–child activities are not a valued aspect of play across some cultures because they run counter to issues of relatedness and separateness, and the convergence of participation in rough play between mothers and fathers in some groups in North America could be attributed to more egalitarian childrearing practices that expose children to dominance and cooperation (see Fletcher, St George, & Freeman, 2013). Rough play remains a viable socialization mechanism for fathers in western developed societies (see volume by Smith & Roopnarine, 2019).

As with rough stimulating activities, mother–father differences are rather mixed when it comes to participation in other modes of play. Observations of lower- to middle-income families in New Delhi, India indicate that mothers and fathers did not differ in their engagement in object-mediated play with infants (Roopnarine et al., 1990), but mothers did engage in more object play with infants than did fathers in Taiwanese families (Sun & Roopnarine, 1996). Levels of engagement in the game "peek-a-boo" were noticeably low in both societies, with mothers in India showing a greater tendency to participate in peek-a-boo than did fathers. In German families the intensity of play was similar between fathers and mothers (Ahnert et al., 2017), and in Israeli families there were no significant differences between father and mother playfulness (Menashe-Grinburg & Atzaba-Poria, 2017). Among Thai families with preschool-aged children, there were no significant differences between mothers and fathers in constructive play with children (Tulananda & Roopnarine, 2001). On the whole, in Asian societies, parent–child play activities were very low compared with other modes of stimulation – hugging and kissing, holding, touching, tickling, teasing, laughing and smiling (Rogoff et al., 1993; Roopnarine et al., 1994). Socialization goals in some of the Asian cultural communities are probably achieved through diverse means rather than through heightened parent–child play activities (see Holmes, 2011; Keller, Borke, Chaud-hary, Lamm, & Kleis, 2010).

In spite of the importance placed on fantasy play for the development of social and cognitive skills (Johnson, Christie, & Wardle, 2005; Neumann, Hood, & Neu-mann, 2009; Christie & Roskos, 2015; Roskos, 2019; Smith & Roopnarine, 2019), there are only a handful of studies on father–child fantasy play. A few studies have found that in European American families, mothers initiated more fantasy and joint play with preschoolers in a laboratory setting than did fathers (Roopnarine & Mounts, 1985). A different laboratory study (Farver & Wimbarti, 1995) demon-strated that fantasy play occurred more frequently when the father and child were together than when the child was playing alone, underscoring the facilitative role of the father in play. Substantiating the lack of emphasis on play in some Asian societ-ies, Thai fathers and mothers engaged in low levels of fantasy play with preschoolers (Tulananda & Roopnarine, 2001).

Book reading

Across developed societies, there is strong emphasis on book reading to foster early language skills development in young children. Early language stimulation through reading out aloud and exposure to print-rich materials introduce opportunities to learn vocabulary and more complex language (Christie & Roskos, 2015). These early reading activities are associated with children's language development (Duursma, Pan, & Raikes, 2008), literacy, and cognitive skills (Mol & Bus, 2011). Factors such as family sociodemographic characteristics, child gender, fathers' residential status, knowledge about and access to books, age of onset of book reading, and language proficiency can all affect frequency of book reading (Dede Yildirim & Roopnarine, 2017; Roskos, 2019). As you may have guessed, within the resource-rich developed countries, paternal literacy rates are high and access to reading materials is more readily available than in developing countries. Hence, one might expect higher rates of father–child reading in the developed as compared to the developing societies.

As Figure 4.3 shows, father–child book reading is on the low end in developing countries. If we consider the African and Caribbean and Latin American countries only, there was remarkable variability in reading to preschool-aged children. About 35% of fathers in Uruguay to 5% in Suriname, and from 17% of fathers in Tunisia to less than 2% in Mali, Guinea-Bissau, and Madagascar read to children within the last three days. In 50% of the African countries surveyed, less than 25% of fathers read to children at all. Within these resource poor countries, far higher percentages of mothers read to children than did fathers. It is not clear why this is the case. A few contributing factors may include fathers' limited knowledge about the importance of reading to young children, their low educational attainment, few opportuni-ties to read to children, and the number of literacy related materials such as chil-dren's books and other print-rich materials available in the home environments. An inventory of literacy materials in the home environment revealed that in the poorer nations in the Caribbean and Latin America such as Belize, Dominican Republic,

FIGURE 4.3 Percentage of fathers who read books to children

Source: Derived from UNICEF MICS, 2009–2016.

and Suriname, many homes (36%, 57%, and 62% respectively) did not have books (Dede Yildirim & Roopnarine, 2017).

In developed countries, paternal book reading is a little higher than in the developing societies of Africa, Asia, and the Caribbean, but rates are considerably lower than maternal book reading. In the UK Millennium Study (McMunn et al., 2015), mothers were twice as likely to read to children as were fathers. Roughly, 50% of fathers read to 4-year-olds and 40% read to 7-year-olds. The figures were lower for fathers (8%) in the Netherlands (Duursma, 2014). Using data from Early Head Start Study sites in the United States, Duursma (2014) examined paternal and maternal book reading to children at 14, 24, 36, and 60 months of age in low-income families from diverse family structural arrangements. Maternal daily and weekly book reading increased from 77% at 14 months to 87% at 24 months, and remained high at 5 years. Based on maternal reports, a third of fathers read to children daily, 21% read to children weekly, and about half of the fathers read monthly or rarely to children at 14 months, and 26% of fathers read daily, 32% read weekly, and 42% read to children monthly or rarely at 24 months. Paternal reading to children at 36 months closely resembled the distribution obtained at 24 months and did not change appreciably when children were 5 years old (24% read daily and 36% read weekly). Surprisingly, there were negligible differences in the frequencies of reading between residential and nonresidential fathers.

Telling stories and singing songs

Storytelling and singing to children are other viable ways of enhancing language and literacy skills development in children (Isbell, Sobel, Lindauer, & Lowrance, 2004), and are not as dependent on educational attainment or material resources as is book reading. Both activities are interactive and permit children to co-create with the parent or adult caregiver (Roney, 1996). Several societies, such as those in Africa, that are historically steeped in oral traditions, have used storytelling and singing as a central vehicle for conveying cultural and other information to children. As has been advanced by researchers in the education field, storytelling invites children's social participation, ignites visual imagination, and is associated with children's listening skills and comprehension of material presented (Isbell et al., 2004; Morrow, 1985; Sobel & Weisberg, 2014). Here, the focus is primarily on paternal storytelling and singing in developing nations.

Figures 4.4 and 4.5 display the percentages of fathers across 57 countries who told stories and sang songs to children during the last three days. As with reading, fathers did not appear that enthusiastic about telling stories or singing to children either. Fathers in Uruguay (35.4%) seem the most and those in Swaziland (2.4%) the least inclined to sing songs to children, and fathers in Montenegro (40.1%) were most likely and those in Swaziland (2.1%) the least likely to tell stories to children. A pattern that seems to repeat itself in the UNICEF data is the low level of cognitive investment by fathers in Africa and the Caribbean region. Of the countries surveyed, fathers in these two regions of the world had some of the lowest rates of telling stories and singing to children.

Support for early learning

Fathers play a vital role in facilitating early learning and enhancing the early cognitive development of children during their formative years (Cabrera et al., 2004; Roopnarine et al., 2005; Dede Yildirim & Roopnarine, 2017a). As per the sustainable

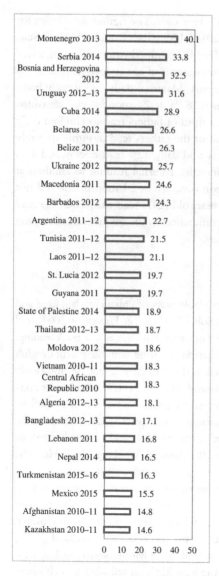
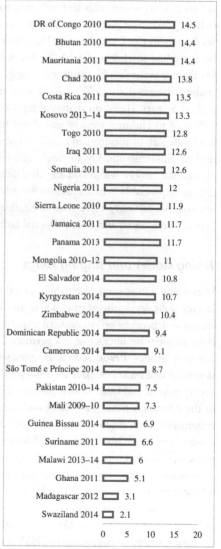

Country	Value
Montenegro 2013	40.1
Serbia 2014	33.8
Bosnia and Herzegovina 2012	32.5
Uruguay 2012–13	31.6
Cuba 2014	28.9
Belarus 2012	26.6
Belize 2011	26.3
Ukraine 2012	25.7
Macedonia 2011	24.6
Barbados 2012	24.3
Argentina 2011–12	22.7
Tunisia 2011–12	21.5
Laos 2011–12	21.1
St. Lucia 2012	19.7
Guyana 2011	19.7
State of Palestine 2014	18.9
Thailand 2012–13	18.7
Moldova 2012	18.6
Vietnam 2010–11	18.3
Central African Republic 2010	18.3
Algeria 2012–13	18.1
Bangladesh 2012–13	17.1
Lebanon 2011	16.8
Nepal 2014	16.5
Turkmenistan 2015–16	16.3
Mexico 2015	15.5
Afghanistan 2010–11	14.8
Kazakhstan 2010–11	14.6

Country	Value
DR of Congo 2010	14.5
Bhutan 2010	14.4
Mauritania 2011	14.4
Chad 2010	13.8
Costa Rica 2011	13.5
Kosovo 2013–14	13.3
Togo 2010	12.8
Iraq 2011	12.6
Somalia 2011	12.6
Nigeria 2011	12
Sierra Leone 2010	11.9
Jamaica 2011	11.7
Panama 2013	11.7
Mongolia 2010–12	11
El Salvador 2014	10.8
Kyrgyzstan 2014	10.7
Zimbabwe 2014	10.4
Dominican Republic 2014	9.4
Cameroon 2014	9.1
São Tomé e Príncipe 2014	8.7
Pakistan 2010–14	7.5
Mali 2009–10	7.3
Guinea Bissau 2014	6.9
Suriname 2011	6.6
Malawi 2013–14	6
Ghana 2011	5.1
Madagascar 2012	3.1
Swaziland 2014	2.1

FIGURE 4.4 Percentage of fathers who told stories to children

Source: Derived from UNICEF MICS, 2009–2016.

development goals outlined by the United Nations, fathers are in a position to improve social capital, reduce poverty rates, address gender inequality, and increase educational opportunities for children across the world. Particularly troublesome are the poverty rates and the low preschool enrollment patterns in much of Africa (less than 30% in most countries) and the poorer nations of Asia (10% in Bhutan and 13% in Bangladesh) and the Caribbean (40% in the Dominican Republic and 34%

Dominican Republic 2014	11.5
Jamaica 2011	11.2
Lebanon 2011	11.1
Iraq 2011	10.5
Togo 2010	10.4
Kazakhstan 2010–11	9.9
Ukraine 2012	9.3
Bangladesh 2012–13	9.3
Moldova 2012	8.9
Suriname 2011	8.5
Nigeria 2011	8.4
Mauritania 2011	8.4
Chad 2010	8.4
Kosovo 2013–14	7.9
Cameroon 2014	7.8
Zimbabwe 2014	7.4
Kyrgyzstan 2014	7.2
Sao Tome and Principe 2014	6.9
Afghanistan 2010–11	6.8
Turkmenistan 2015–16	6.6
Somalia 2011	6.3
Ghana 2011	6.1
Pakistan 2010–14	6
Malawi 2013–14	5.9
Madagascar 2012	4.6
Guinea Bissau 2014	4.3
Mali 2009–10	2.5
Swaziland 2014	2.4

Uruguay 2012–13	35.4
Montenegro 2013	32.7
Serbia 2014	30.9
Bosnia 2011–12	28.8
Barbados 2012	26.2
Belize 2011	25.1
Argentina 2011–12	23.2
Cuba 2014	21.3
St. Lucia 2012	21.3
Costa Rica 2011	19.3
Thailand 2012–13	18.6
Vietnam 2010–11	18.5
Laos 2011–12	18.4
Macedonia 2011	18.3
Belarus 2012	17.9
Mexico 2015	16.3
Bhutan 2010	15.7
State of Palestine 2014	15.3
Guyana 2011	15.2
Tunisia 2011–12	15.2
Central African Republic 2010	15.1
Algeria 2012–13	13.6
El Salvador 2014	13.5
Sierra Leone 2010	13.2
Mongolia 2010–12	12.4
DR of Congo 2010	12.2
Panama 2013	12
Nepal 2014	11.5

FIGURE 4.5 Percentage of fathers who sang to children

Source: Derived from UNICEF MICS, 2009–2016.

in Suriname). Amidst uneven access to preschool education and growing numbers of nonresidential fathers, especially in the developing world, fathers can assume an essential role in offering support for early learning activities with children across different countries. As is demonstrated in Figure 4.6, father support for learning was exceedingly low in the poorer nations. Not unlike participation in reading, paternal support for learning may be severely hampered by economic circumstances, low paternal education, and the lack of learning materials in the home in low-income countries (Dede Yildirim & Roopnarine, 2018).

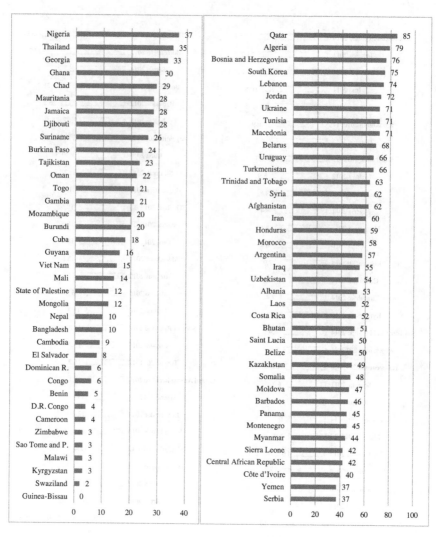

FIGURE 4.6 Father support for learning

Source: Derived from UNICEF MICS, 2009–2016.

Fathers in some cultural communities were more inclined to be involved in children's school-related activities such as attending parent–teacher meetings and school functions and to assist children with educational activities at home, than in providing direct care to them. Fifty percent of Indian fathers in Mumbai assisted children with homework (58% of mothers), 51% helped children learn (47% of mothers) sometimes or frequently (Saraff & Srivastava, 2010), and among older children, 57% of fathers in Baroda, Gujarat attended parent–teacher meetings and school activities, 53% monitored the child's progress in school, and 74% exposed children to reading materials (Sriram & Sandhu, 2013). Similarly, Chinese fathers were involved in making decisions about the schools their children attended (Xu & Zhang, 2008) and participated in taking children to museums (Ho et al., 2010).

Although paternal childcare among the Kalenjin, Abagusii, Lou, Kamba, and Gikuyu in Kenya was low, fathers across all groups paid school fees and bought learning materials for children (Mwoma, 2014). Abagusii and Gikuyu fathers attended their children's school functions and Lou and Gikuyu fathers assisted with children's academic activities at home. In Turkish Cyprus, over half of all fathers attended children's school functions and a majority assisted children with homework (Erdogan, 2011). An identical pattern was observed in a longitudinal study of young children in Turkey (Alici, 2012), and in Brazil, where mothers and fathers shared the task of assisting children with school-related activities (Wagner, Predebon, Mosmann, & Verza, 2005). Fifty-three percent of fathers in Lebanon, 23% in Egypt, 42% in Palestine, and 35% in Morocco assisted children with homework (El Feki et al., 2017). Fathers in Bulgaria, Georgia, Lithuania, Romania, and the Russia Federation mostly shared the task of doing homework with children with wives or others in the household. Across all five countries, educational involvement was low, with fathers in Georgia and Romania showing the lowest interest in working with children on their homework (Kravchenko & Robila, 2015).

Engagement in quantitative skills and technology use

To meet the demands of a technological world, there is greater emphasis on teaching children science, technology, engineering, and mathematics (STEM). Immediately above, we discussed ways in which fathers engaged in homework and other learning activities with children at home. These attempts do not preclude fathers' engagement in STEM activities with children. However, data on paternal engagement in STEM activities are slowly emerging. Once again, we rely on the UNICEF MICS data to elucidate fathers' levels of involvement in quantitative skills activities with preschool-aged children. The MICS asked fathers whether they engaged in counting and naming objects with children, activities that are an important aspect of numeracy development. As can be gleaned from Figure 4.7, paternal engagement in counting ranged from 41.9% in Uruguay to 3.5% in Guinea Bissau. Less than 20% of fathers in most of the African countries and several Caribbean and Latin American countries counted and named objects with children.

Parents and children are spending substantial amounts of time using technological devices for entertainment, play activities, reading, doing homework, communication, and connecting socially with family members and friends. Even in the most techno-savvy societies in the world, the digital skills of parents may lag behind those of their children and this becomes exacerbated in developing countries due to the digital divide (media-rich versus media-poor homes; digital natives or digital immigrants). In a survey of media use among parents ($N = 2,300$) in the United States, about 27% of parents were classified as media-centric with high use of technological devices, 47% were classified as media-moderate, and 26% as media-light (Wartella, Rideout, Lauricella, & Connell, 2014). Eighty-one percent of parents in

FIGURE 4.7 Percentage of fathers who engaged in counting and naming objects with children

Source: Derived from UNICEF MICS, 2009–2016.

the 27 EU countries were online compared to 60% of 6–10 year-olds. Parental co-engagement in using different devices with children was moderately low (28% used iPads, etc., with 2–5 year-olds, 11% with 6–8 year-olds) (Wartella et al., 2014). As children age they seem to spend more time online than do parents (e.g., Estonia, Slovenia, Malta, Hungary, Poland) (Livingstone & Haddon, 2009).

There is fair documentation of children's use of technology, parental monitoring/restriction of internet use, and the threats (content, conduct, contact risk) of internet use on children's safety and well-being (see Livingstone & Haddon, 2009).

While parents have concerns about heavy technology use, most see it as a convenient and efficient means of preparing children for twenty-first-century skills (e.g., social responsibility and justice, global awareness, digital communication). Mindful of the concept of living together but using technology independently, researchers are mapping the impact of technology use on parenting and the mediation strategies parents use with children. The goal here is to provide a brief glimpse into what we know about fathers' involvement in children's technology use. Not unexpectedly, because this is a relatively new frontier, few studies have explicitly examined paternal parenting and technology use in young children across cultures.

When mothers and fathers with children 0–8 years of age in the United states were asked whether smartphones and tablets made parenting easier, only 3% strongly agreed, 26% somewhat agreed, and 70% strongly or somewhat disagreed. Seventy-seven percent of parents said that negotiating media use in their homes did not lead to conflicts, nor to disagreements between spouses. There were slight disagreements between mothers and fathers on issues related to their child's technology use. Different types of mediation strategies (restrictive, passive, and monitoring) in technology use have been identified (Haddon, 2012). The Eurobarometer survey, one of the largest to be conducted so far, examined parental mediation (52.2% mothers, 41.8% fathers) and online risks to children in Austria, Belgium, Bulgaria, the Czech Republic, Denmark, Estonia, France, Germany, Greece, Ireland, Italy, the Netherlands, Poland, Portugal, Slovenia, Spain, Sweden, and the United Kingdom. In Belgium, Denmark, Ireland, the Netherlands, Sweden, and the United Kingdom where individualistic childrearing practices are valued, restricting children's time online increased risks online. Among countries with a collectivistic orientation such as Bulgaria, the Czech Republic, Estonia, Poland, and Portugal, more restriction by parents led to less online risk. A culture's orientation to childrearing (co–use, autonomy granting, self-directed behavior) may dictate which type of strategy is effective in warding off online risk (e.g., use of filtering mechanisms and monitoring software, restrictions) (Kirwil, 2009).

Parental mediation that entails the use of restrictions are more likely to be imposed when children are younger, and girls are monitored more than boys. Mothers were far more supportive and communicated more often with children about technology use than did fathers (Eastin, Greenberg, & Hofschire, 2006). A small percentage of children felt they could talk to their parents about some online experiences (27% in the EU 27 asked for help with some difficulty online). More specifically, a small percentage of children who saw pornography online and were troubled by it, those who were bullied online, those who received a text message and were troubled by it, and those who met an online contact offline and were troubled by the experience, talked to their mother or father about these experiences (Haddon, 2012).

Our fast-paced world is defined by rapid technological and scientific advances. The ubiquity of smartphones and tablets is evident even in the poorest countries, but a divide exists between parents and children in technology use in most cultural communities. On their part, fathers and mothers in the developed world have moved beyond issues of restricting children from technology use to ensuring that their children use technology in productive and safe ways that are beneficial to learning about and communicating with the world. For those in the developing world, technology use remains elusive or exposure occurs through paternal and maternal use of cellphones or centers that offer children services at a cost. At the same time, schools in the developing world often lack resources to offer children adequate access to technology use. This scenario most certainly hinders opportunities for STEM activities in the poorer nations.

Paternal involvement and engagement and gender of child differences

Not the explicit focus of most studies reviewed herein, gender of child differences in paternal care and cognitive and social engagement were inconsistent across cultural communities. The differential treatment of boys and girls was more apparent in the areas of discipline, technology use, and playful interactions. Perhaps socioeconomic changes and women's employment patterns, greater emphasis on gender equality and scrutiny of gender inequality, family policies, and increased expectations connected to parental responsibilities may have led to more egalitarian social participation with children. There is also limited evidence of the differential treatment of young boys and girls in some of the more traditional societies with patriarchal traditions. As has been argued elsewhere, the differential treatment of boys and girls in more traditional societies where parents use indulgent approaches to childrearing may become more evident as children move into early and middle childhood (Jankowiak, Joiner, & Khatib, 2011; Roopnarine, 2011). Alternatively, it may be that in reality fathers are beginning to treat boys and girls more equitably, as is seen in a few son-preference cultural communities (e.g., in China).

Factors associated with paternal involvement

A lot of ground has been covered in this chapter with respect to the factors that influence paternal involvement with children. The more salient ones are related to family relationships (e.g., personal and interpersonal functioning), community stability and economic factors (e.g., neighborhood factors, economic opportunities, paternal leave policies), and characteristics of children themselves (e.g., age, gender, temperament, agency, behaviors). Economic circumstances, the quality of marital/couple relations and in cases of nonresident fathers the relationship with the child's mother, and the complex nature of new family forms can be formidable barriers to paternal investment and involvement with children (Ball & Moselle, 2015; Clark et al., 2015). Repartnering on both the man's and woman's part can complicate the level of economic support offered to children and hinder access to and involvement with children from prior unions. Time constraints, family type, and level of education predicted involvement in childcare by gay fathers (Farr & Patterson, 2013; Tornello, Sonnenberg, & Patterson, 2015).

General summary

We would like to conclude this chapter by reiterating a few issues about paternal involvement with children. Taken together, the variations in the levels and quality of paternal involvement in caring for and nurturing children's social and cognitive skills development across cultural communities are striking. Fathers in the developed world are far more likely to meet the demands of parenting children than those in the developing societies, but time and energy devoted to caring for children are far from egalitarian across all societies. This state of affairs may reflect differences in emphasis placed on early parental involvement in the home environment and community. Equally plausible is that rates of paternal involvement in the developing world are deeply tied to ideological beliefs about what it means to be a man and father, poor economic conditions, lack of knowledge about the importance of male parenting for family and child well-being, and poor neighborhood conditions.

While the increasing levels and quality of father involvement with children in developed societies are encouraging, the low rates of father involvement in so many of the world's developing nations raise some serious concerns. In the developing countries where home and neighborhood environments may not always be ideal for the promotion of early cognitive and social skills, quality paternal involvement and engagement could insulate children from well-known early risk factors associated with poor social and school outcomes. Along with essential material resources (e.g., books, transportation costs) they provide to children for learning, fathers' consistent sensitive care of children and their engagement in diverse cognitive and social activities with them may be crucial for setting a path to minimizing behavioral and social difficulties as children navigate their way through challenging home, neighborhood, and school environments. A discussion of the connections between father involvement and developmental outcomes in children follows next.

5

FATHER INVOLVEMENT AND CHILDHOOD OUTCOMES

As has been emphasized, there are wide variations in the different ways in which fathers are involved with children across cultural communities. Of paramount importance is how the levels and quality of paternal involvement influence different aspects of children's development. Are the patterns of influence consistent across cultural groups, and what factors might influence the connections between father involvement and different aspects of childhood development? As with most of the research on fathering, data are only now emerging on paternal involvement and childhood outcomes in recently developed societies (e.g., China), Islamic-based societies in the Middle East (Jordan, Saudi Arabia), and other developing nations in Asia, Africa, and Latin America and the Caribbean. A review is provided of the empirical literature on the associations between different facets of father involvement and children's social and cognitive development across cultural communities. An attempt is made to include unpublished studies to avoid the so-called file drawer effect. When possible, moderators and mediators of the links between paternal involvement and engagement activities and children's social and cognitive skills in different family constellations are specified.

There is satisfactory evidence from meta-analyses and careful reviews of fathering studies to state that the levels and quality of father–child involvement are associated with children's socio-emotional, behavioral, and cognitive skills across cultural communities (Adamson & Johnson, 2013; Connell & Goodman, 2002; Kim & Hill, 2015; McWayne, Downer, Campos, & Harris, 2013). A host of factors such as material resources, educational attainment, residential status, child gender, childhood characteristics (e.g., personal agency, temperament), relationship with the spouse/partner, ideological beliefs about parenting, and intrapersonal and interpersonal functioning can moderate and/or mediate the associations between the level and quality of father involvement and childhood development. Of course, children influence fathers' functioning and well-being, and mothers and fathers have joint or complementary and separate influences on childhood development through bidirectional or transactional socialization processes (Schermerhorn & Cummings, 2008).

Conceivably, the most frequent criticisms of this body of work are that the cultural pathways between father involvement and common childhood outcomes are not sufficiently delineated from one cultural community to the next, and that there is no clear specification of the direction of influence in most studies. For example, it is uncertain whether the cultural pathways themselves or the factors associated with specific pathways affect social and cognitive outcomes in children (Astone & Peters, 2014). Whatever the concerns about the equivalence of definitions of involvement across cultural communities and direction of influence, there are some fairly consistent findings on the links between paternal warmth and sensitivity, harsh parenting practices, and paternal risk factors and developmental outcomes in children (Harris, 2016; Khaleque & Rohner, 2013; Rohner & Khaleque, 2013; Ahmed et al., 2016; Sorkhhabi, 2005). While paternal time involvement per se is not a good predictor of childhood outcomes, both longitudinal and cross-sectional studies demonstrate that the quality of paternal involvement (e.g., warmth and sensitivity, attentiveness, and nurturance) has a positive influence on childhood development. Turning to examples of studies in the area, we commence with research on paternal sensitivity and father–child attachment.

Importance of father sensitivity and attachment security

As indicated in Chapter 2, fathers' ability to read and process children's cues in an attentive, reliable, and consistent manner is central to the formation of secure emotional bonds with offspring (DeWolff & van IJzendoorn, 1997; Lucassen et al., 2011). Paternal sensitivity, which broadly refers to warmth and responsiveness, the quality of interactions, and positive regard for the child, appears stable during the early childhood years (Braungart-Rieker et al., 2014) and is linked to father–child attachment security. Findings from studies carried out in Europe and North America point to the relations between paternal and maternal sensitivity across the early childhood years (Daniel, Madigan, & Jenkins, 2015; Hallers-Haalboom et al., 2017; von Wyl et al., 2008).

Higher levels of paternal sensitivity were associated with secure infant–father attachment across 16 observational studies involving 1,355 families with infants from mostly developed countries (Lucassen et al., 2011). This is in agreement with a previous meta-analysis on father–child attachment (van IJzendoorn & De Wolff, 1997). As also suggested in Chapter 2, the strength of the association between paternal sensitivity and father–child attachment was weaker than the association between maternal sensitivity and mother–child attachment in both meta-analyses, suggesting that other proximal and distal factors may potentially play a role in influencing the associations between paternal sensitivity and infant–father attachment security. Marital quality and couple/partner harmony appear key among them (Belsky, Fish, & Isabella, 1991; Lundy, 2002).

Paternal sensitivity provides a basis for increasing behaviors such as hugging, smiling, touching, playful activities, and eye contact during father–child interactions (Lamb & Lewis, 2010; 2013). Moreover, the degree of supportive presence, structure and limit setting, quality of instruction, confidence in engagement as well as the absence of paternal hostility, generational boundary dissolution, and intrusiveness (Brown, Mangelsdorf, & Neff, 2012), and supportive co-parenting and relationship quality can all affect paternal sensitivity and interactions with children (Luz, George, Vieux, & Splitz, 2017; Pudasainee-Kapri & Razza, 2015). Even a cursory inspection of studies in this area suggests that paternal sensitivity is foundational to meaningful engagement with children and that these interactions may strengthen parent–child closeness. For instance, paternal interactions strengthened father–infant closeness and paternal attunement to infant vocalizations and emotional expressions in Greek families (Kokkinaki, 2009; Kokkinaki & Vasdekis, 2015) and Portuguese fathers who had a secure attachment with their children reported higher levels of involvement in childcare tasks, play, and leisure activities (Fuertes, Faria, Beeghly, & Lopes-dos-Santos, 2016; Monteiro et al., 2010). Finnish fathers who had more autonomous representations and favorable childhood relationships with their attachment figure were more likely to have a secure attachment with their children (Kouvo, Voeten, & Silven, 2015).

Because of their implications for father–child relations and infant development, there is increasing interest in skin-to-skin (S2S) contact and father–infant attachment security. A review of the findings of 12 qualitative and quantitative studies conducted between 1995 and 2015 in Sweden, India, Germany, Canada, the United States, Denmark, and Colombia, concluded that father engagement in S2S contact with both pre-term and full-term infants enhanced fathers' understanding of their role as fathers, led to higher levels of paternal engagement in childcare activities, vocal communication, and paternal sensitivity, and lessened parenting stress and anxiety (Shorey, Hong-Gu, & Morelus, 2016). Positive outcomes of S2S as reflected in higher father–child attachment scores (FCAS) three days postpartum were also recorded for Taiwanese father–infant pairs (Chen, Gau, Liu, & Lee, 2017). An attempt to reduce cortisol levels in premature infants using S2S contact with Iranian fathers in the Neonatal Intensive Care Unit was less successful (Mirnia, Bostanabad, Asadollahi, & Razzaghi, 2016).

A central question is: how do close father–child bonds influence childhood development? As has been stated already, father–child attachment security lays the groundwork for building trust and for developing social relationships with others (Schneider, Atkinson, & Tardif, 2001). Paternal bonding assessed at six months was associated with lower levels of paternal parenting stress at 24 months, which in turn predicted lower levels of executive functioning problems in children in the Netherlands (de Cock et al., 2017). Father–child attachment was associated with social competence and less internalizing behaviors in boys in the United States (Marcus & Mirle, 1990), to enhanced self-efficacy in Chinese children (Lu & Zhang, 2008), to less anxious/withdrawn behavior problems but not children's positiveness in Belgian children (Verschueren & Marcoen, 1999), and to reciprocal friendships in Portuguese children (Verissimo et al., 2011). Among children (74 published and unpublished manuscripts $N = 55,537$ participants) in several western countries (e.g., Belgium, Germany, Portugal, the Netherlands, United Kingdom, and the United States), poor father–child attachment was significantly associated with delinquent behaviors but it was stronger for mothers ($r = .21$) than for fathers ($r = .19$) and was stronger for parent and child with the same sex (Hoeve et al., 2012).

Few would doubt that secure father–child attachment is a powerful mechanism for charting a postive course for meaningful involvement with children. The trust children build in the process of developing secure relationships with their fathers enhances social competence and reduces behaviorial risks in children. Based mostly on research conducted in North America and Europe, a major mechanism in the development of father–child attachment is sensitivity. We venture to speculate it may have the same significance for paternal parenting in cultural communities in the developing world as well.

Father involvement and children's social skills

There have been sophisticated discussions on the levels and quality of paternal care and children's social development (see Harris, 2015; Lamb & Lewis, 2010, 2013; Li & Lamb, 2015; Roopnarine & Hossain, 2013). While there is good support for the contention that the quality of father involvement in social activities is positively associated with children's behavioral skills, the influence of routine forms of paternal care on childhood social development is less convincing. Nevertheless, there is increasing evidence that fathers may have as much influence in some areas of children's social development as do mothers, but the associations are inconsistent across cultural communities.

Enough studies infer that fathers' attentiveness and nurturance are associated with positive social skills in children. Warmth, responsiveness, and appropriate limit setting are integral properties of the more desirable authoritative parenting style that espouses democratic principles in childrearing. The consistent use of different aspects of attributes in the authoritative style of parenting seems to encourage the positive development of social skills across cultural communities. Fathers in the United States who are warm and emotionally responsive had children who were less emotionally reactive (Byrd-Craven, Auer, Granger, & Massey, 2012) and were better at extending social overtures to other children (Baker, Fenning, & Crnic, 2011). Father–child relationship quality at 54 months predicted children's emotional regulation and sustained attention in first grade, which in turn were related to better peer functioning in third grade (NICHD Early Child Care Research Network Study, 2009). A Canadian study (Daniel, Madigan, & Jenkins, 2015) showed that children's prosocial behavior and maternal and paternal warmth when children were 18 months of age predicted prosocial behavior at 36 months of age, which in turn was associated with children's prosocial behavior at 54 months of age after controlling for child age and gender, maternal and paternal education, and family assets and income (see also Kroll, Carson, Redshaw, & Quigley, 2016). These trends were not restricted to children in heterosexual families. Quality parenting by gay fathers was related to better social outcomes in children in England and the United States (Golombok, 2010; Golombok et al., 2014).

Similarly, among Chinese children, paternal involvement was associated with better cooperativeness and social skills (Liu & Li, 2013) and paternal warmth, understanding, and nonpunitiveness were associated with better social skills and mental health outcomes (see reviews by Li & Lamb, 2013, 2015; Yang, 2010). In Japanese families, children with good emotional regulation had fathers who imposed structure and limits during play, showed respect for autonomy, and were sensitive to children's talk (Kato & Kondo, 2007) and father participation in childrearing was related to social abilities in preschoolers (Kato, Ishii-Kuntz, Makino, & Tsuchiya, 2002). A meta-analysis of 16 studies ($N = 1,521$) from developed societies revealed weak to moderate associations between father–child physical play and childhood aggression, self-regulation, social competence, and emotional skills (St George & Freeman, 2017). By contrast, there were few significant associations between composite routine forms of care and children's behaviors in the UK Millennium Study, which is similar to what was discovered for Australian fathers and children (Baxter & Smart, 2011), fathers and children in the Avon Longitudinal Study of Parents and Children (ALSPAC) in the southwest of England (Opondo, Redshaw, & Quigley, 2017), and in different family constellations in communities in the developing nations of Barbados, Belize, Guyana, the Dominican Republic, Jamaica, and Suriname (Dede Yildirim & Roopnarine, 2017). However, a lack of father involvement in childcare during infancy predicted children's susceptibility to adverse mental health at the age of nine in families in the United States (Boyce et al., 2006).

A meta-analysis (Khaleque & Rohner, 2012) of 66 studies on parental acceptance – rejection (23 published and 43 unpublished) with a total of 19,511 participants in 21 countries and a commonwealth of the United States (Bangladesh, Barbados, Colombia, Czechoslovakia, Egypt, Estonia, India, Iran, Jamaica, Korea, Kuwait, Mexico, Nigeria, Pakistan, Peru, Puerto Rico, Romania, Spain, Sweden, St. Kitts, Turkey, and the United States), and a review of studies on family relationships in Middle Eastern countries (Ahmed et al, 2016) confirm the positive contribution of paternal warmth to children's social skills. As might be expected, caring and accepting paternal and maternal parenting practices were associated with good social adjustment in children and adolescents across a number of societies and in some cases the associations were better for fathers than for mothers (see also Ahmed, Rohner, & Carrasco, 2012; Groh, Roisman, van IJzendoorn, Bakermans-Kranenberg, & Fearon, 2012; Hughes, Blom, Rohner, & Britner, 2005; Li & Lamb, 2013, 2015).

It is also the case that positive paternal parenting offers a protective function against negative childhood behavioral outcomes. A systematic review (Sarkadi, Kristiansson, Oberklaid, & Bremberg, 2008) of 16 longitudinal studies involving 22,300 father–child dyads concluded that consistent father involvement with offspring led to a decrease in delinquency and economic disadvantage in low-income families (see also Flouri & Malmberg, 2012). Another meta-analysis involving 13 studies with samples from diverse ethnic backgrounds (e.g., African American, Caribbean immigrants in the United States) surmised that active (e.g., communication, engaging in activities) and passive father involvement (general presence and financial support) led to lower socio-emotional problems in children (Harris, 2015).

Positive psychological and the emotive qualities of involvement, but not quantity of direct involvement by fathers early in a child's life or security in role as parent and partner, reduced the odds of depressive symptoms when children in the United Kingdom were 9 and 11 years of age, after controlling for children's age, gender, family socioeconomic status, parity, and maternal and paternal depressive symptoms (Opondo et al., 2017). In a like manner, children's internalizing behavior was negatively related to quality of father–child play interactions in Austrian and German families (Ahnert et al., 2017) and in the Dutch cohort study Generation R (N = 1,523), paternal responsibility was related to lower behavioral difficulties in toddlers after controlling for family sociodemographic variables, parental psychopathology, and levels of stress and conflict in the family (Keizer, Lucassen, Jaddoe, & Tiemeier, 2014; see also Sarkadi et al., 2008). Higher levels of paternal and maternal playfulness were associated with lower negativity in children in Israeli families (Menashe-Grinberg & Atzaba-Poria, 2017). Among older children from 12 school districts in Taipei, Taiwan, higher levels of father involvement (perception of paternal support, supervision, and warmth) were associated with lower levels of internalizing and externalizing behaviors and higher self-esteem (Su, Kubricht, & Miller, 2017), and paternal devotion was associated with fewer externalizing and higher prosocial behaviors in 6–10 year-old children of Korean immigrants in New Zealand (Lee et al., 2016). Japanese adolescents who experienced intimate father–child relationships had a lower propensity to delinquency (Obokata & Muto, 2005).

Data from the Pacific Islands Families Study too showed that father involvement (e.g., school encouragement, support, attentiveness) was associated with lower levels of internalizing and externalizing behaviors in 6-year-old children controlling for paternal age and education, race/ethnicity, maternal relationship, weekly household income, and potential mental disorder (Tautolo et al., 2015). In two different samples of families in Spain, maternal and paternal warmth were negatively associated with children's and adolescents' depressive symptoms concurrently and longitudinally but the effect was weaker for fathers than for mothers (del Barrio, Holgado-Tello, & Carrasco, 2016), and higher paternal involvement was associated with less paternal rejection, which in turn, was associated with lower levels of internalizing and externalizing behaviors in children (Ruiz, Holgado-Tello, & Carrasco, 2017).

In an attempt to assess the cross-lagged links between paternal involvement and childhood socioemotional difficulties, Flouri and colleagues (Flouri, Midouhas, & Narayanan, 2016) explored the extent to which English fathers' involvement was related to children's hyperactivity, conduct problems, emotional symptoms, and peer problems at ages 3, 5, and 7, controlling for fathers' education level, mothers' and fathers' emotional disturbance, interparental relationship, family poverty, ethnicity, sibship size, and mothers' involvement. The association between father involvement and lower behavioral difficulties was weak at age 3, but father involvement at age 5 was negatively linked to children's peer problems at age 7, whereas conduct problems and hyperactivity at age 3 were linked to increasing levels of fathers' involvement at age 5, suggesting that children's behavioral difficulties may have instigated more paternal investment over time. Put differently, out of necessity children's behavioral difficulties may have recruited more paternal attention.

Most existing studies have focused on resident biological fathers and childhood behavioral outcomes. A fair amount of energy has gone into examining how fathers' relationship stability with the child's mother and frequency of contacts postdivorce and post-separation among couples who lived together affect childhood functioning (see reviews by Amato & Gilbreth, 1999; Adamsons & Johnson, 2013). As laid out in Chapter 3, there are several factors (e.g., interpersonal and sociodemographic) that influence fathers' contacts with children after relationship dissolution (Cheadle et al., 2010). In a meta-analysis of 52 studies of nonresident father involvement and childhood outcomes, paternal involvement showed the strongest associations with child social and emotional well-being and was associated with social adjustment, and academic achievement. Paternal involvement in child-related activities, positive father–child relationship, and being involved in multiple activities were related to child well-being. Paying child support and overall contact were not associated with child well-being (Adamsons & Johnson, 2013). In the UK Millennium Cohort Study, nonresident father involvement was not related to later childhood behavior, but early and later nonresident father involvement were related (Flouri & Malmberg, 2012).

Nonresident fathers' support and contact (e.g., in person, telephone) after divorce were associated with children's short-term and long-term behavior problems (Choi & Jackson, 2011). By using latent profile analysis, Elam, Sandler, Wolchik, and Tein (2016) were able to determine the heterogeneity that exists among non-resident fathers in the United States based on levels of support, contact, and interparental conflict and childhood outcomes. Four distinct father involvement and interparental conflict groups were identified: high contact–moderate conflict–moderate support; low contact–moderate conflict–low support; high conflict–moderate contact–moderate support; and low conflict–moderate contact–moderate support. Children whose fathers fell into the low contact–moderate conflict–low support group had higher levels of internalizing and externalizing behaviors in the 6 years following divorce compared with children whose fathers fell into the high conflict–moderate contact–moderate support group. Other studies (Modecki, Hagan, Sandler, & Wolchik, 2015) have also documented that father–child contact and relationship quality were significantly associated with interparental conflict and children's well being in German families, and that marital hostility, difficulties in co-parenting, and ineffective discipline were good predictors of childhood aggression in Israeli and Palestinian families (Feldman, Masalha, & Derdikman-Eiron, 2010).

Men also parent children before, during, and after extended periods of separation from them due to military service. Military deployments to Iraq, Afghanistan, and other countries have increased dramatically after the September 11 attacks in the United States (Murphey & Mae Cooper, 2015). Deployed fathers not only face several immediate and long-term personal challenges (e.g., mental health, substance abuse), they find it difficult to stay involved and engaged with their children (e.g., communication). An analysis of 26 studies on the impact of military deployment on families and children showed that frequent and extended deployments increased parenting stress and depressive symptoms, affected couple and family functioning, and had a negative impact on general well-being. Young children whose parents were deployed exhibited more emotional and behavioral difficulties than children who did not experience deployment separation. Family reunification posed other threats to children's social adjustment as well (Trautmann, Alhusen, & Gross, 2015).

Maladaptive parenting

There is no denying that fathers' maladaptive behaviors, such as hostility, rejection, neglect, and being overly controlling have direct and indirect effects on children's behavioral difficulties. Two sets of studies shed light on this issue: one deals with maladaptive parenting practices and childhood behavioral difficulties and the other focuses on paternal psychopathology and childhood behavioral difficulties. It is beyond the scope of this chapter to discuss how parental psychopathology affects parenting or psychological functioning in fathers. What we do know is that maladaptive paternal parenting practices are affected by psychopathology in men themselves, but somewhat modestly, as demonstrated in a meta-analysis of 28 studies (Wilson & Durbin, 2010). However, subsequent studies have found stronger negative associations between paternal depressive symptoms and positive parenting, and positive associations between paternal depressive symptoms and inconsistent discipline in German families (Dette-Hagenmeyer & Reichle, 2014), to child maltreatment tendencies such as not feeding the child, yelling, spanking, slapping, or hitting the child, leaving the child alone in the house or car among Japanese fathers (Takehara, Suto, Kakee, Tachibana, & Mori, 2017), and to less social and cognitive engagement (e.g., singing, reading, telling stories) with infants in the United States (Paulson, Dauber, & Leiferman, 2006).

Starting with maladaptive paternal parenting practices, overcontrol was positively associated with children's and adolescents' anxiety levels in the Netherlands (Verhoeven, Bögels, & van der Bruggen, 2012), inept discipline at age 10 was directly associated with externalizing behavior at age 13 in Belgian children (Slagt et al., 2012), and paternal discipline was inversely related to social competence in Brazilian children after controlling for maternal discipline (Benetti & Roopnarine, 2006). Paternal hostility was associated with internalizing behavior problems among Italian children with disruptive behavioral disorders (Cerniglia et al., 2017), fathers' punitive, rejecting, and overprotective behavioral styles predicted behavioral difficulties, and paternal intrusiveness was associated with internet addiction in Chinese children (e.g., Guo & Wang, 2009; Shen, Wu, & Zhou, 2006; Xie, Zhang, & Li, 2009; Zhang, Chen, Zhang, Zhou, & Wu, 2008).

Other aspects of paternal functioning such as persistent father–child conflict, power control, and inflexibility increase the risk of behavioral difficulties in children. Among mainland Chinese families, father–child conflict was negatively associated with preschoolers' social competence over time (Zhang, 2013), and the frequency and intensity of father–child conflicts in Taiwanese families were directly and positively associated with adolescents' internalizing behavior, aggression, and deviant behavior (Yeh, Tsao, & Chen, 2009). Social isolation among Japanese adolescents was attributed to paternal strictness and inflexibility (Hanashima, 2007; Igarashi & Hagiwara, 2004) and children with authoritarian fathers were seen as more aggressive by their teachers compared with children whose fathers were authoritative or permissive (Nakamichi & Nakazawa, 2003). Likewise, Italian adolescents who perceived their fathers as neglectful, as determined by their acceptance/involvement and strictness/supervision, reported higher levels of externalizing behaviors and lower levels of satisfaction with the family than adolescents who perceived their fathers as authoritative, authoritarian, or indulgent (Di Maggio & Zappulla, 2014; see also Rinaldi & Howe, 2012).

There are situations in which the associations between paternal hostility and rejection and childhood difficulties are not as strong or may be affected by the normativeness of control in childrearing. Associations between paternal rejection and adolescent psychological disorders were mixed in France, Poland, and Argentina compared with adolescents in Kuwait, Algeria, Saudi Arabia, Israel (Bedouin), Jordan, and India where parental control in childrearing is routine. Relative to those in the Middle East and India, adolescents in France, Poland, and Argentina seem particularly susceptible to paternal rejection (Dwairy, 2009). Father control was only associated with children's psychological disorder in the western but not the other countries. It was opined, and we agree, that this may be due to the normative use of control in childrearing in the Middle East and India than in France, Poland, and Argentina (Dwairy, 2009; see also Roopnarine et al., 2013).

What we find especially interesting is that the associations between parental acceptance–rejection and childhood behaviors appear quite stable across some cultural groups over time. This was demonstrated in a cross-cultural longitudinal study (Putnick et al., 2015) of families and 7–10 year-old children in China, Colombia, Italy, Jordan, Kenya, the Philippines, Sweden, Thailand, and the United States. Over a 3-year period, higher levels of paternal and maternal rejection were associated with internalizing and externalizing behavioral difficulties and lower prosocial behaviors after controlling for within-wave relations, stability across waves, parental age, educational attainment, and social desirability bias. Pathways of associations between maternal parenting and childhood outcomes and paternal parenting and child outcomes were not significantly different across the nine countries (see also Khaleque, 2017; Ahmed et al, 2016).

The genetic transmission of mental health disorders in mothers and fathers, risks associated with prenatal development, and stressors within the family and neighborhood all affect the associations between psychological disturbance in fathers and childhood development (see Connell & Goodman, 2002; Phares, 2010). From authoritative reviews and meta-analyses on paternal psychopathology and childhood social outcomes (e.g., Connell & Goodman, 2002; Kane & Garber, 2004; Phares & Compass, 1992; Phares, 2010), it is clear that paternal mental health problems (e.g., alcoholism, substance abuse, depression, anxiety disorder, bipolar disorder, schizophrenia) have a negative impact on a range of children's social behaviors that in some cases approximate what was determined for mothers (Connell & Goodman, 2002; Goodman & Brand, 2008; Phares & Compass, 1992) and become worse as children age (Scourfield et al., 2016). As an illustration, fathers' externalizing difficulties such as alcoholism and antisocial behavior increased the risk of behavioral difficulties (anxiety sensitivity, conduct problems) in children (Eiden, Colder, Edwards, & Leonard, 2009; Goodman & Brand, 2008). Because paternal depression and interpartner violence have received increased attention in the area of fathering studies, the focus here is solely on these two paternal risk factors and their implications for childhood functioning.

Within a developmental psychopathology framework, paternal depression and intimate partner violence are two major risk factors that can create a formidable barrier to optimal parenting and adequate social adjustment in childhood. Depression can severely impair parents' ability to address and meet the emotional and cognitive needs of their children (Field, 1998, 2010; Malphurs et al., 1996; Paulson et al., 2006), affect parent–child interactions (Parfitt, Pike & Ayers, 2013), heighten the odds of child neglect (Lee, Taylor & Bellamy, 2012) and disrupt marital harmony through negative communication and interactions and social withdrawal from spouse/partner (Papp, Goeke-Morey, & Cummings, 2007; Ramchandani et al., 2011). Worse yet, interpartner violence exposes children to potential physical injury in attempts to protect a parent, enduring feelings of isolation through the controlling behavior of the perpetrator, constant stress and tensions, and being the recipient of violence directly (DeBoard-Lucas & Grych, 2011; Gewirtz & Edelson, 2007; see meta-analysis by Kitzmann, Gaylord, Holt, & Kenny, 2003).

Paternal depression increases the odds of behavioral difficulties in children twofold in developed countries (Ramchandani et al., 2008). A meta-analysis of 21 studies outlined the associations between prenatal and postnatal depression and later behavioral difficulties in children (Sweeney & MacBeth, 2016). Paternal depression during the immediate post-birth period had sustaining effects on behavioral difficulties during the early childhood years among Japanese children (Takehara et al., 2017), and paternal depression during the first year of a child's life was linked to behavioral difficulties at school entry in Australian children (Fletcher et al., 2011), but paternal antenatal depression and anxiety did not increase the risk of anxiety and depression in children in the United Kingdom (Capron et al., 2015). In other studies, paternal prenatal symptoms (depression, anxiety, PTSD) were associated with paternal unresponsiveness and infant passivity, while paternal postnatal symptoms were associated with difficulties in father–child interactions in families in Sussex, England (Parfitt et al., 2013) and fathers' anxiety-depression and aggression was related to oppositional defiant disorder in Spanish children (Antúnez et al., 2018). Paternal psychopathology (depression/anxiety symptoms) was related to children's internalizing and externalizing behaviors in a mixed-ethnic sample in the United States and in cultural communities elsewhere (Breaux, Harvey, & Lugo-Candales, 2014; Kane & Garber, 2004; Ramchandani & Psychogiou, 2009; Weitzman, Rosenthal, & Liu, 2011).

Under certain conditions, paternal parenting practices (e.g. positive parenting, warmth) and social support can mediate the negative consequences of depression on children's behavioral difficulties (Dette-Hagenmeyer & Reichle, 2014). Among older children paternal support seems to lessen depressive symptoms in Italian (Graziano, Bonino, & Cattelino, 2009) and Japanese adolescents (Oshima, 2013). This mediating function has not been consistently demonstrated in different ethnic (e.g., African Americans, Hispanic Americans, European Americans) and cultural groups in the developed world (Germany, England, and the United States) (e.g., Roopnarine & Dede Yildirim, 2017).

Violence perpetrated by men against their spouse/partner can have direct effects on children's mental health and well-being (DeBoard-Lucas & Grych, 2011). Exposure to intimate partner violence is related to externalizing behaviors in children (Holmes, 2013), to trauma symptoms in infancy (Bogat, DeJonghe, Levendosky, Davidson, & von Eye, 2006), and to child neglect (Hamby, Finkelhor, Turner, & Ormrod, 2010). An analysis of data from the Building Strong Families Study, a large-scale intervention that provided relationship skills education to European American, Hispanic American, and African American fathers across eight sites, revealed a direct association between interpartner violence by fathers and children's internalizing and externalizing behaviors for men in the noncomplier (offered intervention services but did not attend) and control groups (Roopnarine & Dede Yildirim, 2017). For fathers in the complier group who received intervention services, avoidance of destructive conflict behavior mediated the association between interpartner violence and children's externalizing behavior. Paternal warmth did not mediate the associations between interpartner violence and children's behavioral difficulties for any group, suggesting that intimate partner violence may have more direct effects on childhood functioning.

From this selective review of studies conducted mostly in developed societies, the quality of father involvement had positive associations with children's social skills and seems to offer a protective function against behavioral difficulties. Maladaptive paternal parenting behaviors, and fathers' depressive symptoms and interpartner violence, have more severe consequences for childhood functioning. Of course, one may very well argue that the effect sizes for the associations across some studies and meta-analyses are rather small – a concern that raises it head consistently in research on fathers.

Father engagement and cognitive outcomes

Models of human development (Bronfenbrenner & Morris, 2006) and early learning (Epstein, 1990) stress the nexus between the home and school environments as important for children's early intellectual development. Sufficient studies in the child development and early childhood education literature point to the nature of the home learning environment (HLE) as essential for fostering the development of early literacy skills and for the successful transition to formal schooling (Bus, van IJzendoorn, & Pellegrini, 1995; Martini & Sénéchal, 2012; Rodriguez & Tamis-LeMonda, 2011). By virtue of their rich properties, father–child activities, such as building things together, playing, shared book reading, and telling stories can stimulate cognitive growth in children (Adamson & Johnson, 2013; Dede Yildirim & Roopnarine, 2018) and paternal involvement in school-related activities can enrich children's learning (Hill & Taylor, 2004; Wilder, 2014). Data from the developed and developing world indicate that different modes of paternal cognitive engagement are associated with children's intellectual functioning, both directly and indirectly.

Analyzing 21 studies conducted primarily in the United States (five studies were conducted in Turkey, New Zealand, Wales, the Netherlands, and Canada) over a 10-year period (1998–2008), McWayne, Downer, Campos, and Harris (2013) found that the overall quantity of fathers' positive engagement activities (e.g., physical and pretend play, reading to child, assisting with homework) was positively linked to children's cognitive/academic skills (grades, emergent literacy/numeracy, standardized achievement scores), and that the quality of father engagement such as positive parenting (e.g., authoritative, use of explanations, responsiveness, cognitive stimulation) was also favorably associated with children's cognitive/academic skills. Father ethnicity and residential status tempered the associations between paternal engagement and children's cognitive/academic skills.

The aforementioned associations were confirmed in a different meta-analysis of 66 studies which found that the positive effects of father engagement on children's cognitive skills extended beyond the early childhood years (Jeynes, 2015). There was a stronger association between father engagement and cognitive/academic outcomes for residential (sample consisted of 70% or more residential fathers) than nonresidential fathers (sample consisted of 70% or more nonresidential fathers) or mixed-status fathers and for white than non-white fathers (McWayne et al., 2013), but the race/ethnicity differences were inconsistent across studies and in different meta-analyses (see Jeynes, 2015). Nonresident fathers' contact frequency, support, and father–child relationship closeness were associated with children's cognitive skills, after considering the role of household resources such as the number of books in the home, maternal educational attainment and occupation, and household income (Tanskanen & Erola, 2017). Nonresident fathers' contributions to families' economic well-being, such as paying child support and buying goods and services, were related to better cognitive outcomes among low-income children (Amato & Gilbreth, 1999; Carlson & Magnuson, 2011).

A later review of 19 studies all conducted in the United States over a 20-year period (1994–2014) focused more specifically on paternal involvement and literacy and language outcomes in children (Varghese & Wachen, 2016). African American fathers' home literacy involvement was related to children's reading and mathematics scores (Baker, 2013). Father book reading was associated with cognitive and language skills, and book knowledge in low-income toddlers (Duursma, Pan, & Raikes, 2008). Pancsofar and Vernon-Feagans (2006) also reported that fathers' vocabulary use during book-reading activities was positively associated with children's communication development at 15 months and children's expressive language development at 36 months in families in the United States.

Beyond rates of engagement, the quality of paternal parenting and the complexity of involvement in cognitive activities provide more support for the contributions of fathers to children's intellectual development. Fathers' observed sensitivity, positive regard, and cognitive stimulation were positively associated with children's language and cognitive skills among low-income families in the United States (Tamis-LeMonda, Shannon, Cabrera, & Lamb, 2004) and fathers' warmth, support, and supervision were related to higher academic performance among older children in Taiwan (Su, Kubricht, & Miller, 2017), and to effortful control in Chinese children (Liang et al., 2013). Using data from the Early Childhood Longitudinal Study in the United States ($N = 6,270$ infants), Bronte-Tinkew, Carrano, Horowitz, and Kinukawa (2008) found that engagement in cognitively stimulating activities (e.g., reading, telling stories, and singing), physical care (e.g., changing diapers, preparing meals, feeding), caregiving activities (e.g., bathing, dressing,), nurturing activities (e.g., soothing infants, taking to doctor), and paternal warmth (e.g., holding, tickling) were less likely to be associated with delayed babbling and exploring objects with a purpose. Paternal language complexity was also positively associated with children's picture vocabulary and applied problem scores (Baker & Vernon-Feagans, 2015; Fagan, Iglesias, & Kaufman, 2016).

Whereas positive paternal involvement is associated with desirable cognitive outcomes in children, controlling and negative paternal parenting can impede children's intellectual development. Chinese fathers in Hong Kong who were indifferent and dictatorial had children who performed less well on measures of academic performance, interest in school work, aspiration for education, involvement in extracurricular activities, and efficacy for self-regulated learning than their counterparts whose fathers were determined to be inductive and indulgent (Tam & Lam, 2003). Building on her earlier study, Tam (2009) further assessed the associations between maternal and paternal nurturance and psychological control, parental involvement in education, parental academic efficacy and the academic performance of grades 3–5 in Hong Kong. Fathers' academic efficacy was positively associated with academic performance for girls, whereas mothers' psychological control was negatively associated with academic performance for boys.

In agreement with the above, Tynkkynen, Vuori, and Salmela-Aro (2012) reported that higher paternal psychological control was related to lower educational aspirations and lower grade point average among school-aged Finnish children. Harsh paternal parenting predicted children's emergent metacognition problems and inhibitory self-control problems at age 4 in families in Rotterdam, the Netherlands after controlling for children's gender, gestational age at birth, parents' and children's age, household income, maternal and paternal stress, and child behavior problems and cognitive functioning at age 3 (Lucassen et al., 2015). Paternal authoritarian parenting at age 11 was indirectly associated with adolescents' academic competence at age 13 via adolescents' engagement with school in a Swiss study (Stutz & Schwarz, 2014), and higher levels of father rejection were associated with lower academic performance in children in China, Colombia, Italy, Jordan, Kenya, the Philippines, Sweden, Thailand, and the United States over a 3-year period (Putnick et al., 2015). High frequencies of paternal spanking at age 5 was related to suppressed receptive vocabulary scores at age 9 in low-income families in the United States (MacKenzie et al., 2013).

Along with harsh and inappropriate parenting, father's mental health can have unfavorable effects on children's school performance. A large-scale study (Shen et al., 2016) conducted on 1,124,162 children (48.9% female) born in Sweden determined the associations between paternal and maternal depression assessed before birth, after birth, and during ages 1–5, 6–10, 11–16, and before children's final year of schooling and academic performance. Depression was based on the International Classification of Diseases (8th, 9th Revisions, ICD 8 and ICD 9) and the International Statistical Classification of Diseases (10th Revision, ICD 10) diagnoses from inpatient records from 1969 and outpatient records starting in 2001. Paternal and maternal depression at different periods had a negative impact on school performance. Maternal depression had more severe effects on the performance of girls than that of boys.

From a methodological standpoint, it is not sufficient to determine associations between paternal engagement and cognitive outcomes in children without considering maternal input into children's lives. Do fathers contribute to children's cognitive functioning beyond what mothers do in families? Roopnarine, Krishnakumar, Metindogan, and Evans (2006) examined the individual and joint effects of maternal and paternal parenting styles, parent–child academic involvement at home, and parent–school interaction on children's academic skills among Caribbean immigrant parents and their preschool-aged children living in the northeastern United States. Mothers' parenting styles, involvement in academic activities, and parent–school contact were not associated with children's academic skills. When the associations between maternal and paternal variables and academic outcomes were analyzed separately, father's authoritarian parenting style was negatively, and father–school contact was positively associated with children's vocabulary skills. After including fathers' and mothers' parenting styles in the same model, fathers' authoritarian parenting was found to negatively predict children's vocabulary skills above and beyond maternal parenting styles and maternal involvement. The unique contribution of fathers to children's cognitive development has been reported in other studies (see Tamis-LeMonda, Baumwell, & Cabrera, 2013).

In their meta-analysis, Dede Yildirim and Roopnarine (2018) used datasets from the Multiple Indicator Cluster Surveys (UNICEF, 2015) to assess whether maternal and paternal engagement in play, book reading, and storytelling were associated with children's literacy skills in the developing nations of Africa. The sample consisted of 50,005 preschool-aged children and their caregivers from 18 African countries (Algeria, Central Africa, Chad, the Democratic Republic of Congo, Guinea-Bissau,

Kenya, Madagascar, Malawi, Mauritania, Nigeria, Sao Tome, Sierra Leone, Somalia, Swaziland, Togo, Tunisia, and Zimbabwe). A goal was to assess the relative contributions of playing with the child, book reading, and storytelling to children's early literacy skills such as identifying letters, reading words, and rcognizing symbols. Although paternal engagement in play, book reading, and storytelling with children was low across these African countries, fathers' book reading was linked to identifying letters in Algeria, Central African Republic, Chad, Malawi, Nigeria, Somalia, Togo, and Tunisia, and to reading words in Chad, the Democratic Republic of Congo, Malawi, Nigeria, Somalia, Tunisia, and Zimbabwe, and it was linked to recognizing symbols in Chad, Malawi, Nigeria, Somalia, and Togo. Fathers' storytelling was linked to identifying letters in Ghana, to reading words in Chad, Nigeria, and Togo, and to recognizing symbols in Algeria. Fathers' engagement in play was associated with identifying letters, reading words, and recognizing symbols in Nigeria and to recognizing symbols in Zimbabwe. From these associations, it is tempting to conclude that paternal book reading was more effective in promoting early literacy skills than storytelling or play among children in African families.

Another set of analyses (Dede Yildirim & Roopnarine, 2017) that relied on the MICS data explored the associations between paternal and maternal cognitive engagement (reading, telling stories, and counting) and preschoolers' (N = 11,473) literacy skills in the Caribbean countries of Barbados, Belize, the Dominican Republic, Jamaica, Guyana, and Suriname. Maternal cognitive engagement was related to children's literacy skills in Belize, Guyana, and the Dominican Republic, while paternal cognitive engagement was related to children's literacy skills in Barbados and Guyana. It is likely that the low levels of cognitive engagement across countries may have contributed to these inconsistent findings. Of note is that compared to paternal cognitive engagement, household wealth and number of books in the home were the most reliable predictors of children's early literacy skills across Caribbean countries. It is entirely possible that in poor ecological niches in the developing world where fathers have low educational attainment, preschool education and literacy materials provide other more sustained opportunities for cognitive engagement than paternal parenting alone. Indeed, studies in the United States show that educational attainment and income disparities affected parents use of language with children (see the classic study by Hart & Risley, 1995).

Broadly conceived, other investigations carried out in the developing world paint a similar picture of the associations between paternal involvement and engagement and children's cognitive skills. A small-sample study of families in Nairobi county, Kenya showed that preschool-aged children performed better on number, word, and language activities if their fathers were engaged in assisting them with academic related work at home compared with those whose fathers were preoccupied with paying school fees and buying school materials such as books (Wanjiku, 2016). A close trend emerged from a study conducted in the Gucha District of Kenya, where a small but significant positive relationship was found between paternal involvement in education and preschoolers' academic performance and the type of school children attended (Mwoma, 2009; 2015). Research from elsewhere in the developing world demonstrates associations between paternal availability and children's mathematics and language skills and school readiness at age 6 in Turkish children (Alici, 2012) and grade point average among Turkish children in Cyprus (Erdogan, 2011), between paternal availability and encouragement (asking about school, attending school activities, arranging for a tutor) and children's test scores on national examinations in Bangladesh (Hossain, 2013; Hossain et al., 2005), and between father acceptance and Kuwaiti and Saudi children's language development (see Ahmed, 2013).

As researchers continue to draw links between the level and quality of paternal involvement and children's cognitive skills, some pancultural trends are emerging. Fathers' engagement in literacy-based activities such as book reading and academic activities at home are associated with positive cognitive outcomes in children in several cultural settings and in families from different socioeconomic backgrounds across the world. Probably a major drawback is that the correlations and effect sizes are rather small and mothers' contributions to the associations between paternal engagement and children's cognitive skills were not teased out in a number of investigations. Even so, we wish to stress that the practical significance of paternal engagement for advancing children's early intellectual skills in different ecological niches appears compelling.

Benefits to fathers

Much of the preceding has focused primarily on how father involvement influences childhood development. It is appropriate to briefly consider the benefits men accrue from fathering. Paternal involvement with children brings several benefits to men, their communities, and workplace. From the developed and developing world, men report feeling moved and elated after learning about pregnancy and after being present at the birth of their child and sharing the childbirth experience (Howart et al., 2017; Yogman & Garfield, the Committee on the Psychological Aspects of Child and Family Health, 2016). For example, men report physiological symptoms and behavioral changes during the transition to fatherhood in different cultural communities (Brennan et al., 2007; Finnbogadóttir et al., 2003; Plantin et al., 2011), find it rewarding to be involved with their children (Cabrera, Fagan, & Farrie, 2008; Fagan, 2014), and view having children as a way of leaving copies of themselves behind (Marsiglio, 2009) and as investing in social capital (Astone, Nathanson, Schoen, & Kim, 1999).

Fathers derive more direct benefits from involvement with children (Eggebeen & Knoester, 2001; Levtov et al., 2015). Men who have close relationships with their children enjoy better mental health, have healthier lifestyles, and are more productive at work (Burgess, 2006). Perhaps this is due to their social connectedness with family members and their communities and their avoidance of risk-taking behaviors (Eggebeen, Dew, & Knoester, 2010; Eggebeen & Knoester, 2001; Knoester & Eggebeen, 2006; Knoester, Petts, & Eggebeen, 2007; Nomaguchi & Milkie, 2003; Astone & Peters, 2014). These associations likely vary by family constellation and residential status. Divorced fathers tend to maintain more contact with children over time than never-married fathers (Adamsons & Johnson, 2013), and paternal involvement by itself may work in conjunction with other factors to bring greater satisfaction and longevity to men who bear children.

Summary

Knitting together this body of work on paternal influences on childhood development across cultural communities, there are some definite pan-cultural trends in the associations between the levels and quality of paternal involvement in social and cognitive activities and children's social and intellectual skills. No matter the culture, paternal sensitivity, warmth and nurturance, and limit setting, all hallmarks of authoritative parenting, contribute to children's social and cognitive competence and appear to inoculate children from behavioral difficulties. The negative consequences of harsh and restricting paternal parenting are also consistent across cultural communities. A number of studies did not control for maternal contributions in determining these outcomes. Nevertheless, the findings laid out in this chapter provide some convincing evidence of the role of fathers in facilitating children's cognitive and social development. That this is the case in different cultural settings and in different family constellations is informative in and of itself. We should not forget that most of the findings are from the developed societies. Economic conditions, paternal education and parenting competence, family dynamics, and neighborhood quality among other factors may temper these associations in much of the developing world.

6

FATHERING INTERVENTION PROGRAMS

Participating in intervention programs can boost fathers' sensitivity and cognitive stimulation (Benzies, Magill-Evans, Harriso, McPhail, & Kimak, 2008), father–child interactions (Julion, Breitenstein, & Waddell, 2012), fathers' understanding of child development (Lawrence, Davies, & Ramchandani, 2013), and the quality of mother–father relationships in families (Cowan et al., 2009), while also lessening paternal distress (Roy & Dyson, 2010) and family conflicts (Fletcher, 2009) including violence in the family (McAllister et al., 2012). Aside from the fact that intervention programs have mainly focused on parents in North America, Australia, and Europe, there are a few programs in other parts of the world (e.g., ACEV Father Support Program in Turkey, UNICEF Papa Schools in Ukraine, Sonke Gender Justice, RWAMREC in Rwanda) that seek to reach fathers to encourage engagement with children, to strengthen parenting skills, and to improve men's intrapersonal and interpersonal relationships (e.g., spouse/partner relationship, reducing interpartner violence).

Judging from the increase in the number of randomized control trails (RCT) studies, father intervention programs have improved measurably over the last two decades. Having said that, most programs tend to be rather brief. Perhaps an even more serious problem is the fact that studies in the developing world rarely conduct systematic follow-up assessments of the efficacy of programs that included a control group. The presentation here concentrates on the stated goals and objectives of primary and secondary fathering intervention programs that focus on strengthening parenting and childhood development, improving marital/partner relationships, and addressing violence in families. The impact of select programs on the functioning of fathers, spouses/partners, and children are outlined. As raised earlier, the effect sizes of most of these programs are often small, but their importance for enhancing paternal involvement and childhood development, fathers' and women's well-being and mental health should not be taken lightly.

Parenting programs

A global overview of interventions delivered to fathers across countries (Panter-Brick et al., 2014) declares that programs focus on a wide array of issues with the objective of strengthening family functioning and child well-being: father–infant attachment, infant-caregiver interactions, fathers' involvement in school-related activities, positive parenting strategies, father–child play, physical and mental health, parenting stress and aggravation, anger control, harsh parenting, awareness of child abuse and neglect, domestic violence and sexual abuse, alcohol and drug use, couple relationship quality, and co-parenting. Because overwhelming emphasis has been placed on the importance of the early onset and intensity of family interventions for ameliorating cognitive and social risks to children (Shonkoff, 2010; Shonkoff & Phillips, 2000), we first describe programs that are introduced during the transition to parenthood and during early infancy.

A few intervention programs have offered services to families whose children were in the intensive care unit due to unexpected hospitalization (Turan, Basbak-kal, & Ozbek, 2008; Van der Pal, Maguire, Cessie, Wit, Walther, & Bruil, 2007). An individualized 5-step support program that focused on diverse issues (e.g., provision of detailed information about the NICU; coping with grief and changes in infant's condition; interpreting condition and signals of infant and developing strategies to interact with infant; transition of infant to home environment, and planning family discharge) was delivered by a psychologist in the neonatal intensive care unit to Spanish families with pre-term infants. The program lasted 4 weeks. Parents in the treatment and control groups expressed the same levels of anxiety and stress before the intervention. After 15 days, no father or mother in the treatment group showed any anxiety compared with 2.5% of mothers and 10.3% of fathers in the control group. At the time of discharge, 50% of mothers and 80% of fathers in the treatment group reported no depression but all mothers and fathers in the control group did (Cano Giménez & Sanchez-Luna, 2015). Related studies show similar outcomes. Turkish fathers who received support when their infants were hospitalized in the neonatal intensive care unit (NICU) showed less parenting stress over time (Ozdemir & Alemdar, 2017) and Iranian fathers who received education about support and care while their infants were in the NICU showed reduced anxiety post-intervention (Bostanabad, Areshtanab, Balila, Jafarabadi, & Ravanbakhsh, 2017). Taiwanese fathers who received information about early childcare and parenting skills, the importance of breastfeeding, and the ways in which fathers support infants and mothers during and after hospitalization, as well as one-to-one guidance from the hospital nurse during visits with their preterm infants, showed increased fathering ability compared with fathers in the control group (Lee, Wang, Lin, & Kao, 2012).

Data from the Creating Opportunities for Parent Empowerment (COPE) program, a neonatal intensive care unit intervention in the United States, provide additional support for the effectiveness of in-hospital programs for parents. COPE offered mothers and fathers four sessions (three in-hospital and one at home) composed of audiotaped and written materials aimed at increasing knowledge and beliefs about pre-term infants, the role of parents in attending to pre-term infants, and quality of parent–child interactions. Another goal of the program was to reduce parenting stress, anxiety, and depression (Melnyk et al., 2006). In this randomized controlled trial intervention, assessments were conducted before delivery, after receiving intervention, and when infants were two months old. There were no significant differences between the intervention and control group on fathers' reports of stress in the neonatal intensive care unit. Fathers' anxiety and depressive symptoms decreased over time irrespective of whether or not they received intervention services. However, fathers in the intervention group reported greater knowledge and beliefs about pre-term infants, higher levels of involvement in infant care, and became more sensitive to infants' needs over time than did fathers in the control group. These types of program are also known for reducing the length of hospital stay (Melnyk et al., 2006; Melnyk, Fineout-Overholt, & Mays, 2008).

Yet another aspect of early father–child relationship intervention involves physical contact with neonates in hospital settings. As was stated previously, S2S contact can play a pivotal role in the development of father–infant attachment relationship. In a randomized controlled trial study, the efficacy of S2S contact on father–child attachment was evaluated among Taiwanese families (Chen, Gau, Liu, & Lee, 2017). The intervention consisted of three assisted S2S 15-minute contact sessions within 24 hours of childbirth, without interfering in the initiation of breastfeeding. Participants in the intervention group were instructed on how to hold their infants and were invited to the nursery room to learn bathing techniques. Fathers in both the intervention and control groups were provided with a pamphlet that explains the importance of early childcare upon hospital admission, and they were asked to fill out a pre-test father–infant attachment survey. There were no significant differences between intervention and control group fathers on sociodemographic characteristics, participation in prenatal education, time spent with infant during hospitalization, infant feeding method, parity, infant gender or birth weight, delivery type, and initial mother S2S contact. Following completion of the program, fathers in the intervention group had significantly higher scores on the exploring, talking, touching, and caring subscales of attachment relationship with their infants than did fathers in the control group.

It is considerations of findings such as those discussed above that have led some researchers to evaluate the effectiveness of intervention programs that are designed to boost father involvement with newborn children during the transition to fatherhood. Using a randomized experimental design, one program provided eight group-based education parenting classes (e.g., awareness of parenting issues, changes in the transition to parenthood, positive father involvement, co-parenting and couple relationship) to expectant middle-income European American married or cohabiting couples with the hope of improving the quality of father–child interactions and father involvement with children later on (Doherty, Erikson, & LaRossa, 2006). At six-months postpartum, fathers in the intervention group showed more warmth and emotional support, intrusiveness, positive affect, dyadic synchrony, and increases in overall quality of father involvement, and workday involvement than did fathers in the control group. However, the intent to treat estimates showed significant differences between intervention and control groups only for warmth and emotional support, dyadic synchrony, and workday involvement.

A rural program in Vietnam (Bich & Cuong, 2017) evaluated the outcomes of community-based intervention designed to increase fathers' knowledge, attitudes, and involvement in supporting breastfeeding. The intervention program consisted of different components such as mass media communication, group and individual counseling, and a social public event that took place during both the prenatal and postnatal periods. Topics addressed during group and individual counseling sessions included the importance of breastfeeding and the challenges and benefits of fathers' involvement in breastfeeding. Fathers provided data regarding household characteristics, their knowledge of the importance of breastfeeding and exclusive breastfeeding, their attitudes toward initiation of breastfeeding, toward six-month exclusive breastfeeding, toward supporting the wife in breastfeeding, and involvement in supporting exclusive breastfeeding at the delivery of a previous child, during the antenatal period, at delivery, and during the postpartum period. After adjusting for covariates, fathers in the intervention group showed meaningful increments in their knowledge about the importance of exclusive breastfeeding within the first hour after birth, the benefits of exclusive breastfeeding for the newborn and mother in the first month as opposed to fathers in the control group.

Admittedly, it is difficult to disaggregate the effects of parenting programs on paternal competence, paternal interpersonal and personal functioning, and childhood development without strong experimental designs (Furlong et al., 2012; Roopnarine & Dede Yildirim, 2017). Furthermore, assuring program fidelity can be challenging. Nonetheless, a strong impression is that paternal parenting interventions show tremendous promise for strengthening parenting skills among fathers and for boosting childhood development (Furlong et al., 2012). The reality is that most of the parenting intervention programs for fathers were developed and implemented in industrialized, rich countries. We first touch upon a few parenting programs for fathers in the less developed world before discussing those implemented in Canada, the United States, Australia, and Europe.

Plagued by the perennial lack of material resources, parenting programs outside of developed countries often rely on international donor or within-country private agencies for financial support. For instance, World Vision, Promundo, and Sonke Gender Justice Network collaborated to bring workshops to men in Sri Lanka to assist them to fulfill their responsibilities as caregivers and to inform them about issues pertaining to family planning, gender equality, couple communication skills, and women's and children's rights (World Vision, Promundo, & MenCare, 2013). In other situations, UNICEF has assisted in program construction and implementation. One such case is the UNICEF Father Schools in the Ukraine that promote responsible fatherhood by providing safe spaces for fathers to discuss different issues related to fathering. Usually, program topics center on fathers' involvement during pregnancy and delivery, maternal, newborn, and child health, maternity and paternity leave after delivery, breastfeeding, division of household chores, postpartum depression, ages and stages of child development, developmentally appropriate activities, discipline methods, parenting skills, gender equality, family dynamics, violence against women and children, and reproductive health (Berggren et al., 2010).

Two programs in Jordan and Turkey speak to the difficulties of initiating and sustaining parenting interventions in more traditional, hegemonic societies where men have largely remained outside of the parameters of childrearing. The UNICEF Better Parenting Program (BPP) in Jordan sought to promote early child development by increasing parents' knowledge about effective childrearing strategies, importance of play in childhood development, setting appropriate limits, and understanding basic milestones in children's social and language development. Consisting of 16 hours of parent training, the program was delivered in the northern, middle, and southern regions of Jordan. Program group participants received parenting sessions while control group participants were informed that they would receive the program later. Unfortunately, out of a sample of 336 parents, only 18 fathers participated in parenting sessions across the three regions despite vigorous attempts to encourage fathers to get involved in parenting education. From pre-post questionnaires (containing items on discipline, child abuse and neglect, and other parenting issues) and information gathered through focus groups and interviews, the program content was sufficient to increase fathers' knowledge, skills, and practices related to parenting, and their understanding of the importance of father involvement in the lives of their children (Al-Hassan, 2009).

Unlike that of Jordan, the Father Support Program in Turkey was initiated by ACEV (Mother and Child Education Foundation), a private undertaking to enhance fathers' parenting during the early childhood years. This 15-hour group-based parenting curriculum dealt with the role of fathers in children's lives, knowledge about child development, communication skills, problem solving strategies, prevention of child abuse, participation in household chores, importance of involvement in play and book reading, and positive discipline. It was concluded from the pre-post-test assessments and in-depth interviews that fathers who attended the parenting sessions reported having more knowledge about child behavior and they were more likely to use guidance and reasoning during parenting, to show warmth and affection to their children, and to avoid the use of physical discipline post-intervention (Kocak, 2004).

For diverse reasons (e.g., study design features, economics, skilled personnel, and social service infrastructure), parenting programs involving fathers in Canada, Europe, Australia, and the United States yield a little more concrete evidence on the benefits of fathering programs than those in the developing world. During in-home visits, Benzies, Magill-Evans, Harrison, MccPhail, and Kimak (2008) videotaped father–infant interactions in Canadian families during structured play sessions when infants were 5-, 6-, and 8 months old. Based on the videotaped play sessions, feedback was provided to fathers regarding positive father–child interactions: sensitivity to cues, response to distress, and attempts at fostering social-emotional and cognitive growth. At the 8-month home visit, structured interviews were also conducted to evaluate fathers' perceptions of the utility of the program. Most of the fathers did find the program to be helpful and effective in increasing their understanding of observable infant behaviors and specific father–child interactions. Despite such appraisals, a majority of fathers reported no change in their parenting behavior after receiving home visits, 27% reported positive change, and 14% reported negative change. After holding fathers' educational attainment, age, work hours, marital status, and employment status constant, the parenting education program had the greatest impact on fathers who were the least involved with their children. By contrast, in the Dads on Board Program in Australia, a 16-hour group-based intervention whose aim was to assist fathers to read and understand their children's social cues, pre-post intervention changes were documented among men in the quality of attachment, interactions with infants, and paternal hostility (Bunston, 2013).

Intervention programs for families whose children were enrolled in Head Start in the United States also appear to have positive influences on father–child relationships and childhood outcomes (Raikes & Belotti, 2006; Raikes, Summers, & Roggman, 2005). Fathers who participated in more than 21.5 hours of intervention program curricula (e.g., fathers volunteering in the classroom, father-day activities, father–child recreation activities) geared to reading and playing with children demonstrated elevated levels of father–child involvement compared with those in the control group. Moreover, children of fathers in the high dosage intervention group demonstrated better mathematics readiness for early schooling compared with control group children and those in the low dosage intervention group (Fagan & Iglesias, 1999). It may be that the efficacy of programs for low-income fathers depends on the intensity of intervention services offered.

In a more carefully designed intervention, Cowan et al. (2009) examined the impact of the Supporting Father Involvement (SFI) program on 289 low-income Mexican American and European American families across four California counties. Families were randomly assigned to either a 16-week group session for couples, a 16-week group session for fathers, or a single informational meeting. The group sessions focused on the importance of fathers' positive involvement with children. Pre-intervention, post-intervention after 2-month completion of the assignment, and a post-intervention follow-up after 11-month completion of the assignment showed better outcomes in the areas of fathers' psychological involvement with children, fathers' involvement in caregiving activities, couple satisfaction, and lower parenting stress among men who were in the group for fathers as compared with those in the group for couples and control group. A replication attempt of the SFI program with low-income Mexican American and African American families failed to show any significant differences between controls and the group for couples and the group for fathers on measures of father–child interactions, parenting stress, quality of marriage, social isolation, child hyperactivity, and internalizing symptoms in children (Cowan et al., 2014).

An important goal of childrearing is to equip children with the skills necessary to regulate their emotions appropriately, to display empathy toward others, and to navigate their social worlds effectively (see Denham et al., 2003). This process begins early and depends on the emotion-socialization practices of mothers and fathers (modeling of emotions, teaching children how to understand their emotions and those of others) (Grusec & Hastings, 2007). The Australia Dads Tuning in to Kids Parenting Program is a 14-hour group-based parenting intervention that has its sights on improving the emotional-socialization skills (emotion dismissing, emotion coaching, empathy) of fathers in order to facilitate positive outcomes in children during the early childhood period (Wilson, Havighurst, Kehoe, & Harley, 2016). Fathers with preschool-aged children were randomly assigned to a program and control group. Fathers' emotional parenting style, hostility, their sense of parenting efficacy, and children's negative emotions, behavior problems, and prosocial behaviors were assessed before and after the completion of the program. Fathers who received the parenting program showed meaningful gains in their empathy skills and positive parenting and a decrease in emotion-dismissing beliefs and practices relative to fathers in the control group.

Designed to assist parents to improve their parenting skills and thereby attenuating behavioral difficulties in children, the Positive Parenting Program (Triple P) has been adapted and implemented in more than 25 countries, including Hong Kong, Iran, Ireland, Japan, and Switzerland. Having its genesis in Australia, the Triple P is a multi-level program with increasing intensity: communicating positive parenting through diverse media (e.g., television, online) (level 1), brief interventions that involve face-to-face contacts or phone interviews (level 2), 3–4 individual face-to-face sessions or a series of 2-hour group sessions (level 3), 8–10 individual, group, or self-directed sessions (level 4), and sessions to address other problems (level 5). Its effectiveness has been laid out in two reviews and meta-analyses. After analyzing 101 studies conducted across 33 years (Sanders, Kirby, Telligent, & Day, 2014), moderate short-term effects were determined for social, emotional, and behavioral outcomes in children ($d = .47$), parenting ($d = .58$), parenting satisfaction and efficacy ($d = .52$) and parental adjustment ($d = .34$). In an analysis of 28 published journal articles that examined the effectiveness of the Triple P program across countries, the effect size for maternal parenting was .77 and for paternal parenting .51 (Fletcher, Freeman, & Matthey, 2011).

To arrest parenting challenges and childhood difficulties in high-risk populations, the Triple P was implemented in two semi-rural midland counties in Ireland that were witnessing troublesome rises in unemployment rates (Fives, Pursell, Heary, Nic Gabhainn, & Canavan, 2014). More to the point, the primary objective was to determine whether the Triple P would lead to a reduction in the number of children exhibiting social and behavioral problems, elevate parenting competence, decrease parental anxiety and depression, and help individuals feel more supported in their role as parents. Program fidelity and dosage were important considerations in administering the Triple P to parents. Detailed assessments indicated a decrease in parental reports of children's social emotional problems (e.g., hyperactivity, peer problems, conduct problems) over time. Parents showed improvements in the areas of psychological distress, parenting skills, and in their relationships with their children.

In a long-term assessment (Heinrichs, Kliem, & Hahlweg, 2014) of the efficacy of the Triple P program, 280 German families were assigned to a program group ($N = 186$) and a control group ($N = 94$). The intervention participants received group training whereas controls were invited to participate in the program later on. Assessments were conducted at baseline, post-intervention, and at one, two, three, and four years after program completion. Mothers and fathers reported on their dysfunctional parenting (e.g., permissive parenting, authoritarian discipline, display of danger, meanness, irritability, and long reprimands and reliance on talking), positive parenting and encouraging parental behaviors (e.g., cuddling with my child), and children's internalizing and externalizing behaviors. Fathers reported slightly higher behavior problems and less positive parenting behaviors at baseline than did mothers. Although the effect size was larger for mothers compared with fathers, dysfunctional parenting declined significantly from pre- to post-assessment for both mothers and fathers, and the change in dysfunctional parenting was stable over the one-, two-, three- and four-year follow-up assessments. Both mothers and fathers reported a significant reduction in positive parenting over time. However, fathers' positive parenting showed delayed decline at post-assessments. A later re-analysis of these data corroborated the original findings (Heinrichs, Kliem, & Hahlweg, 2017). These results are similar to those found in other studies on German families that indicate a decline in dysfunctional parental behaviors after intervention (e.g., Stemmler, Beelmann, Jaursch, & Losel, 2007).

Thus far, we have focused on intervention programs constructed for two-parent families. Ellis, Caldwell, Assari, and De Loney (2014) assessed the impact of the Fathers and Sons Program in promoting healthy lifestyles among 287 nonresident African American fathers and their 8–12 year-old children ($N = 158$ intervention, $N = 129$ control). The Fathers and Sons Program consisted of 15 family-based intervention sessions with each lasting at least 45 minutes. Workshops and related activities focused on different components of father–child relationship (e.g., communication, guidance, monitoring, role modeling), substance use, risky behavior, and physical and mental health issues. Around 85% of fathers in the intervention group and 70% of fathers in the control group participated in the post-intervention assessments. Attrition analysis showed that fathers' educational attainment and fathers' length of residence with their sons before becoming nonresident fathers were related to completion of post-intervention assessments. The intervention was directly and positively associated with post-test father–son contact, which in turn was associated with the quality of father–son relationship. Fathers' intention to exercise partially mediated the association between father's quality of relationship and sons' intention to exercise. While some intervention programs (e.g. Tyro Dads Program in Ohio, USA) designed for nonresident and low-income fathers have demonstrated similar positive outcomes in father–child activities (Kim & Jang, 2018) others have not (see Levine, Kaufman, Hammar, & Fagan, 2018)

What program characteristics (e.g., content, features, and delivery methods) might recruit fathers' attention to join parenting intervention programs? Information of this nature can more effectively guide and enhance the efficacy of fathering programs. When fathers in New Zealand were asked about their knowledge of parenting programs in focus groups, a paltry 13% of fathers were aware of parenting programs while only 3% reported having attended such programs (Frank, Keown, Sanders, & Dittman, 2015). Fathers showed a penchant for parenting programs that considered building positive relationships with children, increasing children's confidence and social skills, and fathers' influence on positive child development outcomes. They preferred seminar-type programs, followed by fathers-only group programs, television series, web-based, and individually tailored programs. Effectiveness and location of programs, time, and practitioners' training and knowledge were the most important considerations in fathers' decision to engage in parenting programs (see also Tully et al., 2017).

Factors related to men themselves determine paternal participation in intervention programs. An example involves an assessment of factors related to treatment attrition in the Parent Child Interaction Therapy (PCIT) parenting program implemented in Amsterdam, the Netherlands (Abrahamse, Niec, Junger, Boer, & Lindauer, 2016). The PCIT program was delivered in community mental health centers to parents of children who were referred for mental health services related to conduct problems. Of families who participated in the program, 40% dropped out and 60% completed all of the sessions. Distinctions between dropouts and completers were rather clear. Families with non-western backgrounds and child maltreatment histories were more likely to drop out of the program. Furthermore, fathers who were single, younger, and who had less parenting stress were more likely to drop out of the program than fathers who were married, older, and had more parenting stress. Roopnarine and Dede Yildirim (2017) also found that paternal age and marital status were significantly related to low-income African American, Hispanic American, and European American fathers' participation in intervention programs. Across ethnic groups, fathers who were older and married were more likely to complete a higher percentage of relationship skills education classes.

Parenting interventions for fathers are slowly increasing across the world, with emerging programs taking advantage of the ubiquity of technological devices and social media. Other intervention programs, not reviewed here, have focused on the impact of spiritual education on fathers' roles in children's lives (e.g., Korean families, Kim & Queck, 2013) and some have concentrated on fathers' and children's' health (e.g., Australian families, Lloyd, Lubans, Plotnikoff, & Morgan, 2014). For the most part, interventions for fathers have a positive effect on parenting competence and satisfaction but only for the short term. The 4-year follow-up assessments of the Triple P program come the closest to demonstrating the sustained effects of parenting intervention for fathers.

Marriage and relationship education programs

Family-based intervention programs designed to help married and unwed couples form and maintain healthy relationships by improving couples' communication skills, conflict management strategies, relationship quality, family stability, and individual functioning have implications for co-parenting and fathers' involvement with children (Blanchard, Hawkins, Baldwin, & Fawcett, 2009; Cowan et al., 2009; Rienks, Wadsworth, Markman, Einhorn, & Etter, 2011; Wilcox, Doherty, Glenn, & Waite, 2005). A meta-analysis (Hawkins & Erikson, 2015) explored the effectiveness of couple and relationship education programs in improving relationship satisfaction, quality, and stability, commitment, communication and conflict resolution, physical and psychological aggression, and co-parenting quality by controlling for study design, program characteristics, and program participation levels as well as participants' income, education, marital status, and relationship distress. Single-group/ pre-post-test studies revealed that couple and relationship skills education programs had a positive impact on co-parenting, communication skills, and relationship satisfaction and quality, but the outcomes were stronger for low-income, ethnic minority couples, suggesting that the efficacy of intervention programs might vary for different racial/ethnic groups in the United States (Stanley et al., 2014). This is somewhat contrary to the findings of other intervention studies in which couple and relationship skills education program effects were invariant across racial/ethnic groups (Cowan, Cowan, Pruett, Pruett, & Wong, 2009; Cowan, Cowan, Pruett, Pruett, & Gillette, 2014; O'Halloran, Rizzolo, Cohen, & Wacker, 2013).

In the United States, the Administration for Children and Families in the Department of Health and Human Services launched the Building Strong Families (BSF) and Supporting Healthy Marriages (SHM) projects to deliver relationship skills education classes to at-risk families and to evaluate their effectiveness over time. The BSF intervention was implemented at eight locations across the United States and targeted low-income, unmarried couples with newborn children (5,082 couples at baseline). The explicit goals were to strengthen relationship quality, parenting skills, and co-parenting alliance, and to support children's social-emotional development. The curriculum focused on communication skills, conflict management strategies, emotional intimacy, parenting, money management, and job skills training. Couples in the intervention group received 30 or 42 hours of relationship skills education classes, and were offered supplemental parenting and job skills training classes. Baseline data were collected before randomization and impact assessments were conducted when children were 15- and 36-months old to evaluate the effectiveness of the BSF program on both mothers' and fathers' communication and conflict management skills, parenting, and children's socio-emotional development. The response rates for the 15-month assessments were 83% for mothers and 73% for fathers, and for the 36-month assessments they were 80% for mothers and 69% for fathers.

Using complier average causal effect estimates to compare the outcomes of BSF participants in the program group who attended relationship skills education sessions and outcomes of potential participants in the control group who would have attended sessions if the program were offered to them, Roopnarine and Dede Yildirim (2017) calculated whether relationship skills education had an impact on father's mental health. Across a diverse ethnic sample that consisted of African American, European American, and Hispanic American couples (program,

$N = 1,249$ and control, $N = 1,291$), fathers who received at least one hour of relationship skills education classes in the program group showed a significant decrease in depressive symptoms between when their children were 15 months and 36 months old compared with fathers in the control group. Decreases in depressive symptoms as a function of dosage of relationship skills education were inconsistent, with fathers in the program group who received 1% to 20% and 70% to 90% of relationship skills education affected the most by the intervention. These patterns could be due to characteristics associated with the couples themselves and to degree of relationship commitment across family structures.

The SHM project was also a multisite study that offered economically disadvantaged married couples 24 or 30 hours of relationship skills education classes, educational and social events, enrichment activities, and family support services. A total of 6,298 couples who were expecting or had a child were randomly assigned to a program or control group. Program group couples were encouraged to take relationship and marriage education workshops, which focused on effective communication skills, conflict management strategies, and building and strengthening supportive relationships between couples. After randomization and program delivery, assessments were conducted when children were 12- and 30-months old. The 30-month impact assessments revealed that program participation increased fathers' satisfaction with communication, handling of disagreements, time spent together with their partner, sex life, and the division of chores, and decreased disagreements with partners. The program group fathers were also less likely to have problems with job, family, or friends due to alcohol or drug use than did fathers in the control group (Lundquist et al., 2014).

From what was found, fathers' personal and interpersonal functioning should receive equal emphasis as parenting practices in intervention programs. Rarely have these two sets of constructs been considered in tandem in intervention programs for fathers (see Doherty et al., 2006). It would seem that this might increase the efficacy of paternal intervention programs across cultural communities. As indicated earlier, in the developing world, male dominance and interpartner violence are widespread. The dynamic relationships between marital/partner relationship, job satisfaction, mental health, and parenting have been laid out in conceptual models (Belsky, 1984; Bronfenbrenner & Morris, 2006; Cabrera et al., 2007, 2009) and examined in some research studies on parenting (e.g., Roopnarine & Dede Yildirim, 2017).

Violence prevention programs

In view of the substantial negative effects of intimate partner violence on father–child relationships and children's socio-emotional and behavioral adjustment (see Roopnarine & Dede Yildirim, 2017), several intervention programs have been developed for fathers who perpetrate intimate partner violence in developed and developing countries (e.g. White Ribbon Campaign in Peru, Building a Culture of Peace in Nicaragua, GAHO in Panama). There is ample evidence to suggest that intimate partner violence does not occur in isolation and, in fact, co-occurs with other types of abusive behavior, such as hostility, physical and emotional abuse of children, and child neglect (Kimber et al., 2015; Quellet-Morin et al., 2015). According to the International Men and Gender Equality Survey that collects data from developing countries, 17% – 41% of men reported the use of intimate partner violence against their female partners in Brazil, Chile, Croatia, India, Mexico, and Rwanda (Barker et al., 2011). Surveys in the Middle East and North Africa report comparable rates of physical and sexual violence against women as perpetrated by their husbands. For example, in Egypt, 34.8% of men had slapped their wife or thrown something at them with the intent to harm, 38.3% of men had pushed or shoved their wife, 15.3% had hit their wife with their fist or with something else, 10.9% kicked, dragged, beat, choked, or burned their wife, and 16.4% forced their wife to have sex when she did not want to, based on women's reports (El Feki et al., 2017; see also Pulerwitz et al., 2015).

Regional Capacity Building Workshops were organized by Save the Children in Sweden, UNIFEM Regional Office for South Asia, and Instituto PROMUNDO (Bhandari & Karkara, 2006) to assist fathers in Bangladesh, India, Nepal, and Pakistan on multiple fronts. The aims of the workshops were: to discuss and improve ongoing programs, to demonstrate national and international fatherhood programs and policies, to engage diverse groups of fathers (e.g. biological father, stepfather, social father, fathers who live at a distance) in intervention programs, to gain an understanding of effective intervention for men, and to change the views of men as fathers through public policies.

Essentially, the workshops provided training for facilitators along five main themes: "expected roles of men and boys in domestic chores," "expected roles of men and boys in the lives of boys and girls," "roles of men in families apart from being fathers," "expected role of the father with change in the growing age of the child," and "change in father's role in recent years." The workshops also addressed several issues pertaining to fatherhood, including gender discrimination/inequality, masculinity and the socialization processes of boys and men, violence against children and women, responsible sexual behavior, HIV/AIDS, men's active involvement with young children, and children's rights and developmental needs. It was hoped that these joint efforts would result in research data that would inform intervention programs, develop collaborations among community based programs, researchers, media, NGOs and interested stakeholders, and lead to better monitoring of programs and evaluation outcomes over extended periods.

As part of violence prevention, Program H, a 28-hour group education and social marketing campaign, was developed by Promundo and implemented in more than 20 countries (e.g., Tanzania, Namibia, Ethiopia, Mexico, India, the Balkans, Latin America, and the Caribbean). Young men were enrolled in group-based workshops that focused on gender equality, sexual health, family planning, fatherhood and caregiving, violence prevention, and HIV/AIDS prevention (Promundo, Instituto PAPAI, Salud y Género, & ECOS, 2013). Analyses have been conducted to assess the effectiveness of Program H in different countries. For instance, in Brazil, a total of 780 males (in Bangu, Mare, and Morro dos Macacos) aged 14–25 participated in a quasi-experimental study (Pulerwitz, Barker, Segundo, & Nascimento, 2006). Men were assigned to group education only, combined education with a community-wide lifestyle campaign group, and a control group. The control group participants were slated to receive the intervention later. Intervention services were offered over a 6-month period and qualitative and quantitative data were collected before intervention, after intervention, and at 6-month follow-up post-intervention. The response rate was very good initially but dropped off a little at post-intervention. At the six-month follow-up, men who received education only and those in the combined education and community-wide lifestyle campaign groups showed significant decreases in beliefs in statements such as "men need sex more than women do," "I would be outraged if my wife asked me to use a condom," and "changing diapers, giving the kids a bath, and feeding the kids are the mother's responsibility," compared with those in the control group (Pulerwitz et al., 2006).

Attending to negative attitudes toward women prior to men becoming fully entrenched in sexual relationships can serve to reduce violence in interpersonal relationships and to increase awareness of parenting responsibilities. Thus, it is not uncharacteristic for some programs to target young men for enrollment in intervention to confront and reduce gender-based violence and family-related difficulties. To educate young men about gender roles, equality and equity between the sexes to lessen violence, unprotected sex, and substance abuse, the Men Engage Kenya Network (MenKen), the Rwanda Men's Resource Centre (RWAMREC), and the Men's Associations for Gender Equality – Sierra Leone (MAGE – SL) conducted Mengage Tri-Country Projects in Kenya, Rwanda, and Sierra Leone. Each organization spearheaded community outreach activities and workshops to empower men and women to promote gender equality (Sonke Gender Justice, 2015). In a similar manner, the Young Men Initiative (YMI) was introduced in Serbia, Bosnia and Herzegovina, Kosovo, and Croatia to lessen gender-based violence and promote gender equality by providing culturally sensitive enrichment workshops and activities to young boys. Preliminary findings suggest that the YMI program was effective in teaching strategies to transform negative masculine ideologies (Namy et al., 2014).

Staying with programs on the African continent for a moment, two other studies have attempted to tackle violence and gender equality in South Africa and Uganda. Both countries have remained very traditional when it comes to women's roles, and they have high rates of violence against women. The Sonke Gender Justice Network in South Africa conducted semi-structured interviews to evaluate the One Man Can (OMC) program that was applied to prevent violence against women, to lower the risk of HIV/AIDS, and to promote gender equality. Workshops were delivered to men and boys that concentrated on gender, power, violence, human rights, women's rights, and masculinity (Dworkin, Hatcher, Colvin, & Peacock, 2013). After receiving group-based workshops, positive changes were realized in participants' understanding of women's rights, in their perception of the gendered division of labor and masculinity, in their attitudes about decision-making, reduction in the number of sexual partners and risks of unsafe sex, and shifting attitudes about male dominance, violent behavior, and masculine respect.

Favorable outcomes were also accomplished in the Responsible, Engaged, and Loving (REAL) Fathers Initiative in Northern Uganda. Fathers were invited to participate in a 12-week mentoring program to end violence against women and children (Ashburn et al., 2016). REAL curriculum covers such topics as the use of nonviolent discipline methods, conflict resolution strategies, and communication skills for couples to reduce the risk of child maltreatment and intimate partner violence by practicing positive interpersonal skills. Assessments of the effects of REAL among 500 fathers between the ages of 16 and 25 and their young children in Uganda (Ashburn et al., 2016) were conducted at baseline and 10 months after the mentoring sessions. Fathers who received at least one individual or group mentoring session were more likely to use positive parenting strategies, such as warmth and physical affection, and involve themselves in activities including playing, singing songs, naming objects, counting things, to avoid using any form of physical punishment (shaking the child, shouting, yelling, or screaming at child, spanking, hitting, or slapping the child on the bottom with bare hands), and to feel more confident in not using any form of physical punishment to manage undesirable child behaviors compared with fathers who were not exposed to the mentoring sessions. Program fathers also showed a significant reduction in the frequency of use of any form of verbal or psychological intimate partner violence.

Two programs in Sweden and Canada have focused more directly on families who have a history of intimate partner violence and/or hostility and abuse toward children. The Swedish program engaged participants in a 10-week group-based intervention (1.5 hours weekly) aimed at increasing parents' awareness and understanding of children's social and emotional needs, parent–child attachment, and parenting that minimizes the negative effects of intimate partner violence on children (Kamal, Strand, Jutengren, & Tidefors, 2016). A thematic analysis of responses gathered from focus groups one week after the intervention showed that fathers who participated in the intervention program gained better self-control, self-confidence, and communication skills, employed more positive parenting practices, including explanations, reasoning, setting rules and emotional support, and were better able to manage their children's difficult behaviors.

The Caring Dads: Helping Fathers Value Their Children Program implemented in Canada also showed promise in reducing hostility and abusive behavior toward children (Scott & Crooks, 2007). A primary motive of this program was to prevent fathers' abusive behaviors towards their partner and children. Pretest-post-test evaluation of the participants in this 17-week group intervention program revealed that there were significant mean reductions in total stress, emotional unavailability and unresponsiveness, hostility, denigration and rejection of children, and angry arousal in child and family situations, in a subsample of fathers who demonstrated hostility toward their children. Although the lack of randomization limits the generalizability of these findings, programs such as Caring Dads that focus on fathers' abusive behaviors can be effective in attenuating hostile father–child and father–mother interactions.

In closing this section, we call attention to a systematic review (Barker, Ricardo, Nascimento, Olukoya, & Santos, 2010) of the short- and long-term impact of intervention programs in cultural communities in North America (41%), Latin America and the Caribbean (16%), Europe (3%), Sub-Saharan Africa (16%), the Middle East and North Africa (9%), and Asia and the Pacific (16%) that involved men and boys. These programs were broadly related to sexual and reproductive health, father involvement, gender-based violence, and women's and children's health. Although some programs may have been effective in changing gender roles and norms to reduce gender-based violence in the short term, only a few integrated fatherhood programs (e.g., those that combine group education with community outreach, mobilization and mass-media campaigns) were effective in increasing father involvement, care, and support.

Programs for incarcerated fathers

Men who were formerly incarcerated face several challenges related to re-entry into community life, finding employment, reuniting with family members, continued substance abuse, obtaining housing, accessing social support, and gaining access to health care (Woods et al., 2013). As has been pointed out by others (Bonhomme, Stephens, & Braithwaite, 2006; Geller, 2013), the impact of incarceration reaches beyond prison walls to family members and the community. Among fathers in prison, only 26% offered daily care to children. Most fathers in state prison in the United States relied on the other parent (84%), grandparents (15%), and other relatives (6%) to care for their children (Glaze & Maruschak, 2008). Paternal incarceration has short-term and long-term negative influences on interpersonal relationships, father–child relationship, parenting practices, and children's socio-emotional and academic skills (Geller, 2013; Secret, 2012; Travis & Waul, 2003). Children of incarcerated parents in the United States and Denmark were at greater risk of mental health difficulties and antisocial behavior compared with their peers (Murray, Farrington & Sekol, 2012; Oldrup, Frederiksen, Henze-Pedersen, & Olsen, 2016; Thulstrup & Karlsson, 2017), and of experiencing social stigma (Murray, Bijleveld, Farrington, & Loeber, 2014).

Programs (e.g., those based on prevention science that identify universal and selective strategies) have been developed in correctional facilities to ease the transition of incarcerated men from prison to their families and home communities (Gordon et al., 2013; Woods et al., 2013). Major impediments in designing, implementing, and assessing parent–child intervention programs in correctional facilities are wide ranging. Common challenges include gaining access to inmates' children or obtaining informed consent (Loper & Tuerk, 2007), difficulty in assessing the parent–child relationship in correctional institutions, and institutional challenges such as lack of understanding of the importance of parenting programs by prison staff, low literacy levels among inmates, implementing different programs based on the needs of incarcerated fathers, and lost contact of inmates after release. For these reasons, existing efforts to evaluate programs in correctional facilities are limited to small samples and qualitative studies, and thus the short-term or long-term potential impacts of parenting programs on the adjustment of children of inmates are largely unknown. As matter of fact, evidence of the effects of programs for fathers in and out of prison is thin. For illustrative purposes, two programs are considered here.

The InsideOut Dad program, developed by National Fatherhood Initiative in the United States, attempts to enhance father–child relationships through group-based education. This 12-session parenting program covers a variety of topics related to men's lives, including roles of fathers and mothers, parenting differences, co-parenting, showing and handling feelings, grief and loss, stress and anger, physical health, body image, children's growth and discipline, competitive and non-competitive fathering, marriage benefits, spirituality, faith and fatherhood, and child support and visits upon release. Implemented in three correctional facilities in New Jersey, 309 fathers participated in the program. A majority of fathers were African American (71.7% program group and 81.9% control group) and single (56% program group and 59.2% control group). Pre- and post-program assessments were conducted on parenting confidence and self-esteem, knowledge of program content, parenting attitudes, and father involvement (calling, writing, and visiting children). Fathers in the program group had significantly higher mean difference scores on parenting attitudes, parenting confidence and self-esteem, knowledge of program content, and contact with children than those in the control group (Block et al., 2014).

As in the InsideOut Dad program, the Being a Dad Program in Northern Ireland also focused on enhancing father–child relationship, fathers' parenting knowledge, attitudes, and behaviors, and family life and relationships (McCrudden, Braiden, Sloan, McCormack, & Treacy, 2014). This 17-week prison education program permitted men to participate if they were a father, stepfather or father-figure of a child under 11 years of age, received regular visits from the child, and had been in the correctional facility for at least 3 months. Of the 24 fathers who met the criteria for participation, 18 completed the sessions and pre-post assessment surveys. Gains were acquired in fathers' understanding of their child's age, stage of development, and behavior, in their confidence and awareness of their parenting style, and in the influence of incarceration on their children and families. Qualitative evaluations obtained through focus group discussions indicated that after participating in the program fathers had a greater understanding of effective parenting strategies, such as communication skills, the desire to be a better father, and the need for continued contact with their children.

In sum, programs for incarcerated parents cover a variety of topics, including child development, concepts endemic to fathering, communication skills, effective discipline, safety and sensitivity, play skills, stress and anger management, conflict resolution, age appropriate expectations, and limit setting. An analysis of the results of 17 parenting programs for incarcerated parents (5 targeted male inmates, and 12 targeted female inmates) in the United States found that assessment studies that employed an experimental and control group design showed positive change in areas of parenting attitudes, knowledge of child development, and parenting stress at post-test assessments (Loper & Tuerk, 2007). Another evaluation of parenting programs in prisons (Newman, Fowler, & Cashin, 2011) determined that these programs were effective at lessening the approval of physical punishment, and gaining a greater understanding of child development and positive parenting strategies.

Conclusion

Most fatherhood programs were designed with the clear-cut goals of enhancing knowledge and perspectives about child development, parenting, co-parenting, and relationship quality. Yet others aimed to facilitate adjustment after release from incarceration, and to prevent violence against women and children. Across cultural/ethnic groups, fatherhood and marriage and relationship skills education programs include diverse samples of fathers (e.g. residential and nonresidential fathers, step/social fathers and father figures, incarcerated fathers, and fathers with intimate partner violence history), are conducted in different settings (e.g., hospitals, community health centers, schools, religious organizations, and correctional facilities), and are tailored to assist fathers based on their needs and experiences. Programs have also been devised to meet the parenting needs of indigenous groups in Australia and Canada, and Maori in New Zealand (see Ball & Moselle, 2015; Edwards & Ratima, 2014)

Even though existing impact evaluations are limited in terms of adequately addressing the efficacy of intervention programs due to high attrition rates, small sample sizes, lack of randomization, and policy structures (e.g., not supportive of paternity leave, not promoting men's role as caregivers), at a bare minimum different programs were found to be beneficial in changing traditional masculine ideologies, increasing father involvement, supporting a healthy father–child relationship, and assisting children's socio-emotional and cognitive development in the short term. More collaboration is needed between researchers, nongovernment organizations, policymakers, media, and other stakeholders to increase intervention efforts in developing countries, taking into consideration cultural differences and societal expectations about parenting roles and responsibilities. Undoubtedly, assessing the long-term efficacy of different programs would help inform policies designed to promote optimal paternal parenting and childhood development in diverse cultural settings.

7

SOCIAL POLICIES AND FATHERING

Practitioners, policy makers, government bodies, employers, and researchers are increasingly interested in how social policies regarding fathers are linked to families' physical and socioeconomic wellbeing, fathers' transition to parenthood, and father involvement and engagement with children across different cultural communities (Levtov et al., 2015; O'Brien & Moss, 2010; Plantin, 2015). For the most part, family policies formulated for the workplace, childcare, income, and child support have generally favored mothers over fathers. That is, family policies have ensured paid maternity leave and income assistance for childcare. As such, parental policies have historically ignored fathers as caregivers and nurturers of children. That being said, evolving views of fatherhood and shifts in employment patterns (e.g., nonstandard work hours, more women in the labor force, stay-at-home dads) have led to expanded coverage of family-related issues in many countries, particularly in Europe.

But abundant challenges remain with respect to the complexities and obstacles in developing inclusive family policies related to fathers' sociodemographic characteristics such as age (e.g., adolescent fathers), income (e.g., low income), job status (nonstandard work hours, part-time job with no benefits, temporary or seasonal job, military service), union/residential status (not co-residing with mother, immigration status, non-custodial, incarcerated, step/social father), and living arrangements and conditions (e.g., assistance housing, homelessness). In this chapter, we provide a broad overview of policies pertaining to paternity establishment, income and child support, childcare, work and family, and their associations with family and child well-being in different cultural communities.

Paternity establishment and child support policies

It is no secret that there is growing emphasis on paternity establishment and acknowledgement of children born outside of marriage across nations. According to the 2014 OECD report, the proportion of children born in nonmarital unions and relationships is rising in developed countries due to nontraditional households, the growth of single-parent households, teenage pregnancy, male-shifting unions, unstable relationships, the absence of an established relationship, and multiple-partner fertility. It is estimated that a little over a half of the children in France, Norway, Slovenia, Estonia, Bulgaria, and Iceland were born in nonmarital relationships. Seventy percent (69.8%) of births to African American women, 68.1% to American Indian or Alaskan Natives, occurred outside of marriage in 2016 (Martin et al., 2018). These rates are considerably less (10%) for Korean, Japanese, Turkish, Israeli, and Greek families (see Figure 7.1) (OECD, 2014).

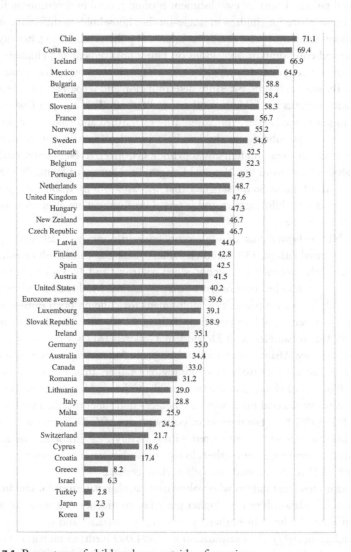

Country	Percentage
Chile	71.1
Costa Rica	69.4
Iceland	66.9
Mexico	64.9
Bulgaria	58.8
Estonia	58.4
Slovenia	58.3
France	56.7
Norway	55.2
Sweden	54.6
Denmark	52.5
Belgium	52.3
Portugal	49.3
Netherlands	48.7
United Kingdom	47.6
Hungary	47.3
New Zealand	46.7
Czech Republic	46.7
Latvia	44.0
Finland	42.8
Spain	42.5
Austria	41.5
United States	40.2
Eurozone average	39.6
Luxembourg	39.1
Slovak Republic	38.9
Ireland	35.1
Germany	35.0
Australia	34.4
Canada	33.0
Romania	31.2
Lithuania	29.0
Italy	28.8
Malta	25.9
Poland	24.2
Switzerland	21.7
Cyprus	18.6
Croatia	17.4
Greece	8.2
Israel	6.3
Turkey	2.8
Japan	2.3
Korea	1.9

FIGURE 7.1 Percentage of children born outside of marriage

Source: Derived from OECD Family Database 2014, www.oecd.org/els/family/SF_2_4_Share_births_outside_marriage.pdf

Higher rates of out-of-marriage births are also seen in families throughout the developing world (see Bucheli & Vigorito, 2017; Cuesta & Myer, 2014). In Mexico it was 55% in 2010 (Institute for Family Studies, 2015) and in 2011, out-of-marriage births reached 70% in Peru (Cabella, Fernández, & Prieto, 2015). Birth to children in visiting relationship unions has been normative in Caribbean and some African cultural communities for some time now (Anderson & Daley, 2015; Makusha & Richter, 2015; Roopnarine & Jin, 2016). The prevalence of nonmarital childbearing around the world notwithstanding, policies necessitate paternity determination and recognition in order to enforce child support payments from noncustodial or nonresidential fathers. Paternity establishment is often crucial in determining financial and other assistance for children in single-mother households in different countries.

Without going into great detail, the impact of policies related to paternity establishment and child support obligations on father involvement and children's socioemotional and cognitive development and economic well-being has ignited active debates. By most accounts, paternity determination and recognition has been associated with benefits to children, mothers, and fathers. Turning to a few examples, fathers in the United States who voluntarily established and recognized their legal and financial responsibilities to children born outside of marriage were more likely to be involved in their children's lives (Mincy, Garfinkel, & Nepomnyaschy, 2005). But analysis of data from the National Longitudinal Survey of Youth (NYLS) 1997 cohort in the United States suggests that the associations among the establishment of paternity, child support, and paternal involvement are a bit more complex (Argys & Peters, 2001).

The NLYS showed that of adolescents born in nonmarital relationships, 33% had unidentified fathers, 53% had their fathers' names on their birth certificate, 9% had fathers who voluntarily acknowledged paternity, and 14.5% had fathers who established paternity by court orders or genetic testing. Mothers who were married were less likely to have paternity establishment for children born outside of marriage and to receive child support from fathers. Men's educational attainment and receiving Aid to Families with Dependent Children (AFDC) predicted establishment of paternity. African American and Hispanic American youths were less likely to receive child support from their nonresident fathers than European American youths. Number of children in the household, mothers' education level, and fathers' marital status were good predictors of whether child support obligations were met (Argys & Peters, 2001). For the sake of policy, receipt of AFDC benefits and genetic testing laws were positively associated with paternity establishment, whereas long-arm statutes (pursuing absent fathers living in another state) were positively associated with child support award and father–child contact.

It remains true that fathers who voluntarily establish paternity for children born in nonmarital relationships have higher paternity confidence and are more likely to invest in their children's lives, thereby preventing mortality and inadequate nutrition (Anderson, 2017). An examination of 4,494,009 births to unmarried mothers taken from the United States Centers for Disease Control and Prevention National Statistics Birth and Natality datasets, which cover the record of all live births, sheds light on this issue. Separate analyses conducted for European American, African American, Alaskan Indian/Alaska Native, Asian American, and Hispanic American children indicated significant differences in the prevalence of paternity establishment across racial/ethnic groups, of which European American and Hispanic American children had higher rates while African American children had lower rates. Maternal education, age, and having private insurance were also linked to the prevalence of paternity establishment across racial/ethnic groups, whereas being a Medicaid recipient decreased the likelihood of paternity establishment. Paternity establishment was linked to lower rates of premature delivery, higher birth weight, higher Apgar scores, lower rates of admittance to neonatal intensive care units, and higher breastfeeding rates.

Most policy wonks would agree that paternity establishment and collaborations between child welfare and child enforcement agencies are critical for the legal system to set up child support enforcement and payments (Xu, Pirog, & Vargas, 2016). Child support enforcement provides mothers with additional income, decreases the likelihood of receiving welfare assistance, and may lift children out of poverty and reduce the poverty gap (Bucheli & Vigorito, 2017; Hakovirta & Jokela, 2018). In most countries, noncustodial parents are obligated to pay child support or child maintenance to custodial parents to help cover the cost of living (OECD, 2010). The factors influencing the payment amount vary by country. In most cases, parents' income, family size and composition, the number of children in a single-parent household, and custodial arrangements play major roles in determining whether payment obligations are fulfilled. Payments are set up by either private agreements between parents, court order (e.g., Belgium, France, Sweden, and the US), or government agencies using formal or informal guidelines; some countries strictly enforce child support payments and ensure advance payments (e.g., Austria, Denmark, Finland, France, and Ireland). However, in some countries, there are discrepancies between child support orders and actual payments. The United States stands out in this regard. Paternity establishment may be required for child support obligations, but half of eligible mothers did not receive child support from the father in 2008 (Grall, 2009; Huang & Han, 2012). When fathers meet child support obligations, they are more likely to be involved in childrearing decisions because they are more inclined to monitor the use of the money (Huang, 2006). A backlash is that child support enforcement may increase the number of work hours needed among low-income fathers to afford payments. What this means is that increased time spent at work can have a negative impact on the frequency of father–child contact (Gunter, 2016).

The types of child support (e.g., formal cash, in-kind) that mothers receive from nonresident fathers are dependent on the type of relationship structure that was established between the couple. Utilizing data from the Fragile Families and Child Wellbeing Study and the Public Use Microdata Samples of the 2000 census in the United States, Nepomnyaschy and Garfinkel (2010) found that ever-cohabited mothers with the child's father received more informal cash support and total cash support than did never-cohabited mothers. Fathers were also more likely to make contributions of money and other material things during pregnancy, to visit the mother in the hospital, and express intention to contribute in the future among ever-cohabited than never-cohabited mothers. Fathers who contributed money and other things during pregnancy, African American fathers, fathers with at least a high school diploma, those who were 21 years or older, and who were employed were more likely to provide informal cash support. Mothers who lived in cities with strong child support enforcement received less informal but more formal cash support than mothers who lived in areas with an average level of child support enforcement. Mothers who had ever cohabited with the child's father received higher total cash support regardless of city-level child support enforcement policies.

In a comparative analysis of child maintenance policies in Canada, Denmark, Finland, Germany, Norway, Sweden, the United Kingdom, and the United States, only 22% of never-married single parents received child maintenance in the UK, while the rates were higher in the other countries: 38% in Canada, 94% in Denmark, 77% in Finland and Germany, 56% in Norway, 100% in Sweden, and 30% in the United States (Hakovirta, 2011). A more recent study that tapped into the Luxembourg Income Study (LIS) data from 2013 showed that payments to lone-mother families receiving child maintenance in Finland, Germany, Spain, United Kingdom, and the United States were up somewhat (Hakovirta & Jokela, 2018). The relative contribution of child support payments to custodial parents' average gross income was highest in Germany (42.8%) and lowest in Denmark (9.6%). The reduction in the rate of poverty as a result of child maintenance in all families with children ranged from 1.4% to 3% across Canada, Denmark, Germany, Norway, Sweden, the United Kingdom, and the United States. Finland witnessed the highest rate (15.3%) of reduction in the poverty gap after payments. The rate of reduction in the poverty gap is associated with the receipt of higher child maintenance in single parent households: 23.9% in Canada, 13.5% in Denmark, 15.8% in Finland, 5.2% in Germany, 16.6% in Norway, 15.7% in Sweden, 30% in the United Kingdom, and 20.5% in the United States (see also Skinner, Cook, & Sinclair, 2017). A recent analysis showed that European mothers in the lowest income quintile benefitted less from child maintenance than those in the highest income quintile (Hakovirta & Jokela, 2018).

Assuming that support payments may have a more substantial effect in improving the standard of living and reducing rates of poverty for single mothers and children in developing societies with unstable economic conditions, we now look at assessments of the function of child support payments on custodial mothers' financial wellbeing and childhood poverty in Colombia (Cuesta & Meyer, 2014), Peru (Rios-Salas & Meyer, 2014), and Uruguay (Bucheli & Vigorito, 2017). Because of economic conditions and underdeveloped judicial systems, payments may be modest and enforcement lax in some developing societies (see UNIFEM, 2008 for the Caribbean region). Legal costs and transportation can also make a dent in the economic resources of lone-mother families in poor rural communities (Hernández Breña, 2011). In Colombia, child support does not entirely rest with the court system. Custodial parents may enter into a voluntary agreement with the non-custodial parent or utilize the Colombian Child Support System (C-CSS) (Cuesta & Meyer, 2014). In the Peruvian system, child support payment is based on a legal relationship between a parent and the child irrespective of marital status. It normally covers the cost of child maintenance (e.g., housing, medical and educational costs, etc.) (Rios-Salas & Meyer, 2014).

As in the developed world, most families who qualify for child support in Colombia are single-parent mothers. In 2008, only 28% of custodial mothers, 67% of whom lived below the poverty line, received child support from nonresident fathers. Of single mothers who lived below the poverty line, child support contributed to 62% of their income while 31% came from labor. Receiving child support from nonresident fathers reduced the poverty gap by 39% among mothers who lived below the poverty line, and the effect went up to 50% among mothers who lived in extreme poverty (Cuesta & Meyer, 2014). Child support and assistance payments halved the post-separation income loss for mothers with school-aged children in Uruguay (Bucheli & Vigorito, 2017). Among mothers in Peru, child support payments were associated with ties to the ex-partner and children – a pattern found in the developed countries. The most disadvantaged Peruvian mothers were more likely to receive child support than those with better resources (Rios-Salas & Meyer, 2014). Again, these trends underline the significance of connections to the ex-partner and between the ex-partner and children for receiving child support, and the strong impact of child support in reducing childhood poverty in some developing countries.

Paternal attitudes to child support should not be ignored either. Physical contact with children and the quality of relationship with the child's mother also affect attitudes toward child support. A study conducted in Norway (Skevik, 2006) surveyed attitudes toward child support payments among fathers drawn from a national registry of nonresident parent database. It is important to mention that while previously the child support maintenance policy in Norway required payments from non-custodial parents to custodial parents based on their ability to pay, the reforms of 2001 now include consideration of the actual costs of children, the joint income of the parents, and the non-custodial parent's social contact with the child. Most Norwegian fathers indicated that "Liable parents who have much contact should pay less maintenance," "Child maintenance should not be so high it makes the recipient better off than reliable person," "Mothers who deny fathers contact with their children should not receive child maintenance," and "Child maintenance awards should not exceed the costs of having children in the household." When fathers' sociodemographic characteristics, the quality of fathers' relationship with the child, and mothers' and fathers' partnering statuses were used as predictors of fathers' attitudes toward child payments, fathers who had no contact with their child for three months and who had unfriendly relationships with their child's mother were more likely to state that fathers should not pay child support. Fathers who had new partners but no new children and fathers who had frequent contact with their children over the past month were more likely to state that fathers who have a lot of contact should pay less child support.

In short, establishing paternity and child support payments have an appreciable impact on:

- Reducing poverty and narrowing the poverty gap in lone-mother families, though variations exist in the degree to which this happens in the developed and developing countries;
- Father–child contacts and involvement in childrearing decisions;
- Attitudes toward child support payments, which influence the quality of and relationship with the child's mother and fathers' social contacts with children.

Paternity leave policies

A general claim is that parental leave policies are designed to provide more advantages and time allowance to mothers due to the benefits they bring to infants, families, and society. Maternity leave uptake is associated with less maternal stress during pregnancy and maternal postpartum depression (Avendano, Berkman, Brugiavini, & Pasini, 2015), lower infant and child mortality rates (Rossin, 2011; Ruhm, 2000; Heymann et al., 2011), longer breastfeeding and time spent with infant (Huang & Yang, 2015), and less low birthweight and premature births (Rossin, 2011; Stearns, 2015; Tanaka, 2005) in developed countries. Present European Union legislation suggests that women should take at least two weeks mandatory, and up to 14 weeks optional, paid maternity leave (Koslowski, Blum, & Moss, 2016). Regulations, eligibility, duration, and additional benefits of maternity leave vary across countries. The United States is one of the few western countries that does not offer paid maternity leave.

Workplace policies in many European countries have centralized the idea of gender equality by implementing opportunities to benefit new mothers, such as nurseries, childcare rooms, and breastfeeding time allowance. As important as these advances are, maternity leave is also one of the main sources of workplace discrimination against women across cultures. Pregnant women are less likely to be hired and promoted, and they are perceived as more emotional and less committed to work than their non-pregnant counterparts (Correll, Benard, & Paik, 2007). On average, women earn less than men with the same education and qualifications, and maternity leave widens the pay gap due to lost earnings (see Evertsson, 2016).

Expectations of motherhood, as well as women's biological role in childbearing, consistently determine mothers' and fathers' respective roles after childbirth and how much time they spend in caregiving. As has been mentioned on different occasions, women spend more time with children and do significantly more household labor than men, regardless of their work hours. Documenting time spent with children and in household labor, taking into account educational attainment, age, work hours, employment status, and uptake of parental leave, Baxter and Smart (2011) calculated that Australian mothers spent 30% more time with infants and preschool-aged children during weekdays than did fathers. The divide in childcare between mothers and fathers lessened on weekends, but mothers still cared for their children significantly more than did fathers. There were glaring gender discrepancies in household work as well. Mothers were involved in 3.5 hours of domestic work during the day, while fathers spent 1.3 hours. Interestingly, fathers who spoke English as a second language, cohabited with the child's mother, and worked less than 35 hours provided significantly more childcare than other men based on mothers' reports. Fathers who worked 55 hours or more a week were less likely to assist their children with eating, change their diaper, get them ready for bed, give them a bath, help them get dressed, or help them with brushing their teeth, than did fathers who worked 35–44 hours on average a week.

Ethnotheories or cultural scripts about gender roles can be a factor in the use of paternal leave across countries (Levtov et al., 2015). Annually, the International Social Survey Programme (ISSP) solicits perceptions about gender roles, division of household labor, and the use of parental leave across 41 cultures. Data from the 2012 ISSP Family and Changing Gender Roles IV survey revealed persistent perceived differences between men and women in terms of work roles and responsibility for childcare. When participants were asked to choose the best way for families with a child under school age to organize their family and work life, more than 40% of participants in Argentina, Bulgaria, China, Taiwan, the Czech Republic, Hungary, India, Japan, Latvia, Lithuania, Mexico, Philippines, Russia, the Slovak Republic, South Africa, Turkey, and Venezuela stated that the mother should stay at home, and that the father should work full-time. A majority of participants in Belgium, Chile, Denmark, Finland, France, Germany, Iceland, Ireland, Israel, Portugal, Slovenia, Spain, Switzerland, the United Kingdom, and the United States agreed with the statement that the mother should work part time, and the father should work full time. Only in the Netherlands and Sweden did a majority of the participants agree with the statement that both the mother and father should continue to work full time.

Not unexpectedly, in the 2012 ISSP survey, participants' perceptions about parental leave matched their ideas about who should work full time and who should care for children. A gender bias was quite visible when participants were asked "if both [parents] are in a similar work situation and are eligible for paid leave, how should this paid leave period be divided between mother and father?" A majority of participants in Argentina, Bulgaria, China, Croatia, the Czech Republic, Hungary, Israel, Latvia, Lithuania, Mexico, Russia, Slovakia, South Africa, Turkey, and Venezuela indicated that mothers should take the entirety of the paid leave whereas fathers should not take any leave. Most participants in Australia, Canada, Chile, Finland, Iceland, Ireland, Japan, South Korea, Norway, Portugal, Slovenia, Switzerland, and the United Kingdom stated that mothers should take the most and fathers should take just some paid leave. Only in Belgium, France, Germany, the Netherlands, Sweden, and the United States did participants indicate that paid leave should be split equally between mothers and fathers.

In spite of the gender-biased attitudes toward work and childcare reflected in these surveys, family policies by far support both mothers' and fathers' efforts at meeting parenting responsibilities after the child's birth to facilitate the transition to parenthood, but more so in developed than in developing countries. Only in a few

European countries have policies been restructured to scale up paternity leave to foster gender equality at work, to change men's breadwinner role, and to enhance paternal engagement during the care-intensive first year of a child's life. In 2016, the average length of paid father-specific leave was 8.4 weeks in the OECD countries, while the average length of paid maternal and parental leave was 55.2 weeks, though eligibility and additional benefits vary significantly between countries (see Table 7.1 for leave allocation for specific EU countries). Based on their eligibility and allowance of paternity leave, 90% of fathers in Denmark took two weeks or more paternity leave, with 60% of fathers in Australia taking the same allocation. By contrast, fathers in the United Kingdom and United States took less time off around childbirth: 33% of fathers in the United States took more than two weeks, with 24% taking less than one week off; 25% of fathers in the United Kingdom took more

TABLE 7.1 Duration of paid parental leave in EU countries, 2016

Country	Mother (weeks)*	Father (weeks)†
Austria	60	8.7
Belgium	32.3	19.3
Czech Republic	110	0
Denmark	50	2
Estonia	166	2
Finland	161	9
France	42	28
Germany	58	8.7
Greece	43	0.4
Hungary	160	1
Ireland	26	0
Italy	47.7	0.4
Latvia	94	1.4
Luxembourg	42	26.4
Netherlands	16	0.4
Poland	52	2
Portugal	30.1	22.3
Slovak Republic	164	0
Slovenia	52.1	2.9
Spain	16	2.1
Sweden	55.7	14.3
United Kingdom	39	2

Note: * Length of paid maternity and parental leave available to mothers in weeks
† Length of paid paternity and parental leave reserved for fathers in week

Source: From OECD, 2016, www.oecd.org/policy-briefs/parental-leave-where-are-the-fathers.pdf

than ten days, 37% taking between 6 to 10 days, and 39% taking less than five days off (Huerta et al., 2013). Some countries ensure father-specific parental leave to increase uptake, while others allow fathers to share parental leave. For example, in Finland, maternity leave is 17.5 weeks and paternity leave is 3 weeks, while shared parental leave is 26.5 weeks. Of course, fathers in developed countries take leave after a child is born in the absence of leave policies as well (Huerta et al. 2014).

In sharp contrast to the EU countries, most developing countries have no provisions for paternal leave. Among Caribbean countries only a handful (e.g., the Bahamas, 7 days and the Dominican Republic, 2 days) offer paternal leave. Few countries in Asia and the Middle East have policies on paternal leave. Two countries, China and India, with the world's largest numbers of fathers, have no paternity leave. In the poorer nations of Africa, things look a lot different compared to other low- and middle-income countries. Benin, Burkina Faso, and Cameroon, the Central African Republic, Chad, Cote d'Ivoire, Gabon, and Madagascar offer 10 days of paternal leave; Kenya offers 14 days and Burundi 15 days of paternal leave. Likewise, most Latin American countries have paternal leave policies (e.g., 2 days in Guatemala, 5 days in Chile, 8 days in Colombia, 10 days in Ecuador, and 14 consecutive days in Venezuela) (For a complete list see Levtov et al., 2015). It is not clear how many fathers take advantage of paternal leave in developing countries. Economic conditions (labor market, drop in household income), cultural beliefs about gender roles, and the availability of affordable childcare, fathers' knowledge about paternity leave policies, and the work culture all affect fathers' uptake of paternal leave in developing societies.

Attempts to determine what predicts men's use of paternity leave in the developed countries are instructive. Månsdotter, Fredlund, Hallqvist, and Magnusson (2010) assessed factors related to paternity leave uptake in Sweden using data from the Stockholm County Council's Public Health Survey. Paternity leave was categorized as fathers who took zero days (12.8%), 1–30 days (15.1%), 31–60 days (20.1%), 61–90 days (17.2%), 91–155 days (21.4%), and those who took more than 155 days (13.4%). Fathers who did not take any paternity leave were more likely to have been born outside Sweden, less likely to live with their partner or children, and more likely to smoke and have high levels of alcohol consumption than fathers who took at least one day of paternity leave. Fathers who were more educated, had higher incomes, had permanent jobs, were living with their partner and children, and had higher social reliance (e.g., support in crises situations, confidence in the health care system) were more likely to take at least 91 days of paternity leave. In estimating the relative chances of taking at least 60 days of paternity leave, several key factors emerged. Among the more salient ones, fathers who had university-level positions, public employment, and received higher levels of social support were more likely to take at least 60 days of paternity leave.

Reduction in earnings, workplace characteristics, and social networks too are associated with paternity leave uptake in European countries. Data from the Norwegian registry indicated that nontransferable paternity leave negatively affected fathers' earnings (Rege & Solli, 2013). On average, fathers experienced a 1–3% drop in their income relative to the amount of paternity leave they take. Peer effects and knowledge of the workplace also affected paternity leave uptake decision-making in Norway (Dahl, Løken, & Mogstad, 2014), and in Sweden, the percentage of women in the father's workplace, size of workplace, percentage of other male employees in the workplace to have previously taken parental leave, fathers' age, education, and income were all positively associated with first-time fathers' length of parental leave (Bygren & Duvander, 2006). Fathers in the United Kingdom who were older than 25 years, had a higher level of education, were white, married, worked between 34 and 44 hours per week, earned more than £10,400 p.a., owned a house, and were present at delivery had a higher likelihood of taking leave around childbirth than their less advantaged counterparts.

A qualitative study of Spanish families (Romero-Balsas, Muntanyola-Saura, & Rogero-Garcia, 2013) further highlights the role of job security and other sources of support for childcare and household work in amount of leave fathers are likely to take. Recall that fathers have the right to take 15 days paid paternity leave in Spain. From in-depth interviews with Spanish fathers, four main themes were identified in decision-making regarding the amount of time taken off from work following childbirth. Fathers in the study were divided into three groups: those who took less than 5 days, those who took 15 days, and those who took more than 1 month of paternity leave. Fathers who took 5 days off work saw paternity leave as a right, not as a duty, were more likely to have job insecurity and work-related obligations, and to view mothers as the main caregiver due to breastfeeding. Fathers who took 15 days off work saw paternity leave as a right and benefit, were more likely to have highly qualified jobs, and more willing to help mothers recover from birth and lessen maternal responsibility for childcare. Fathers in this group saw 15 days of leave as sufficient, often relying on continued care from relatives. Fathers who took 1 month or more of parental leave were more likely to see parental leave as a right and duty that enabled them to fulfill their parental responsibilities. These fathers were more likely to work in the public sector or large private companies, and felt less work obligations during parental leave. They generally accepted that their primary responsibility was that of childcare during the leave, but they also relied on other family members to provide care, and sought paid help for household chores.

What happens when policy emphasis is placed on increasing paternal uptake of leave by introducing special provisions for fathers? Ekberg, Eriksson, and Friebel (2013) evaluated the Swedish "Daddy Month" reform, a parental leave policy introduced on January 1, 1995 that allows fathers to take 1 month off from work per child, with benefits. This was meant to foster father participation in childcare in the first year of the child's life, decrease the inequality in division of household labor, and increase women's labor market participation. The parental leave policy in Sweden provides paid maternal and paternal leave after the birth of the child and paid leave for the care of sick children. Before the reform, fathers were allowed to take (1) 2 weeks leave during the first 60 days after the childbirth, with proportional income benefits; (2) 90 days of leave with an hourly wage; or (3) a maximum of 360 days leave with a wage replacement of 80%. The policy had a "use it or lose it" stipulation whereby parental leave of 90 days or 360 days can be used until the child turns 8 years old or finishes first grade in school. Leave uptake increased in fathers of children born after compared with fathers of children born before the reform. A revealing aspect of these data were the seasonal patterns in the uptake of paternal leave. That is, fathers showed a preference for taking days off during the summer months and in December during the holiday season. Fathers were more likely to take days off during the child's second year and the last year of their paternity leave allowance. The reform did not have a significant effect on fathers' care of sick children (see also Hagqvist, Nordenmark, Pérez, Alemán, & Gådin, 2017 for changes in gender roles as result of change in parental leave over two decades).

Perhaps an equally weighty question is: how does the duration of fathers' leave from work around childbirth and during the child's first year of life predict time spent with infants during weekdays and weekends? Findings of studies conducted in Australia, Spain, the United States, the United Kingdom, and Denmark provide a partial answer to this question. Beginning with Australia, fathers are allowed to take 2 weeks paid leave with benefits (eligibility criteria differ by individuals) and up to 52 weeks transferable leave with no pay, but with job security (see Whitehouse, Baird, Brennan, & Baxter, 2017 for a detailed discussion of leave policies in Australia). Only 24.1% of fathers in Australia took paid parental leave, whereas 45.5% took annual leave around the birth of a child (Martin et al., 2014). Using weekday and weekend diary accounts of time use in the Growing up in Australia: Longitudinal Study of Australian Children (LSAC), Hosking, Whitehouse, and Baxter (2010) were able to determine whether the duration of fathers' leave from work affected their involvement with infants in three areas: fathers' presence, time with infant, and caregiving activities, including feeding, changing diapers, and bathing. Duration of fathers' leave was divided into five categories: no leave (22%), less than 2 weeks (32%), 2–3 weeks (22%), 3 weeks (6%), and 4 weeks and longer (17%). Fathers' type of employment, frequency of weekend and evening work, existence of weekend work, self-employment, holding multiple jobs, gross weekly income, age and education, as well as maternal employment, maternity leave uptake, breastfeeding status, and marital status were used as control variables in the study.

Overall, 35.9% of infants were awake with only father near them for a duration of 24 minutes, while 93.4% of infants were awake with only mother near them for a duration of 4.5 hours on weekdays. On weekends, almost 45% of infants were awake with only father within proximity of them for an average duration of 36 minutes, while 77.2% of infants were awake with only mother within proximity of them for an average duration of 2.3 hours between 6:00 a.m. and 9:30 p.m. Fathers' workday hours and weekly income were negatively associated with their care involvement, while fathers' irregular and regular weekend work were positively associated with fathers' time with infant during work days. Fathers' work hours, irregular and regular weekend work, and nonstandard work hours were negatively associated with fathers' time with their child on weekends, but fathers' weekly income was positively associated with duration of fathers' time with infants during weekends. Duration of leave was not associated with sole father care on weekdays, but infants whose fathers took 2 weeks leave or 4 or more weeks leave were more likely to receive 1 hour of sole fatherly care during the weekends than those whose fathers did not take any paternity leave.

Expanding on the theme explored in Australian families, Romero–Balsas (2015) examined the links between paternity leave uptake and father involvement in childcare using data from The Social Use of Parental Leave in Spain – 2012 survey. A major focus was to determine the associations between paternity leave uptake and fathers' engagement in childcare and domestic tasks, and whether the percentage of fathers' involvement in childcare and domestic tasks were different by the number of children in the family. The ratio of paternity leave uptake was similar among fathers with one child and those with more than one child. There were no differences between fathers who took and did not take paternity leave with respect to involvement in different categories of child-related activities: care for an ill child, playing, bathing, dressing, putting the child to bed or getting the child up, staying with the child, taking the child to school or picking the child up from school, and helping with homework. Nor were there significant differences in engagement in domestic tasks, such as cleaning the house, washing clothes, preparing lunch/dinner, and doing the shopping between those who did and did not take leave. Fathers who had one child were more likely to define themselves as non-traditional when it comes to engaging in childcare and carrying out domestic tasks than did fathers with more than one child.

As you may have gathered, there is no orderliness to the findings on amount of paternal leave and involvement in child-related activities in developed countries. Data on fathers in Australia, Denmark, the United Kingdom, and the United States provide more consistent links between leave uptake and fathers' care investment with children. Danish fathers who took leave when children were less than a year old were more likely to feed and change diapers daily, and play with their infant at least a few times a week compared with fathers who did not take any leave – findings that mirror those found for Australian fathers. Fathers in the United Kingdom who took leave were more likely to feed their child, get up for the child at least once per night, give the child a bath, and to read to the child at least a few times per week; and in the United States, fathers who took leave were more likely to help their child get dressed and change diapers at least once a day and read to their child a few times a week compared with fathers who did not take any leave. This pattern held for the first 3 years of children's lives (Huerta et al., 2014).

The last point we wish to make here is that paternity leave uptake is associated with different aspects of family functioning and childhood outcomes. After the "daddy-quota" was implemented in Norway, there was a reduction in spousal conflicts emanating from the division of household work (Kotasadam & Finseraas, 2011). Paternal leave uptake reduced gendered time use in Sweden and Spain (Hagqvist et al., 2017), and in Quebec, Canada, fathers were more likely to engage in household work following father leave reforms (Pattnaik, 2013). Although it is difficult to say whether they are a direct result of paternal leave or not, Swedish couples were less likely to break up when fathers took in excess of 2 weeks leave during the birth of the first child (Olah, 2001), paternal leave had a positive effect on work–life balance in European countries (OECD, 2016), and there was less violence in families where fathers took paternal leave (Holter et al., 2008). Paternal leave uptake was also associated with postpartum depression in mothers. A French study (Sejourne, Vaslot, Beaume, Goutaudier, & Chabrol, 2012) found that perceived social support was not associated with maternal depression, but paternal involvement in childcare was negatively associated with maternal depression at 2 months postpartum.

There is evidence that children too benefit when fathers take leave. Paternity leave was related to the greater likelihood of breastfeeding during the first year of the child's life (Flacking et al., 2010), lower rates of child injury among 0–4 year-olds in Sweden (Laflamme et al., 2012), and to more contact with Swedish children post-separation (Duvander & Jans, 2009). Extended paternal leave was positively linked to father–child bonding in Sweden (Haas & Hwang, 2009), cognitive functioning in Australian children (Huerta et al., 2013), and to examination scores in Norwegian children (Cools, Fiva, & Kirkebøen, 2015). Again, it is possible that increased paternal leave leads to higher levels of engagement and monitoring of children on the part of fathers, which may then have favorable effects on children's cognitive and social functioning and their overall well-being. In other words, paternal investment in children likely moderate and/or mediate the associations between paternal leave uptake and childhood functioning. Controlling for maternal involvement in childcare while determining these associations would make a stronger case for the impact of employment leave policies on paternal investment in caring for children and on childhood development (see Huerta, et al., 2014).

Summary and recommendations

Despite the limited number of evaluation studies on the long-term effects of social policies on children and families across cultures, those pertaining to paternity establishment, child support, and paternity leave seem to have a positive influence on fathers' involvement in caregiving and on children's well-being. More specifically, paternity leave uptake boosts father's level of involvement in care during the first year of children's lives in a number of developed societies. Paternity establishment and child support enforcement provide more financial resources to children while influencing father–child contacts in developed and developing countries. Among children born out of marriage, child support payments increase fathers' emotional engagement with children and significantly reduce childhood poverty and the poverty gap.

From what has been discussed above, cultural expectations, views about motherhood and fatherhood, fathers' sociodemographic characteristics, fathers' work-related obligations, the work organization culture (peers, receptiveness to fathers' caregiving concerns), and the lack of awareness about the use and benefits of paternity leave mitigate against men taking time off from work after childbirth. This aside, better educated, economically privileged fathers with job security are more likely to exploit leave opportunities than are their less economically privileged peers (Huerta et al., 2013). Moreover, fathers who take maximum time off around childbirth tend to have more flexible attitudes toward gender roles and the division of caregiving responsibilities than those who take no or limited leave (Månsdotter et al., 2010; Romero-Balsas et al., 2013).

After more than two decades of work in this area, policies that offer compensation and consider flexibility and eligibility seem to work for families in the European countries (Van Belle, 2016). Persuasive arguments have been made for more liberal entitlements, bonuses in cash or time, and active information campaigns to increase leave uptake (Van Belle, 2016). A few countries (e.g., Sweden) already offer bonuses and cash to mothers and fathers, beyond what they receive for parental leave, only if they take full leave. In the Nordic countries, reserving part of parental leave for fathers (the "daddy quota") seems to pay dividends because this has contributed to an increase in the uptake of paternal leave (Rege & Solli, 2013). In the economically strapped countries of the developing world, the cash incentives may well be out of reach for most, but active public campaigns (e.g., through the use of technology) about voluntary paternal leave and its impact on women's employment and the entire family's health and well-being, could hold tremendous sway in encouraging men to become more responsible and engaged caregivers (Van Belle, 2016; Levtov et al., 2015). At the same time, more inclusive policies are needed to acknowledge and enhance the parenting roles of noncustodial, nonresident fathers, step/social fathers, incarcerated fathers, fathers of children with disabilities, and gay fathers.

REFERENCES

Abrahamse, M. E., Niec, L. N., Junger, M., Boer, F., & Lindauer, R. L. (2016). Risk factors for attrition from an evidence-based parenting program: Findings from the Netherlands. *Children and Youth Services Review*, 6442–6450. doi: 10.1016/j.childyouth.2016.02.025

Adamsons, K., & Pasley, K. (2013). Refining identity theory to better account for relationships and context: Applications to fathering. *Journal of Family Theory and Review*, *5*(3), 241–261. doi: 10.1111/jftr.12014

Adamsons, K., & Johnson, S. K. (2013). An updated and expanded meta-analysis of non-resident fathering and child well-being. *Journal of Family Psychology*, *27*(4), 589–599. doi: 10.1037/a0033786

Ahmed, R. A. (2005). Egyptian families. In J. L. Roopnarine & U.P. Gielen (Eds.), *Families in global perspective* (pp. 151–168). Boston, MA: Pearson.

Ahmed, R. A. (2013). The father's role in the Arab world: Cultural perspectives. In D. W. Shwalb, B. J., Shwalb, & M. E. Lamb (Eds.), *Fathers in cultural context* (pp. 122–150). New York: Routledge.

Ahmed, R. A., Rohner, R. P., & Carrasco, M. A. (2012). Relations between psychological adjustment and perceived parental, sibling, best friend, and teacher acceptance among Kuwaiti adolescents. In K. Ripoll-Nuñez, A. L. Comunian & C. M. Brown (Eds.), *Expanding horizons: Current research on interpersonal acceptance* (pp. 1–10). Boca Raton, FL: Brown Walker Press.

Ahmed, R. A., Rohner, R. P., Khaleque, A., & Gielen, U. P. (2016). Parental acceptance and rejection in the Arab world: How do they influence children's development? In U. P. Gielen & J. L. Roopnarine (Eds.), *Childhood and adolescence: Cross-cultural perspectives and applications* (pp. 121–150). Santa Barbara, CA: Praeger/ABC-Clio.

Ahmeduzzaman, M., & Roopnarine, J. (1992). Sociodemographic factors, functioning style, social support, and fathers' involvement with preschoolers in African-American families. *Journal of Marriage and the Family*, *54*, 699–707.

Ahn, S. M., Lee, K. Y., & Lee, S. M. (2013). Fathers' parenting participation and time. *Korean Family Resource Management Associations*, *17*(2), 93–119.

Ahnert, L., Pinquart, M., & Lamb, M. (2006). Security of children's relationships with nonparental care providers: A meta-analysis. *Child Development*, *77*(3), 664–679. doi: 10.1111/j.1467-8624.2006.00896.x

Ahnert, L., Teufl, L., Ruiz, N., Piskernik, B., Supper, B., Remiorz, S., Gesing, A., & Nowacki, K. (2017). Father–child play during the preschool years and child internalizing behaviors: Between robustness and vulnerability. *Infant Mental Health Journal, 38*(6), 743–756. doi: 10.1002/imhj.21679

Ainsworth, M. D. (1962). The effects of maternal deprivation: A review of findings and controversy in the context of research strategy. In *Deprivation of maternal care: A reassessment of its effects* (WHO Public Health Papers, no. 15, pp. 87–195). Geneva, Switzerland: World Health Organization.

Ainsworth, M. D. S. (1967). *Infancy in Uganda: Infant care and the growth of love.* Oxford: Johns Hopkins University Press.

Ainsworth, M. D. S. (1989). Attachments beyond infancy. *American Psychologist, 44,* 709–716.

Ainsworth, M. D. S., & Bell, S. M. (1970). Attachment, exploration, and separation: Illustrated by the behavior of one-year-olds in a strange situation. *Child Development, 41,* 49–67.

Ainsworth, M. D. S., Blehar, M. C., Waters, E., & Wall, S. (1978). *Patterns of attachment: A psychological study of the strange situation.* Hillsdale, NJ: Erlbaum.

Ainsworth, M. D. S., & Wittig, B. A. (1969). Attachment and exploratory behavior of one-year-olds in a strange situation. In B. M. Foss (Ed.), *Determinants of infant behavior* (vol. 4, pp. 111–136). London: Methuen.

Al-Hassan, S. (2009). *Evaluation of the Better Parenting Program: A study conducted for UNICEF.* Amman, Jordan: UNICEF.

Alici, C. (2012). Paternal contributions to children's cognitive functioning and school readiness. Unpublished master's thesis. Koc University, Istanbul.

Al-Krenawi, A. (2013). Mental health and polygamy: The Syrian case. *World Journal of Psychiatry, 3*(1), 1–7. doi: 10.5498/wjp.v3.i1.1

Al-Yagon, M. (2011). Fathers' coping resources and children's socioemotional adjustment among children with learning disabilities. *Journal of Learning Disabilities, 44*(6), 491–507. doi: 10.1177/1087054710378582

Amato, P. R. (1994). Father child relations, mother child relations, and offspring psychological well being in early adulthood. *Journal of Marriage and the Family, 56,* 1031–1042.

Amato, P. R. (1998). *More than money? Men's contributions to their children's lives.* New York: Lawrence Erlbaum Associates.

Amato, P. R., & Gilbreth, J. (1999). Nonresident fathers and children's well-being: A meta-analysis. *Journal of Marriage and the Family, 61,* 557–573.

Amato, P. R., & Keith, B. (1991). Parental divorce and the well-being of children: A meta-analysis. *Psychological Bulletin, 110*(1), 26–46.

Anderson, K. G. (2015). Father absence, childhood stress, and reproductive maturation in South Africa. *Human Nature, 26*(4), 401–425. doi: 10.1007/s12110-12015-9243-9246

Anderson, K. G. (2017). Establishment of legal paternity for children of unmarried American women: Tradeoffs in male commitment to paternal investment. *Human Nature, 28*(2), 168–200. doi: 10.1007/s12110-12017-9284-0

Anderson, P. (2007). The changing roles of fathers in the context of Jamaican family life. (Working Paper no. 10). Kingston: Planning Institute of Jamaica.

Anderson, P., & Daley, C. (2015). African-Caribbean fathers: The conflict between masculinity and fathering. In J. L. Roopnarine (Ed.), *Fathers across cultures: The importance, roles, and diverse practices of dads* (pp. 13–62). Santa Barbara, CA: Praeger/ABC-Clio.

Anderson, S., Qiu, W., & Wheeler, S. J. (2017). The Quality of father–child rough-and-tumble play and toddlers' aggressive behavior in China. *Infant Mental Health Journal, 38*(6), 726–742. doi: 10.1002/imhj.21675

Antúnez Z., de la Osa, N., Granero, R., & Ezpeleta, L. (2018). Reciprocity between parental psychopathology and oppositional symptoms from preschool to middle childhood. *Journal of Clinical Psychology, 74*(3), 489–504. doi: 10.1002/jclp.22504

Argys, L. M., & Peters, H. E. (2001). Interactions between unmarried fathers and their children: the role of paternity establishment and child-support policies. *American Economic Review, 91*(2), 125–129. doi: 10.1257/aer.91.2.125

Ashburn, K., Kerner, B., Ojamuge, D., & Lundgren, R. (2016). Evaluation of the responsible, engaged, and loving (real) fathers initiative on physical child punishment and intimate partner violence in northern Uganda. *Prevention Science, 18*(7), 854–864. doi: 10.1007/s11121-016-0713-9

Astone, N. M., & Peters, H. E. (2014). Longitudinal influences on men's lives: Research from the Transition to Fatherhood project and beyond. *Fathering, 2,* 161–177.

Astone, N. M., Nathanson, C. A., Schoen, R., & Kim, Y. J. (1999). Family demography social theory and investment in social capital. *Population and Development Review, 25*(1), 1–31.

Astone. N. M., Karas, A., & Stolte, A. (2016). *Father's time with children: Income and residential differences.* Washington, DC: The Urban Institute.

Australian Bureau of Statistics (2013). *Australian social trends.* Catalogue no. 4102.0. Canberra: ABS.

Australian Bureau of Statistics (2016). *ABS census of population and housing.* Canberra: ABS.

Avendano, M., Berkman, L., F., Brugiavini, A., & Pasini, G. (2015). The long-run effect of maternity leave benefits on mental health: Evidence from European countries. *Social Science and Medicine, 132,* 45–53. doi: 10.1016/j.socscimed.2015.02.037

Awong-Persaud, D. (2003). The impact of involvement and characteristics of fathers on male adolescents' self-esteem in Port-of-Spain, Trinidad. M.Sc. thesis. University of the West Indies, St. Augustine, Trinidad.

Bailey, W., Branche, C., McGarrity, G., & Stuart, S. (1998). *Family and the quality of gender relations.* Kingston, Jamaica: Institute of Social and Economic Research.

Baker, C. E. (2013). African American fathers' depression and stress as predictors of father involvement during early childhood. *Journal of Black Psychology, 40*(4), 311–333.

Baker, C. E. (2015). African American and Hispanic fathers' work characteristics and preschool children's cognitive development. *Journal of Family Issues, 37*(11), 1514–1534.

Baker, C. E., & Vernon-Feagans, L. (2015). Fathers' language input during shared book activities: Links to children's kindergarten achievement. *Journal of Applied Developmental Psychology, 36,* 53–59. doi: 10.1016/j.appdev.2014.11.009

Baker, J. K., Fenning, R. M., & Crnic, K. A. (2011). Emotion socialization by mothers and fathers: Coherence among behaviors and associations with parent attitudes and children's social competence. *Social Development, 20*(2), 412–430.

Ball, J., & Moselle, S. (2015). Indigenous fathers' journeys in Canada: Turning around disrupted circles of care. In J. L. Roopnarine (Ed.), *Fathers across cultures: The importance, roles, and diverse practices of dads* (pp. 205–228). Santa Barbara, CA: Praeger/ABC-Clio.

Ball, J., & Wahedi, M.O.K. (2010). Exploring fatherhood in Bangladesh. *Childhood Education, 86,* 366–370. doi: 10.1080/00094056.2010.10523171

Barber, N. (2008). Explaining cross-national differences in polygyny intensity: Resource-defense, sex ratio, and infectious diseases. *Cross-Cultural Research, 42*(2), 103–117. doi: 10.1177/1069397108314587

Barker, G., Contreras, J.M., Heilman, B., Singh, A.K., Verma, R.K., & Nascimento, M. (2011). *Evolving men: Initial results from the International Men and Gender Equality Survey (IMAGES).* Washington, DC: International Center for Research on Women (ICRW) and Rio de Janeiro: Instituto Promundo.

Barker, G., Ricardo, C., Nascimento, M., Olukoya, A., & Santos, C. (2010). Questioning gender norms with men to improve health outcomes: Evidence of impact. *Global Public Health, 5*(5), 539–553. doi: 10.1080/17441690902942464

Bastos, A. C. S., Pontes, V. V., Brasileiro, P. G., & Serra, H. M. (2013). Fathering in Brazil: A diverse and unknown reality. In D. W. Shwalb, B. J. Shwalb, & M. E. Lamb (Eds.), *Fathers in cultural context* (pp. 228–249). New York and London: Routledge.

Baumrind, D. (1969). Authoritarian vs. authoritative parental control. *Adolescence, 3*, 255–272.

Baumrind, D. (1996). Parenting: The discipline controversy revisited. *Family Relations, 45*, 405–414.

Baumrind, D. B. (1967). Child care practices anteceding three patterns of preschool behavior. *Genetic Psychology Monographs, 75*(1), 43–88.

Baxter, J. (2017). *Stay-at-home dads (facts sheet).* Melbourne: Australian Institute of Family Studies.

Baxter, J., & Smart, D. (2011). *Fathering in Australia among couple families with young children.* Department of Families, Housing, Community Services and Indigenous Affairs, Occasional Paper no. 37. Canberra: Australian Government.

Becker, G. S. (1981). *A treatise on the family.* Cambridge, MA: Harvard University Press.

Belsky, J. (1979). The interrelation of parental and spousal behavior during infancy in traditional nuclear families: An exploratory analysis. *Journal of Marriage and Family, 41*, 749–755.

Belsky, J. (1984). The determinants of parenting: A process model. *Child Development, 55*(1), 83–96.

Belsky, J., Fish, M., & Isabella, R. A. (1991). Continuity and discontinuity in infant negative and positive emotionality: Family antecedents and attachment consequences. *Developmental Psychology, 27*, 421–431.

Belsky, J., Steinberg, L., & Draper, P. (1991) Childhood experience, interpersonal development, and reproductive strategy: An evolutionary theory of socialization. *Child Development, 62*, 647–670. doi: 10.2307/1131166

Benetti, S. P., & Roopnarine, J. L. (2006). Paternal involvement with school-aged children in Brazilian families: Association with childhood competence. *Sex Roles, 55*, 669–678.

Benzies, K., Magill-Evans, J., Harrison, M. J., MacPhail, S., & Kimak, C. (2008). Strengthening new fathers' skills in interaction with their 5-month-old infants: Who benefits from a brief intervention? *Public Health Nursing, 25*(5), 431–439. doi: 10.1111/j.1525-1446.2008.00727.x

Berggren, M., Eremin, N., Kazansky, S., Martsenyuk, V., Motygin, V., & Turovets, A. (2010). *Father school: Step by step.* Moscow: BEST-Print Printing House.

Berry, J. W. (1980). Acculturation as varieties of adaptation. In A. M. Padillo (Ed.), *Acculturation: Theories, models, and some new findings* (pp. 9–25). Boulder, CO: Westview Press.

Berry, J.W. (1997). Immigration, acculturation and adaptation. *Applied Psychology, 46*, 5–68.

Berry, J. W. (1999). Intercultural relations in plural societies. *Canadian Psychology/Psychologie Canadienne, 40*(1), 12–21. doi: 10.1037/h0086823

Berry, J. W. (2013). Global psychology. *South African Journal of Psychology, 43*, 391–401. doi: 10.1177/0081246313504517

Berry, J. W. (2016). Ecocultural perspective on human behaviour. In A. Uskul & S. Oishi (Eds.), *Socioeconomic environment and human psychology.* Oxford: Oxford University Press.

Berry, J. W. (2017a). Migration and intercultural relations in the Caribbean region. *Caribbean Journal of Psychology, 9*, 97–109.

Berry, J. W. (2017b). Theories and models of acculturation. In S. J. Schwartz & J. B. Unger (Eds.), *Oxford handbook of acculturation and health* (pp. 15–27). New York: Oxford University Press.

Berry, J. W., & Sabatier, C. (2011). Variations in the assessment of acculturation attitudes: Their relationships with psychological wellbeing. *International Journal of Intercultural Relations, 35*(5), 658–669. doi: 10.1016/j.ijintrel.2011.02.002

Berry, J. W., Phinney, J.S., Sam, D.L., and Vedder, P. (2006). *Immigrant youth in cultural transitions: Acculturation, identity, and adaptation across national contexts.* Mahwah, NJ: Erlbaum.

Bhandari, N., & Karkara, R. (2006). *Regional capacity building workshop on men, caring and fatherhood.* Kathmandu: Save the Children Sweden.

Biblarz, T., & Stacey, J. (2010). How does the gender of parents matter? *Journal of Marriage and Family, 72*(1), 3–22. doi: 10.1111/j.1741–3737.2009.00678.x

Bich, T. H., & Cuong, N. M. (2017). Changes in knowledge, attitude and involvement of fathers in supporting exclusive breastfeeding: A community-based intervention study in a rural area of Vietnam. *International Journal of Public Health, 62*(1), 17–26. doi: 10.1007/s00038-016-0882-0

Björk, S. (2013). Doing morally intelligible fatherhood: Swedish fathers' accounts of their parental part-time work choices. *Fathering, 11*(2), 221–237.

Blanchard, V. L., Hawkins, A. J., Baldwin, S. A., & Fawcett, E. B. (2009). Investigating the effects of marriage and relationship education on couples' communication skills: A meta-analytic study. *Journal of Family Psychology, 23*(2), 203–214. doi: 10.1037/a0015211

Block, S., Brown, C. A., Barretti, L. M., Walker, E., Yudt, M., & Fretz, R. (2014). A mixed-method assessment of a parenting program for incarcerated fathers. *The Journal of Correctional Education, 65*(1), 50–67.

Bogat, G. A., DeJonghe, E., Levendosky, A. A., Davidson, W. S., & von Eye, A. (2006). Trauma symptoms among infants exposed to intimate partner violence. *Child Abuse and Neglect, 30*(2), 109–125.

Bonhomme, J., Stephens, T., & Braithwaite, R. (2006). African-American males in the United States prison system: Impact on family and community. *Journal of Men's Health and Gender, 3*(3), 223–226. doi: 10.1016/j.jmhg.2006.06.003

Bornstein, M. H., & Cote, L. R. (2004). Mothers' parenting cognitions in cultures of origin, acculturating cultures, and cultures of destination. *Child Development, 75*, 1–15.

Bornstein, M. H., Putnick, D. L., Lansford, J. E. Pastorelli, C., Skinner, A. T., Sorbring, E., & . . . Oburu, P. (2014). Mother and father socially desirable responding in nine countries: Two kinds of agreement and relations to parenting self-reports. *International Journal of Psychology, 50*(3), 174–185. doi: 10.1002/ijop.12084

Bossardi, C. N., Gomes, L. B., Vieira, M. L., & Crepaldi, M. A. (2013). Engajamento paterno no cuidado a crianças de 4 a 6 anos [Paternal engagement in the care of 4–6 years old children]. *Psicologia Argumento, 31*(73), 237–246.

Bostanabad M. A., Areshtanab H. N., Balila M, Jafarabadi M. A., & Ravanbakhsh K. (2017). Effect of a supportive-training intervention on mother–infant attachment. *Iranian Journal of Pediatrics, 27*(6): e10565. doi: 10.5812/ijp.10565

Bowen, M. (1974). Toward the differentiation of self in one's family of origin. In F. Andres & J. Lorio (Eds.), *Georgetown family symposia: Volume I.* Washington, DC: Department of Psychiatry, Georgetown Medical Center.

Bowlby, J. (1969), *Attachment and loss, Vol. 1: Attachment.* New York: Basic Books.

Bowlby, J. (1973). *Attachment and loss, Vol. 2: Separation.* New York: Basic Books.

Bowlby, J. (1982). *Attachment and loss. Vol. 1: Attachment* (2nd ed.). New York: Basic Books.

Boyce, P., Condon, J., Barton, J., & Corkindale, C. (2007). First-time fathers' study: psychological distress in expectant fathers during pregnancy. *Australian and New Zealand Journal of Psychiatry, 41*(9), 718–725. doi: 10.1080/00048670701517959

Boyce, T., Essex, M., Alkon, A., Goldsmith, H. H., Kraemer, H., C., & Kupfer, D., J. (2006). Early father involvement moderates biobehavioral susceptibility to mental health problems in middle childhood. *American Academy of Child and Adolescent Psychiatry, 45*(12), 1510–1520.

Braungart-Rieker, J., Zentall, S., Lickenbrock, D. M., Ekas, N. V., Oshio, T., & Planalp, E. (2014). Attachment in the making: Mother and father sensitivity and infants' responses during the Still-Face Paradigm. *Journal of Experimental Child Psychology, 125*, 63–84.

Breaux, R. P., Harvey, E. A., & Lugo-Candelas, C. I. (2014). The role of parent psychopathology in the development of preschool children with behavior problems. *Journal of Clinical Child and Adolescent Psychology, 43*(5), 777–790.

Brennan, A., Marshall-Lucette, S., Ayers, S., & Ahmed, H. (2007). A qualitative exploration of the couvade syndrome in expectant fathers. *Journal of Reproductive and Infant Psychology, 25*(1), 18–39. doi: 10.1080/02646830601117142

Bretherton, I. (2010). Fathers in attachment theory and research: A review. *Early Child Development and Care, 180*(1–2), 9–23. doi: 10.1080/03004430903414661

Bretherton, I., Lambert, J. D., & Golby, B. (2006). Modeling and reworking childhood experiences: Involved fathers' representations of being parented and of parenting a preschool child. In O. Mayseless, & O. Mayseless (Eds.), *Parenting representations: Theory, research, and clinical implications* (pp. 177–207). New York: Cambridge University Press. doi: 10.1017/CBO9780511499869.007

Brodzinsky, D., & Pertman, A. (Eds.) (2011). *Adoption by lesbians and gay men: A new dimension in family diversity.* New York: Oxford University Press.

Brodzinsky, D. M. (2011). Adoption by lesbians and gay men: A national survey of adoption agency policies and practices. In D. Brodzinsky & A. Pertman (Eds.), *Adoption by lesbians and gay men: A new dimension in family diversity* (pp. 436–456). New York: Oxford University Press.

Bronfenbrenner, U. (1979). *The ecology of human development: Experiments by nature and design.* Cambridge, MA: Harvard University Press.

Bronfenbrenner, U., & Morris, P. A. (2006). The bioecological model of human development. In W. Damon & R. M. Lerner (Eds.), *Handbook of child psychology, Vol. 1: Theoretical models of human development* (6th ed.) (pp. 793–828). New York: Wiley.

Bronte-Tinkew, J., Carrano, J., Horowitz, A., & Kinukawa, A. (2008). Involvement among resident fathers and links to infant cognitive outcomes. *Journal of Family Issues, 29*(9), 1211–1244.

Bronte-Tinkew, J., Horowitz, A., & Scott, M. E. (2009). Fathering with multiple partners: Links to children's well-being in early childhood. *Journal of Marriage and Family, 71*(3), 608–631. doi: 10.1111/j.1741-3737.2009.00622.x

Brown, G., Mangelsdorf, S. C., & Neff, C. (2012). Father involvement paternal sensitivity, and father–child attachment security in the first 3 years. *Journal of Family Psychology, 26*(3), 421–430.

Brown, J., Newland, A., Anderson, P., & Chevannes, B. (1997). Caribbean fatherhood: Under researched, misunderstood. In J. L. Roopnarine, & J. Brown (Eds.), *Caribbean families: Diversity among ethnic groups* (pp. 85–113). Westport, CT: Ablex.

Bucheli, M., & Vigorito, A. (2017). *Separation, child-support and well-being in Uruguay.* Instituto de Economía, Facultad de Ciencias Económicas y Administración. Uruguay: Universidad de la República.

Bunston, W. (2013). What about the fathers? Bringing "Dads on Board" with their infants and toddlers following violence. *Journal of Family Studies, 19*(1), 70–79.

Bureau of Labor Statistics. (2014). *American time use survey.* Washington, DC: U.S. Department of Labor, Bureau of Labor Statistics.

Burgess, A. (2006). *The costs and benefits of active fatherhood: Evidence and insights to inform the development of policy and practice.* Available at www.fatherhoodinstitute.org/index.php?id= 0&cID=586

Burton, L. M., Bonilla-Silva, E., Ray, V., Buckelew, R., & Hordge Freeman, E. (2010). Critical race theories, colorism, and the decade's research on families of color. *Journal of Marriage and Family, 72*(3), 440–459.

Bus, A. G., van IJzendoorn M. H., & Pellegrini A. D. (1995). Joint book reading makes for success in learning to read: A meta-analysis on intergenerational transmission of literacy. *Review of Educational Research, 65*(1), 1–21. doi: 10.3102/00346543065001001

Bygren, M., & Duvander, A. (2006). Parents' workplace situation and fathers' parental leave use. *Journal of Marriage and Family, 68*(2), 363–372. doi: 10.1111/j.1741–3737.2006.00258.x

Byrd-Craven, J., Auer, B. J., Granger, D. A., & Massey, A. R. (2012). The father–daughter dance: The relationship between father–daughter relationship quality and daughters' stress response. *Journal of Family Psychology, 26*(1), 87–94. doi: 10.1037/a0026588

Cabella, W., Fernández, M., & Prieto, V. (2015). Las transformaciones de los hogares uruguayos vistas a través de los censos de 1996 y 2011. *Atlas sociodemográfico y de la desigualdad del Uruguay 6*, Uruguay: Instituto Nacional de Estadística.

Cabinet Office. (2013). *Gender equality white book in 2013.* Available at www.gender.go.jp/about_danjo/whitepaper/h25/gaiyou/index.html

Cabrera, N., Aldoney, D., & Tamis-LeMonda, C. (2013). Latino fathers. In N. J. Cabrera & C. S. Tamis-LeMonda (Eds.), *Handbook of father involvement: Multidisciplinary perspectives* (2nd ed.) (pp. 244–260). Mahwah, NJ: Lawrence Erlbaum Associates.

Cabrera, N. J., Fagan, J., & Farrie, D. (2008). Explaining the long reach of fathers' prenatal involvement on later paternal engagement with children. *Journal of Marriage and the Family, 70*, 1094–1107. doi: 10.1111/j.1741–3737.2008.00551.x

Cabrera, N., Fitzgerald, H. E., Bradley, R. H., & Roggman, L. (2007). Modeling the dynamics of paternal influences on children over the life course. *Applied Development Science, 11*(4), 185–189.

Cabrera, N. J., Fitzgerald, H. E., Bradley, R. H., & Roggman, L. (2014). The ecology of father–child relationships: An expanded model. *Journal of Family Theory and Review, 6*, 336–354. doi: 10.1111/jftr.12054

Cabrera, N. J., Karberg, E., Malin, J. L., & Aldoney, D. (2017). The magic of play: Low-income mothers' and fathers' playfulness and children's emotion regulation and vocabulary skills. *Infant Mental Health Journal, 38*(6), 757–771.

Cabrera, N. J., Ryan, R., Shannon, J. D., Brooks-Gunn, J., Vogel, C., Raikes, H., Tamis-LeMonda, C. S., et al. (2004). Fathers in the Early Head Start National Research and Evaluation Study: How are they involved with their children? *Fathering, 2*, 5–30.

Cabrera, N. J., Shannon, J. D., & La Taillade, J. J. (2009). Predictors of coparenting in Mexican American families and links to parenting and child social emotional development. *Infant Mental Health Journal, 30*(5), 523–548.

Cabrera, N., Shannon, J., & Tamis-LeMonda, C. (2007). Fathers' influence on their children's cognitive and emotional development: From toddlers to pre-k. *Applied Developmental Science, 11*(4), 208–213.

Cabrera, N., & Tamis-LeMonda, C. (Eds.) (2013). *Handbook of father involvement.* New York: Routledge.

Cancian, M., Meyer, D. R., & Cook, S. (2011). The evolution of family complexity from the perspective of children. *Demography, 48*, 957–982.

Cano Giménez, E., & Sánchez-Luna, M. (2015). Providing parents with individualized support in a neonatal intensive care unit reduced stress, anxiety and depression. *Acta Paediatrica, 104*(7), e300 – e305. doi: 10.1111/apa.12984

Cappa, C., & Khan, S. M. (2011). Understanding caregivers' attitudes towards physical punishment of children: Evidence from 34 low- and middle-income countries. *Child Abuse and Neglect, 35*, 1009–1021.

Capron, L. E., Glover, V., Pearson, R. M., Evans, J., O'Connor, T. G., Stein, A., Murphy, S. E., & Ramchandani, P. G. (2015). Associations of maternal and paternal antenatal mood with offspring anxiety disorder at age 18 years. *Journal of Affective Disorders, 187*, 20–26.

Caragata, L., & Miller, W. (2008). *What supports engaged fathering? Employment and family supports.* Guelph: University of Guelph.

Carlson, M., & Magnuson, K. A. (2011). Low-income fathers' influence on children. *American Academy of Political and Social Science, 635*, 95–116.

Carlson, M. J., & McLanahan, S. S. (2010). Fathers in Fragile Families. In M. E. Lamb (Ed.), *The role of the father in child development* (5th ed.) (pp. 241–269). Hoboken, NJ: Wiley.

Carlson, M. J., VanOrman, A. G., & Turner, K. J. (2017). Fathers' investments of money and time across residential contexts. *Journal of Marriage and Family, 79*, 10–23. doi: 10.1111/jomf.12324

Carpenter, B., & Towers C. (2008) Recognising fathers: The needs of fathers of children with disabilities. *Support for Learning, 23*, 118–125.

Carter, M.W., & Speizer, I. (2005). Salvadoran fathers' attendance at prenatal care, delivery, and postpartum care. *Revista Panamericana de Salud Pública/Pan American Journal of Public Health, 18*(3), 149–156.

Carvalho, A. M. A., Moreira, L. V. C. & Gosso, Y. (2015). Fathering in Brazil. In J. L. Roopnarine (Ed.), *Fathers across cultures: The importance, roles, and diverse practices of dads* (pp. 39–62). Santa Barbara, CA: Praeger/ABC-Clio.

Carvalho, A. M. A., Moreira, L. V. C., & Rabinovich, E. P. (2010) Olhares de crianças sobre a família: Um enfoque quantitativo [Children's conceptions of family: a quantitative approach]. *Psicologia, Teoria e Pesquisa, 26*(3), 417–426.

Cerniglia, L., Cimino, S., Tafà, M., Marzilli, E., Ballarotto, G., & Bracaglia, F. (2017). Family profiles in eating disorders: Family functioning and psychopathology. *Psychology Research and Behavioral Management, 10*, 305–312. doi: 10.2147/PRBM.S145463

Chaleby, K. (1985). Women of polygamous marriages in an inpatient psychiatric service in Kuwait. *Journal of Nervous and Mental Disease, 173*(1), 56–58.

Chao, R. K. (1994). Beyond parental control and authoritarian parenting style: Understanding Chinese parenting through the cultural notion of training. *Child Development, 65*(4), 1111–1119.

Chaudhary, N. (2013). The father's role in the Indian family. In D. Shwalb, B. Shwalb & M. E. Lamb (Eds.), *Fathers in cultural context* (pp. 68–94). New York: Routledge.

Cheadle, J., Amato, P. R., & King, V. (2010). Patterns of nonresident father contact. *Demography, 47*, 205–225.

Chekki, D. A. (1988). Recent directions in family research: India and North America. *Journal of Comparative Family Studies, 19*, 171–186.

Chen, E., Gau, M., Liu, C., & Lee, T. (2017). Effects of father–neonate skin-to-skin contact on attachment: A randomized controlled trial. *Nursing Research and Practice.* doi: 10.1155/2017/8612024

Chen, S. X., Benet-Martınez, V., & Bond, M. H. (2008). Bicultural identity, bilingualism, and psychological adjustment in multicultural societies: Immigration-based and globalization-based acculturation. *Journal of Personality, 76*, 803–838. doi: 10.1111/j.1467–6494.2008.00505.x

Chen, X., Liu, M., & Li, D. (2000). Parental warmth, control, and indulgence and their relations to adjustment in Chinese children: A longitudinal study. *Journal of Family Psychology, 14*(3), 401–419. doi: 10.1037//0893–083200.14.3.401

Chereji, E., Gatz, M., Pedersen, N. L., & Prescott, C.A. (2013). Re-examining the association between fertility and lifespan: Testing the disposable soma theory in a modern sample of human twins. *Journal of Gerontology: Biological Sciences, 68*, 499–509.

Chesley, N. (2011). Stay-at-home fathers and breadwinning mothers, gender, couple dynamics, and social change. *Gender and Society, 25*(5), 642–664.

Chesley, N. & Flood, S. (2017). Signs of change? At-home and breadwinner parents' housework and child-care time. *Family Relations, 79*, 511–534. doi: 10.1111/jomf.12376

Chevannes, B. (1999). *What we sow and what we reap: Problems in the cultivation of male identity in Jamaica.* Kingston, Jamaica: Grace Kennedy Foundation.

Chevannes, B. (2001). *Learning to be a man: Culture, socialization and gender identity in five Caribbean countries.* Kingston, Jamaica: University of the West Indies Press.

Chevannes, M. (1997). Nurses caring for families: Issues in a multiracial society. *Journal of Clinical Nursing, 6*(2), 161–167.

Chikovore, J., Makusha, T., & Richter, L. (2013). Father involvement in young children's care and education in southern Africa. In J. Pattnaik (Ed.), *Father involvement in young children's lives: A global analysis* (vol. 6) (pp. 261–278). Dordrecht: Springer.

Child Trends Databank. (2002). *Parental warmth and affection.* Available at: www.childtrends.org/?indicators=parental-warmth-and-affection

Choi, M. S., & Cho, S. H. (2005). Adolescent's image about their father. *The Korean Journal of Youth Counseling, 13*(1), 55–69.

Choi, J., & Jackson, A. (2011). Fathers' involvement and child behavior problems in poor African American single-mother families. *Children and Youth Services Review, 33*, 698–704.

Christie, J., & Roskos, K. (2015). Play with a purpose: Creating meaningful environments with children, families, and communities in the United States. In L. Huo, S. Neuman, & M. Abumiya (Eds.), *Early childhood education in three cultures: China, Japan, and the United States* (pp. 39–49). London: Springer.

Clark, S., Cotton, C., & Marteleto, L. (2015). Family ties and young fathers' engagement in Cape Town, South Africa. *Journal of Marriage and Family, 77*(2), 575–589.

Clarke, E. (1957). *My mother who fathered me.* London: George Allen and Unwin.

Clarke-Stewart, K. (1978). And daddy makes three: The father's impact on mother and young child. *Child Development, 49*(2), 466–478. doi: 10.2307/1128712

Coatsworth, J. D., Maldonado-Molina, M., Pantin, H. & Szapocznik, J. (2005). A person-centered and ecological investigation of acculturation strategies in Hispanic immigrant youth. *Journal of Community Psychology, 33*, 157–174. doi: 10.1002/jcop.20046

Collins, W. A., & Russell, G. (1991). Mother–child and father–child relationships in middle childhood and adolescence: A developmental analysis. *Developmental Review, 11*, 99–113.

Connell, A. M., & Goodman, S. H. (2002). The association between psychopathology in fathers versus mothers and children's internalizing and externalizing behavior problems: A meta-analysis. *Psychological Bulletin, 128*(5), 746–773. doi: 10.1037/0033-2909.128.5.746

Cools, S., Fiva, J. H., & Kirkebøen, L. J. (2015). Causal effects of paternity leave on children and parents. *Scandinavian Journal of Economics, 117*(3), 801–828.

Correll, S. J., Benard, S., & Paik, I. (2007). Getting a job: Is there a motherhood penalty? *American Journal of Sociology, 112*(5), 1297–1339.

Cowan, P. A., Cowan, C. P., Pruett, M. K., Pruett, K., & Gillette, P. (2014). Evaluating a couples group to enhance father involvement in low-income families using a benchmark comparison. *Family Relations: An Interdisciplinary Journal of Applied Family Studies, 63*(3), 356–370. doi: 10.1111/fare.12072

Cowan, P. A., Cowan, C. P., Pruett, M. K., Pruett, K., & Wong, J. J. (2009). Promoting fathers' engagement with children: Preventative intervention with low-income children. *Journal of Marriage and the Family, 71*, 663–679.

Craig, L., & Mullan, K. (2011). How mothers and fathers share childcare: A cross-national time-use comparison. *American Sociological Review*, 76(6), 834–861.

Cuesta, L., & Meyer, D. R. (2014). The role of child support in the economic wellbeing of custodial-mother families in less developed countries: The case of Colombia. *International Journal of Law, Policy and the Family*, 28(1), 60–76.

Cummings, E. M., Merrilees, C. E., & George, M. (2010). Fathers, marriages and families: Revisiting and updating the framework for fathering in family context. In M. Lamb (Ed.), *The role of the father in child development* (5th ed.) (pp. 154–176). New York: Wiley.

Cyr, C., Michel, G., & Dumais, M. (2013). Child maltreatment as a global phenomenon: From trauma to prevention. *International Journal of Psychology*, 48, 141–148.

Dahl, G. B., Løken, K. V., & Mogstad, M. (2014). Peer effects in program participation. *American Economic Review*, 104(7), 2049–2074. doi: 10.1257/aer.104.7.2049

Daniel, E., Madigan, S., & Jenkins, J. (2015). Paternal and maternal warmth and the development of prosociality among preschoolers. *Journal of Family Psychology*, 30(1), 114–124. doi: 10.1037/fam0000120

Darling, N., & Steinberg, L. (1993). Parenting style as context: An integrative model. *Psychological Bulletin*, 113(3), 487–496. doi: 10.1037/0033-2909.113.3.487

David, A., Aslan, G., Siedentopf, J.-P., & Kentenich, H. (2009). Ethnic Turkish fathers in birth support roles in a Berlin labour and delivery room: Motives, preparation and incidence in a 10-year comparison. *Journal of Psychosomatic Obstetrics and Gynecology*, 30(1), 5–10.

David, E. J. R., Okazaki, S., & Saw, A. (2009). Bicultural self-efficacy among college students: Initial scale development and mental health correlates. *Journal of Counseling Psychology*, 56(2), 211–226.

de Cock, E. A., Henrichs, J., Klimstra, T. A., Maas, A. M., Vreeswijk, C. M., Meeus, W. J., & van Bakel, H. A. (2017). Longitudinal associations between parental bonding, parenting stress, and executive functioning in toddlerhood. *Journal of Child and Family Studies*, 26(6), 1723–1733. doi: 10.1007/s10826-017-0679-7

Deave, T. & Johnson, D. (2008). The transition to parenthood: What does it mean for fathers? *Journal of Advanced Nursing*, 63(6), 626–633.

DeBoard-Lucas, R. L., & Grych, J. H. (2011). Children's perceptions of intimate partner violence: Causes, consequences, and coping. *Journal of Family Violence*, 26, 343–354.

Dede Yildirim, E., & Roopnarine, J. L. (2017a). Paternal and maternal engagement across six Caribbean countries and childhood outcomes. *Journal of Applied Developmental Psychology*, 53, 64–73. doi: 10.1016/j.appdev.2017.08.007

Dede Yildirim, E., & Roopnarine, J. L. (2017b). Nonviolent discipline, physical assault, and psychological aggression in five Caribbean countries: Associations with preschooler's early literacy and social skills. *International Journal of Psychology*. doi: 10.1002/ijop.12465

Dede Yildirim, E., & Roopnarine, J. L. (2018). The associations between paternal and maternal caregiving and children's literacy skills in African countries: A meta-analysis. Unpublished manuscript.

del Barrio, V., Holgado-Tello, F. P., & Carrasco, M. A. (2016). Concurrent and longitudinal effects of maternal and paternal warmth on depression symptoms in children and adolescents. *Psychiatry Research*, 24275–24281. doi: 10.1016/j.psychres.2016.05.032

Dellman, T. (2004). The best moment of my life: A literature review of fathers' experience of childbirth. *Australian Midwifery Journal*, 17(3), 20–26.

Denham, S. A., Blair, K.A., DeMulder, E., Levitas, J., Sawyer, K., Auerbach-Major, S., & Queenan, P. (2003). Preschool emotional competence: Pathway to social competence? *Child Development*, 74(1), 238–256.

Dette-Hagenmeyer, D. E., & Reichle, B. (2014). Parents' depressive symptoms and children's adjustment over time are mediated by parenting, but differentially for fathers and mothers. *European Journal of Developmental Psychology, 11*(2), 196–210. doi: 10.1080/ 17405629.2013.848789

Devonish, J., & Anderson, P. (2017). Fathering the "outside" child: Differences and shortfalls among urban Jamaican fathers. *Journal of Social and Economic Studies, 66*(1), 33–77.

De Wolff, M., & van IJzendoorn, M. (1997). Sensitivity and attachment: A meta-analysis on parental antecedents of infant attachment. *Child Development, 68*, 571–591.

Dhruvarajan, V. (1990). Religious ideology, Hindu women and development in India. *Journal of Social Issues, 46*, 57–69.

Di Maggio, R., & Zappulla, C. (2014). Mothering, fathering, and Italian adolescents' problem behaviors and life satisfaction: Dimensional and typological approach. *Journal of Child and Family Studies, 23*(3), 567–580. doi: 10.1007/s10826-013-9721-6

Doherty, W. J., Erikson, M. F., & LaRossa, R. (2006). An intervention to increase father involvement and skills with infants during the transition to parenthood. *Journal of Family Psychology, 20*(3), 438–447. doi: 10.1037/0893-3200.20.3.438

Duchesne, S., & Ratelle, C. F. (2014). Attachment security to mothers and fathers and the developmental trajectories of depressive symptoms in adolescence: Which parent for which trajectory? *Journal of Youth and Adolescence, 43*(4), 641–654.

Dutta, M. (2000). Women's employment and its effects on Bengali households of Shillong, India. *Journal of Comparative Family Studies, 31*(2), 217–229.

Duursma, E. (2014). The effects of fathers' and mothers' reading to their children on language outcomes of children participating in early head start in the United States. *Fathering, 12*(3), 283–302.

Duursma, E. (2016). Who does the reading, who the talking? Low-income fathers and mothers in the US interacting with their young children around a picture book. *First Language, 36*(5), 465–484.

Duursma, E., Pan, B.A., & Raikes, H. (2008). Predictors and outcomes of low-income fathers' reading with their toddlers. *Early Childhood Research Quarterly, 23*(3), 351–365. doi: 10.1016/j.ecresq.2008.06.001

Duvander, A. Z., & Jans, A. C. (2009). Consequences of fathers' parental leave use: Evidence from Sweden. *Finnish Yearbook of Population Research 2009*. Helsinki, Finland: Population Research Institute.

Dwairy, M. (2009). Parenting and adolescent psychological adjustment: Toward a systemic approach in parenting research. *The Open Family Studies Journal, 2*, 66–74.

Dworkin, S. L., Hatcher, A. M., Colvin, C., & Peacock, D. (2013). Impact of a gender-transformative HIV and antiviolence program on gender ideologies and masculinities in two rural, South African communities. *Men and Masculinities, 16*(2), 181–202. doi: 10.1177/1097184X12469878

Dyer, W. J., McBride, B. A., Santos, R. M., & Jeans, L. M. (2009). A longitudinal examination of father involvement with children with developmental delays: Does timing of diagnosis matter? *Journal of Early Intervention, 31*, 265–281.

Eastin, M., Greenberg, B., & Hofschire, L. (2006). Parenting the internet. *Journal of Communication, 56*, 486–504.

Eddy, M. M., Thomson-de Boer, H., & Mphaka, K. (2013). *So we are ATM fathers: A study of absent fathers in Johannesburg, South Africa*. Johannesburg: Centre for Social Development in Africa, University of Johannesburg and the Sonke Gender Justice.

Edwards, C. P., & Gandini, L. (2018). The Reggio Emilia approach to early childhood education. In J. L. Roopnarine, J. E. Johnson, S. F. Quinn & M. Patte (Eds.), *Handbook of International Perspectives on Early Childhood Education* (pp. 365–378). New York: Routledge.

Edwards, W., & Ratima, M. (2014). *Engaging Maori fathers: A literature review. Father involvement, Maori parenting and engaging Maori fathers in parenting*. Available at http://thrive.org.nz/ wp-content/uploads/2016/01/Engaging-Maori-Fathers.pdf

Eggebeen, D., & Knoester, C. (2001). Does fatherhood matter for men? *Journal of Marriage and Family, 63*(2), 381–393.

Eggebeen, D. J., Dew, J., & Knoester, C. (2010). Fatherhood and men's lives at middle age. *Journal of Family Issues, 31*(1), 113–130. doi: 10.1177/0192513x09341446

Eiden, R. D., Colder, C., Edwards, E. P., & Leonard, K.E. (2009). A longitudinal study of social competence among children of alcoholic and nonalcoholic parents: Role of parental psychopathology, parental warmth, and self-regulation. *Psychology of Addictive Behaviors, 23*(1), 36–46. doi: 10.1037/a0014839

Ekberg, J., Eriksson, R., & Friebel, G. (2013). Parental leave: A policy evaluation of the Swedish "Daddy-Month" reform. *Journal of Public Economics, 97*, 131–143.

Elam, K. K., Sandler, I., Wolchik, S., & Tein, J. (2016). Non-residential father–child involvement, interparental conflict and mental health of children following divorce: A person-focused approach. *Journal of Youth and Adolescence, 45*(3), 581–593. doi: 10.1007/s10964-015-0399-5

El Feki, S., Heilman, B., & Barker, G. (Eds.) (2017). *Understanding masculinities: Results from the International Men and Gender Equality Survey (IMAGES) – Middle East and North Africa.* Cairo and Washington, DC: UN Women and Promundo-US.

Ellis, K. R., Caldwell, C. H., Assari, S., & De Loney, E. H. (2014). Nonresident African-American fathers' influence on sons' exercise intentions in the Fathers and Sons Program. *American Journal of Health Promotion, 29*(2), 89–98. doi: 10.4278/ajhp.130417-QUAN-179

Ember, C.R., & Ember, M. (2002). Father absence and male aggression: A re-examination of the comparative evidence. *Ethos, 29*(3), 296–314.

Ember, M., Ember, C. R., & Low, B. S. (2007). Comparing explanations of polygyny. *Cross-Cultural Research, 41*(2), 96–122.

Epstein, S. (1990). Cognitive-experiential self-theory. In L. Pervin (Ed.), *Handbook of personality: Theory and research* (pp. 165–192). New York: Guilford Press.

Erdogan, Y. (2011). An investigation of the relationship among parental involvement, socio-economic factors of parents and students' academic achievement. Unpublished doctoral dissertation, Eastern Mediterranean University (EMU), Northern Cyprus.

Escayg, K. (2014). Parenting and pedagogical practices: The racial socialization and racial identity of pre-school Trinidadian children. Unpublished doctoral dissertation. University of Toronto, Canada.

Eurostat (2016), *Gender pay gap statistics.* Available at http://ec.europa.eu/eurostat/statistics-explained/index.php/Gender_pay_gap_statistics

Evertsson, M. (2016). Parental leave and careers: Women's and men's wages after parental leave in Sweden. *Advances in Life Course Research, 29*, 26–40.

Fabricius, W. V., Braver, S. L., Diaz, P., & Velez, C. E. (2010). Custody and parenting time: Links to family relationships and well-being after divorce. In M. E. Lamb (Ed.), *The role of the father in child development* (5th ed.) (pp. 201–240). New York: Wiley.

Fagan, J. (2014). A review of how researchers have used theory to address research questions about fathers in three large data sets. *Journal of Family Theory and Review, 6*(2), 374–389.

Fagan, J., & Iglesias, A. (1999). Father involvement program effects on fathers, father figures, and their head start children: A quasi-experimental study. *Early Childhood Research Quarterly, 14*(2), 243–269. doi: 10.1016/S0885-2006(99)00008-3

Fagan, J., Iglesias, A., & Kaufman, R. (2016). Associations among Head Start fathers' involvement with their preschoolers and child language skills. *Early Child Development and Care, 186*(8), 1342–1356. doi: 10.1080/03004430.2015.1094654

Fägerskjöld, A. (2008). A change in life as experienced by first-time fathers. *Scandinavian Journal of Caring Sciences, 22*(1), 64–71.

Farr, R. H., & Patterson, C. J. (2013). Lesbian and gay adoptive parents and their children. In A. E. Goldberg & K. R. Allen (Eds.), *LGBT-parent families: Innovations in research and implications for practice*. New York: Springer.

Farver, J. A., & Wimbarti, S. (1995). Indonesian children's play with their mothers and older siblings. *Child Development, 66*, 1493–1503. doi: 10.1111/j.1467–8624.1995.tb00947.x

Feldman, R., Masalha, S., & Derdikman-Eiron, R. (2010). Conflict resolution in the parent–child, marital, and peer contexts and children's aggression in the peer group: A process-oriented cultural perspective. *Developmental Psychology, 46*(2), 310–325. doi: 10.1037/a0018286

Fenwick, J., Bayes, S., & Johansson, M. (2012). A qualitative investigation into the pregnancy experiences and childbirth expectations of Australian fathers-to-be. *Sexual and Reproductive Healthcare, 3*, 3–9.

Ferguson, G. M. (2018). Caribbean migration and globalization: Illuminating new global patterns of acculturation and adaptation in the 21st Century. *Caribbean Journal of Psychology, 10*, 192–222.

Field, T. (1998). Maternal depression effects on infants and early interventions. *Preventive Medicine, 27*(2), 200–203.

Field, T. (2010). Postpartum depression effects on early interactions, parenting, and safety practices: A review. *Infant Behavior and Development, 33*(1), 1. doi: 10.1016/j.infbeh.2009.10.005

Filgueiras, M. R., & Petrini, G. (2010). O pai patriarcal segundo Roberto Freyre [The patriarchal father according to Roberto Freyre]. In L.V.C. Moreira, G. Petrini & F. B. Barbosa (Eds.), *O pai na sociedade contemporânea* (pp. 23–39). Bauru, SP: EDUSC.

Finnbogadóttir, H., Svalenius, E., & Persson, E. K. (2003). Expectant first-time fathers' experiences of pregnancy. *Midwifery, 19*(2), 96–105.

Fives, A., Pursell, L., Heary, C., Nic Gabhainn, S., & Canavan, J. (2014). *Parenting support for every parent: A population-level evaluation of Triple P in Longford Westmeath*. Final Report. Athlone: Longford Westmeath Parenting Partnership (LWPP).

Flacking, R., Dykes, F., & Ewald, U. (2010). The influence of fathers' socioeconomic status and paternity leave on breast feeding duration: A population-based cohort study. *Scandinavian Journal of Public Health, 38*, 337–343.

Fletcher, R. (2009). Promoting infant well-being in the context of maternal depression by supporting the father. *Infant Mental Health Journal, 30*(1), 95–102. doi: 10.1002/imhj.20205

Fletcher, R., Freeman, E., & Matthey, S. (2011). The impact of behavioural parent training on fathers' parenting: A meta-analysis of the Triple P-Positive parenting program. *Fathering, 9*(3), 291–312. doi: 10.3149/fth.0903.291

Fletcher, R., St George, J., & Freeman, E. (2013). Rough and tumble play quality: Theoretical foundations for a new measure of father–child interaction. *Early Child Development and Care, 183*, 746–759.

Flinn, M. (1992). Paternal care in a Caribbean village. In B. Hewlett (Ed.), *Father–child relations: Cultural and biosocial perspectives* (pp. 57–84). New York: Aldine De Gruyter.

Flouri, E., & Malmberg, L. (2012). Fathers' involvement and preschool children's behavior in stable single-mother families. *Children and Youth Services Review, 34*(7), 1237–1242. doi: 10.1016/j.childyouth.2012.02.020

Flouri, E., Midouhas, E., & Narayanan, M. K. (2016). The relationship between father involvement and child problem behaviour in intact families: A 7-year cross-lagged study. *Journal of Abnormal Child Psychology, 44*(5), 1011–1021. doi: 10.1007/s10802-015-0077-9

Fomby, P., & Osborne, C. (2017). Family instability, multipartner fertility, and behavior in middle childhood. *Journal of Marriage and Family, 79*(1), 75–93.

Fouts, H. (2013). Fathering in Central and East Africa: Cultural and adaptationist perspectives in small-scale societies. In D. Shwalb, B. Shwalb, & M. E. Lamb (Eds.), *Fathers in cultural context* (pp. 151–172). New York: Routledge.

Fouts, H. N., Roopnarine, J. L., & Lamb, M. E. (2007) Social experiences and daily routines of African American infants in different socioeconomic contexts. *Journal of Family Psychology, 21*(4), 655–664. doi: 10.1037/0893–3200.21.4.655

Fox, N. A., Kimmerly, N. L., & Schafer, W. D. (1991). Attachment to mother/attachment to father: A meta-analysis. *Child Development, 62*, 210–225.

Fraley, R. C., & Spieker, S. J. (2003). Are infant attachment patterns continuously or categorically distributed? A taxometric analysis of Strange Situation behavior. *Developmental Psychology, 39*(3), 387–404. doi: 10.1037/0012–1649.39.3.387

Frank, T. J., Keown, L. J., Dittman, C. K., & Sanders, M. R. (2015). Using father preference data to increase father engagement in evidence-based parenting programs. *Journal of Child and Family Studies, 24*(4), 937–947. doi: 10.1007/s10826-10014-9904-9909

Freud, A. (1963). The concept of developmental lines. *The Psychoanalytic Study of the Child, 18*(1), 245–265. doi: 10.1080/00797308.1963.11822930

Friedman, D., Hecther, M., & Kanazawa, S. (1994). A theory of value of children. *Demography, 31*, 375–401.

Fuertes, M., Faria, A., Beeghly, M., & Lopes-dos-Santos, P. (2016). The effects of parental sensitivity and involvement in caregiving on mother–infant and father–infant attachment in a Portuguese sample. *Journal of Family Psychology, 30*(1), 147–156. doi: 10.1037/fam0000139

Furlong, M., McGilloway, S., Bywater, T., Hutchings, J., Smith, S. M., & Donnelly, M. (2012). Behavioral and cognitive-behavioral group-based parenting programmes for early-onset conduct problems in children aged 3 to 12 years. *Evidence Based Child Health, 2*, 318–692. doi: 10.1002/ebch.1905

Garcia Coll, C., Lamberty, G., Jenkins, R., McAdoo, H., Crnic, K., Wasik, B., & García, H. (1996). An integrative model for the study of developmental competencies in minority children. *Child Development, 67*(5), 1891–1914. doi: 10.2307/1131600

Garfield, C. F., Duncan, G., Rutsohn, J., McDade, T. W., Adam, E. K., Coley, R. L., & Chase-Lansdale, P. L. (2014). A longitudinal study of paternal mental health during transition to fatherhood as young adults. *Pediatrics, 133*(5), 836–843. doi: 10.1542/peds.2013–3262

Gawlik, S., Muller, M., Hoffmann, L., Dienes, A., Wallwiener, M., Sohn, C., Schlehe, B., & Reck, C. (2014). Prevalence of paternal perinatal depressiveness and its link to partnership satisfaction and birth concerns. *Archives of Women's Mental Health, 17*(1), 49–56.

Gaydosh, L. (2017). Beyond orphanhood: parental non-residence and child wellbeing in Tanzania. *Journal of Marriage and Family, 79*(5), 1369–1387.

Geller, A. (2013). Paternal incarceration and father–child contact in Fragile Families. *Journal of Marriage and Family, 75*(5), 1288–1303. doi: 10.1111/jomf.12056

Georgas, J., Berry, J. W., van de Vijver, F. J. R., Kağıtçıbaşı, C., & Poortinga, Y. H. (2006). *Families across cultures: A 30-nation psychological study.* Cambridge: Cambridge University Press.

George, C., Kaplan, N., & Main, M. (1985). Adult attachment interview. Unpublished manuscript, University of California – Berkeley.

Gershoff, E. T. (2002). Corporal punishment by parents and associated child behaviors and experiences: A meta-analytic and theoretical review. *Psychological Bulletin, 128*, 539–579. doi: 10.1037/0033–2909.128.4.539.

Gershoff, E. T., Goodman, G. S., Miller-Perrin, C. L., Holden, J. W., Jackson, Y., & Kadzen, A. E. (2018). The strength of the causal evidence against physical punishment of children and its implications for parents, psychologists, and policymakers. *American Psychologist, 73*(5), 626–638.

Gewirtz, A. H., & Edelson, J. L. (2007). Young children's exposure to intimate partner violence: Towards a developmental risk and resilience framework for research and intervention. *Journal of Family Violence, 22*, 151–163.

Glaze, L. E., & Maruschak, L. M. (2008). *Parents in prison and their minor children.* Bureau of Justice Statistics Special Report. Washington, DC: Bureau of Justice Statistics.

Goetz, E. R., & Vieira, M. L. (2009). Percepções dos filhos sobre aspectos reais e ideais do cuidado parental [Childen's perceptions of real and ideal aspects of parental care]. *Estudos de Psicologia (Campinas), 26*(2), 195–203.

Goldberg, A. E. (2010). Studying complex families in context. *Journal of Marriage and Family, 72*(1), 29–34.

Golombok, S. (2010). Children in new family forms. In R. Gross (Ed.), *Psychology: The science of mind and behavior* (6th ed.) (pp. 510–511). London: Hodder Education.

Golombok, S., Mellish, L., Jennings, S., Casey, P., Tasker, F., & Lamb, M. (2014) Adoptive gay father families: Parent–child relationships and children's psychological adjustment. *Child Development, 85*(2), 456–468. doi: 10.1111/cdev.12155

Goodman, S. H., & Brand, S. R. (2008). Parental psychopathology and its relation to child psychopathology. In M. Hersen & A. M. Gross (Eds.), *Handbook of clinical psychology, vol. 2: Children and adolescents* (pp. 937–965). Hoboken, NJ: John Wiley & Sons.

Goodnow, J. J., & Collins, W. A. (1990). *Development according to parents: The nature, sources and consequences of parents' ideas.* Hillsdale, NJ: Erlbaum.

Gordon, D. M., Hawes, S. W., Perez-Cabello, M. A., Brabham-Hollis, T., Lanza, A. S., & Dyson, W. J. (2013). Examining masculine norms and peer support within a sample of incarcerated African American males. *Psychology of Men and Masculinity, 14*(1), 59–64. doi: 10.1037/a0028780

Gracia, P. (2014). Fathers' child care involvement and children's age in Spain: A time use study on differences by education and mothers' employment. *European Sociological Review, 30*(2), 137–150. doi: 10.1093/esr/jcu037

Grall, T. S. (2009). *Custodial mothers and fathers and their child support: 2007.* Washington, DC: U.S. Census Bureau.

Gray, D. E. (2003). Gender and coping: The parents of children with high functioning autism. *Social Science and Medicine, 56*, 631–642.

Gray, P. & Anderson, K. G. (2010). *Fatherhood: Evolution and human paternal behavior.* Cambridge, MA: Harvard University Press.

Graziano, F., Bonino, S., & Cattelino, E. (2009). Links between maternal and paternal support, depressive feelings and social and academic self-efficacy in adolescence. *European Journal of Developmental Psychology, 6*(2), 241–257. doi: 10.1080/17405620701252066

Greenfield, P. M., Keller, H., Fuligni, A., & Maynard, A. (2003). Cultural pathways through universal development. *Annual Review of Psychology, 54*, 461–490.

Greenstein, T. N. (2009). National context, family satisfaction, and fairness in the division of household labor. *Journal of Marriage and Family, 71*, 1039–1051. doi: 10.1111/j.1741-3737.2009.00651.x

Groh, A. M., Fearon, R. M., van IJzendoorn, M. H., Bakermans-Kranenburg, M. J., & Roisman, G. I. (2017). Attachment in the early life course: Meta-analytic evidence for its role in socioemotional development. *Child Development Perspectives, 11*, 70–76. doi: 10.1111/cdep.12213

Groh, A. M., Roisman, G. I., van IJzendoorn, M. H., Bakermans-Kranenburg, M. J., & Fearon, R. P. (2012). The significance of insecure and disorganized attachment for children's internalizing symptoms: A meta-analytic study. *Child Development, 83*(2), 591–610.

Grusec, J. E., & Hastings, P. D. (2007). *Handbook of socialization: Theory and research.* New York: Guilford Press.

Gunter, S.R. (2016). Child support wage withholding and father–child contact: Parental bargaining and salience effects. *Review of Economics of the Household, 16*(2), 427–452. doi: 10.1007/s11150-11016-9330-9334.

Guo, Z., & Wang, J. (2009). Fumu jiaoyangfangshi yu youer xinlijiankang de guanxi yanjiu. [The relationship between parenting styles and mental health of preschoolers]. *Journal of Cangzhou Teachers' College, 25*(2), 72–73.

Guzzo, K. B. (2014). Trends in cohabitation outcomes: Compositional changes and engagement among never-married young adults. *Family Relations, 76,* 826–842. doi: 10.1111/jomf.12123

Haas, L., & Hwang, C. P. (2009). Is fatherhood becoming more visible at work? Trends in corporate support for fathers taking parental leave in Sweden. *Fathering, 7*(3), 303–321. doi: 10.3149/fth.0703.303

Haddon, L. (2012). Parental mediation of internet use: Evaluating family relationships. In E. Loos, L. Haddon & E. Mante-Meijer (Eds.), *Generational use of new media* (pp. 13–30). Aldershot: Ashgate.

Hagqvist, E., Nordenmark, M., Pérez, G., Alemán, S. T., & Gådin, K. G. (2017). Parental leave policies and time use for mothers and fathers: A case study of Spain and Sweden. *Society, Health and Vulnerability, 8*(1). doi: 10.1080/20021518.2017.1374103

Hakovirta, M. (2011). Child maintenance and child poverty: A comparative analysis. *Journal of Poverty and Social Justice, 19*(3), 249–262.

Hakovirta, M., & Jokela, M. (2018). Contribution of child maintenance to lone mothers' income in five countries. *Journal of European Social Policy.* doi: 10.1177/0958928717754295

Hallers-Haalboom, E. T., Mesman, J., Groeneveld, M. G., Endendijk, J. J., van Berkel, S. R., van der Pol, L. D., & Bakermans-Kranenburg, M. J. (2014). Mothers, fathers, sons and daughters: Parental sensitivity in families with two children. *Journal of Family Psychology, 28*(2), 138–147.

Hallers-Haalboom, E. T., Groeneveld, M. G., van Berkel, S. R., Endendijk, J. J., van der Pol, L. D., Linting, M., & . . . Mesman, J. (2017). Mothers' and fathers' sensitivity with their two children: A longitudinal study from infancy to early childhood. *Developmental Psychology, 53*(5), 860–872. doi: 10.1037/dev0000293

Hamby, S., Finkelhor, D., Turner, H., & Ormrod, R. (2010). The overlap of witnessing partner violence with child maltreatment and other victimizations in a nationally representative survey of youth. *Child Abuse and Neglect, 34,* 734–741.

Hanashima, H. (2007). The father – son relationships as seen from Hikikomori males and their fathers. *Japanese Journal of Family Psychology, 21,* 77–94.

Harkness, S., & Super, C. M. (1992). From parents' cultural belief systems to behavior. In L. Eldering & P. Leseman (Eds.), *Effective early intervention: Cross-cultural perspectives* (pp. 67–90). New York: Falmer Press.

Harris, D. (2015). A meta-analysis on father involvement and early childhood social-emotional development. Available at http://steinhardt.nyu.edu/opus/issues/2010/spring/father_childhood_development

Hart, B., & Risley, T. (1995). *Meaningful differences in the everyday experience of young American children.* Baltimore, MD: Paul H. Brookes Publishing.

Hashem, S. M. M. (2001). A study of determinants of parental child maltreatment. *Faculty of Arts Journal* (Menoufia University, Egypt), *44,* 249–307 (in Arabic).

Hastings, R. P., & Brown, T. (2002) Behavior problems of children with autism, parental self-efficacy, and mental health. *American Journal on Mental Retardation, 107,* 222–232.

Hawkins, A. J., & Erikson, S. E. (2015). Is couple relationship education effective for lower income participants? A meta-analytic study. *Journal of Family Psychology, 29*(1), 59–68. doi: 10.1037/fam0000045

Hawkins, A. J., & Dollahite, D. (Eds.) (1997). *Generative fathering: Beyond deficit perspectives.* Thousand Oaks, CA: Sage.

Heilman, B., Levtov, R., van der Gaag, N., Hassink, A., & Barker, G. (2017). *State of the world's fathers: Time for action.* Washington, DC: Promundo, Sonke Gender Justice, Save the Children, and MenEngage Alliance.

Heinrichs, N., Kliem, S., & Hahlweg, K. (2014). Four-year follow-up of a randomized controlled trial of Triple P group for parent and child outcomes. *Prevention Science, 15*(2), 233–245. doi: 10.1007/s11121-012-0358-2

Henry, I. P., K., Morelli, G. A., & Tronick, E. Z.(2005). Child caretakers among Efe foragers of the Ituri Forest. In B. S. Hewlett and M. Lamb (Eds.), *Hunter-gatherer childhoods: Evolutionary, developmental and cultural perspectives* (pp. 191–213). New Brunswick, NJ: Aldine Transaction.

Hernández Breña, W. (2011). *¿Cuánto le cuesta la justicia a las mujeres?* Lima, Peru: Programa Fortalecimiento de la Institución Democrática de la Agencia Suiza para el Desarrollo y la Cooperación – COSUDE, pp. 1–225.

Hewlett, B. S. (1987). Patterns of parental holding among Aka pygmies. In M. Lamb (Ed.), *The father's role: Cross-cultural perspectives.* Hillsdale, NJ: Erlbaum.

Hewlett, B. S. (1991). Aka pygmies of the Western Congo Basin. In B. S. Hewlett, *Intimate fathers: The nature and context of Aka Pygmy paternal infant care.* Ann Arbor: University of Michigan Press.

Hewlett, B. S. (1992). (Ed.), *Father–child relations: Cultural and biosocial contexts.* New York: Aldine de Gruyter.

Hewlett, B. S., & Lamb, M. E. (Eds.) (2005). *Hunter-gatherer childhoods: Evolutionary, developmental, and cultural perspectives* (pp. 175–213). New Brunswick, NJ: Aldine Transaction Publishers.

Hewlett, B. S., & Macfarlan, S. J. (2010). Fathers' roles in hunter-gatherer and other small-scale societies. In M. E. Lamb (Ed.), *The role of the father in child development* (pp. 413–434). Hoboken, NJ: Wiley.

Heymann, J., Raub, A., & Earle, A. (2011). Creating and using new data sources to analyze the relationship between social policy and global health: The case of maternal leave. *Public Health Reports, 126*(3), 127–134.

Hill, N. E., & Taylor, L. C. (2004). Parental school involvement and children's academic achievement. *Current Directions in Psychological Science, 13*, 161–164.

Hirasawa, A. (2005). Infant care among the sedentarized Baka hunter-gatherers in southeastern Cameroon. In B. S. Hewlett & M. E. Lamb (Eds), *Hunter-gatherer childhoods: Evolutionary, developmental and cultural perspectives* (pp. 365–384). New Brunswick, NJ: Aldine Transaction.

Ho, H.-Z., Chen, W.-W., Tran, C. N., & Ko, C.-T. (2010). Parental involvement in Taiwanese families: Father–mother differences. *Childhood Education, 86*(6), 376–381. doi: 10.1080/00094056.2010.10523173

Hoeve, M., Stams, G. J., van der Put, C. E., Dubas, J. S., van der Laan, P. H., & Gerris, J. R. (2012). A meta-analysis of attachment to parents and delinquency. *Journal of Abnormal Child Psychology, 40*, 771–785.

Hofferth, S., Flood, S., & Sobek, M. (2013). *American Time Use Survey Data Extract System: Version 2.4.* Minnesota Population Center, University of Minnesota. College Park, MD: Maryland Population Research Center, University of Maryland.

Hofferth, S., & Lee, Y. (2015). Family structure and trends in US fathers' time with children, 2003–2013. *Family Science, 6*(1), 318–329. doi: 10.1080/19424620.2015.1082805

Hofstede, G. (1980). *Culture's consequences: International differences in work-related values.* Beverly Hills, CA: Sage.

Holden, G. W., & Miller, P. C. (1999). Enduring and different: A meta-analysis of the similarity in parents' child rearing. *Psychological Bulletin, 125*(2), 223–254.

Holmes, M. R. (2013). The sleeper effect of intimate partner violence exposure: Long-term consequences on young children's aggressive behavior. *Journal of Child Psychology and Psychiatry, 54*, 986–995. doi: 10.1111/jcpp.12071

Holmes, R. M. (2011). Adult attitudes and beliefs regarding play on Lana'i. *American Journal of Play, 3*, 356–384.

Holter, Ø. G , Svare, H., & Egeland, C. (2008). *Likestilling og livskvalitet 2007. AFI-rapport 2008:1.* Oslo: Arbeidsforskningsinstituttet.

Hosking, A., Whitehouse, G., & Baxter, J. (2010). Duration of leave and resident fathers' involvement in infant care in Australia. *Journal of Marriage and Family, 72*, 1301–1316.

Hossain, Z. (2013). Fathers in Muslim families in Malaysia and Bangladesh. In D. W. Shwalb, B. J. Shwalb & M. E. Lamb (Eds.), *Fathers in cultural contexts* (pp. 95–121). New York: Routledge.

Hossain, Z., & Juhari, R. (2015). Fathers across Arab and non-Arab Islamic societies. In J. L. Roopnarine (Ed.), *Fathers across cultures: The importance, roles, and diverse practices of dads* (pp. 368–390). Santa Barbara, CA: Praeger/ABC-Clio.

Hossain, Z., & Roopnarine, J. L. (1994). African-American fathers' involvement with infants: Relationship to their functioning style, support, education, and income. *Infant Behavior and Development, 17*(2), 175–184.

Hossain, Z., Roopnarine, J. L., Ismail, R., Menon, S., Hashmi, S. I., & Sombuling, A. (2008). Fathers' and mothers' reports of involvement in caring for infants in Kadazan families in Sabah, Malaysia. *Fathering, 5*(1), 58–72.

Hossain, Z., Roopnarine, J. L., Masud, J., Muhamed, A. A., Baharudin, R., Abdullah, R., & Jahur, R. (2005). Mothers' and fathers' childcare involvement with young children in rural families in Malaysia. *International Journal of Psychology, 40*, 385–394.

Howarth, A., Scott, K., & Swain, N. (2017). First-time fathers' perception of their childbirth experiences. *Journal of Health Psychology*, 1–12. doi: 10.1177/1359105316687628

Howe, T. S., Sheu, C. F., Wang, T. N., & Hsu, Y. W. (2014). Parenting stress in families with very low birth weight preterm infants in early infancy. *Research in developmental disabilities, 35*(7), 1748–1756.

Huang, C.C. (2006). Child support enforcement and father involvement for children in never-married mother families. *Fathering, 4*(1), 97–111. doi: 10.3149/fth.0401.97

Huang, C. C., & Han, K. Q. (2012). Child support enforcement in the United States: Has policy made a difference? *Children and Youth Services Review, 34*(4), 622–627. doi: 10.1016/j.childyouth.2011.12.006

Huang, R., & Yang, M. (2015). Paid maternity leave and breastfeeding practice before and after California's implementation of the nation's first paid family leave program. *Economics and Human Biology, 16*, 45–59. doi: 10.1016/j.ehb.2013.12.009

Huber, B. R., & Breedlove, W. L. (2007). Evolutionary theory, kinship, and childbirth in cross-cultural perspective. *Cross-Cultural Research, 41*(2), 196–219. doi: 10.1177/1069397106298261

Huerta, M., Adema, W., Baxter, J., Han, J., Lausten, M., Lee, R., & Waldfogel, J. (2013). *Fathers' leave, fathers' involvement and child development: Are they related? Evidence from four OECD countries.* Paris: OECD Publishing.

Huerta, M. C., Adema, W., Baxter, J., Han, W.-J., Lausten, M., Lee, R., & Waldfogel, J. (2014). Fathers' leave and fathers' involvement: Evidence from four OECD countries. *European Journal of Social Security, 16*(4), 308–346. doi: 10.1177/138826271401600403

Hughes, M. M., Blom, M., Rohner, R., & Britner, P. (2005). Bridging parental acceptance-rejection theory and attachment theory in the preschool Strange Situation. *Ethos, 33*(3), 378–401.

Hunter, M. (2006). Father without amandla: Zulu-speaking men and fatherhood. In L. Richter & R. Morell (Eds.), *Baba: Men and fatherhood in South Africa* (pp. 99–107). Cape Town: HSRC Press.

Hyun, J. H. (2013). A study on childrearing and the value of the child in mother's perceptions. *Journal of Child Research Institute in Seoul Theological University, 12*, 41–55.

Hyun, J. H., Nakazawa, J., Shwalb, D. W., & Shwalb, B. J. (2016). Parents and childcare in South Korean and Japanese families. In U. P. Gielen & J. L. Roopnarine (Eds.), *Childhood and adolescence: Cross-cultural perspectives and applications* (pp. 177–206). Santa Barbara, CA: Praeger.

Hyvönen, U. (1993). *Om barns fadersbild.* Umeå, Finland: Umeå Universitet., Inst. för socialt arbete.

Ibrahim, M. A. (2010). Effects of parental power and prestige on children's psychological adjustment. Paper presented at the 3rd International Congress on Interpersonal Acceptance and Rejection, Padua, Italy.

Igarashi, T., & Hagiwara, H. (2004). Junior high school students' tendency toward nonattendance at school and attachment in early childhood. *Japanese Journal of Educational Psychology, 52*, 264–276.

Iliyasu, Z., Abubakar, I. S., Galadanci, H. S., Hayatu, Z., & Aliyu, M. H. (2010). Birth preparedness, complication readiness and fathers' participation in maternity care in a northern Nigerian community. *African Journal of Reproductive Health, 14*(1), 21–32.

ICF. (2006–2016). *Demographic and Health Surveys.* Funded by USAID. Rockville, MD: ICF [Distributor].

Institute for Family Studies. (2015). *World Family Map 2015: Mapping family change and child well-being outcomes.* Available from www.childtrends.org/wp-content/uploads/2015/09/2015-39WorldFamilyMap2015.pdf

Isbell, R., Sobol, J., Lindauer, L., & Lowrance, A. (2004). The effects of storytelling and story reading on the oral language complexity and story comprehension of young children. *Early Childhood Education Journal, 32*(3), 157–163. doi: 10.1023/B:ECEJ.0000048967.94189.a3

Jankowiak, W. (2008). Desiring sex, longing for love: A tripartite conundrum. In W. Jankowiak (Ed.), *Intimacies: Love and sex across cultures* (pp. 1–36). New York: Columbia University Press.

Jankowiak, W., Joiner, A., & Khatib, C. (2011). What observation studies can tell us about single child play patterns, gender, and changes in Chinese society? *Cross-Cultural Research, 45*(2), 155–177.

Jayakody, R., & Kalil, A. (2002). Social fathering in low-income, African American families with preschool children. *Journal of Marriage and Family, 64*, 504–516. doi: 10.1111/j.1741-3737.2002.00504.x

Jeynes, W. H. (2015). The relationship between father involvement and student academic achievement. *Urban Education, 50*(4), 387–423.

Johansson, M., Rubertsson, C., Rådestad, I., & Hildingsson, I. (2012). Childbirth – An emotionally demanding experience for fathers. *Sexual and Reproductive Healthcare, 3*(1), 11–20.

Johnson, J. E., Christie, J., & Wardle, F. (2005). *Play, development, and early education.* Boston: Pearson/Allyn and Bacon.

Juhari, R., Yaacob, S. N., & Talib, M. A. (2013). Father involvement among Malay Muslims in Malaysia. *Journal of Family Issues, 34*(2), 208–227.

Julion, W., Breitenstein, S., & Waddell, D. (2012). Fatherhood intervention development in collaboration with African American non-resident fathers. *Research in Nursing and Health, 35*(5), 490–506.

Jung, K. M., & Kim, M. K. (2012). The recognition of grandmother and mother in the role expectations of child rearing. *Korean Education Inquiry, 30*(3), 63–79.

Kağıtçıbaşı, Ç. (2005). Autonomy and relatedness in cultural context implications for self and family. *Journal of Cross-Cultural Psychology, 20*(10), 1–20.

Kağıtçıbaşı, Ç. (2007). *Family, self, and human development across cultures: Theory and applications* (2nd ed). Mahwah, NJ: Lawrence Erlbaum Associates.

Kakar, S. (1992). *The inner world: A Psychoanalytic Study of Childhood and Society in India.* New Delhi: Oxford University Press.

Kamal, L., Strand, J., Jutengren, G., & Tidefors, I. (2016). Perceptions and experiences of an attachment-based intervention for parents troubled by intimate partner violence. *Clinical Social Work Journal.* doi: 10.1007/s10615-10016-0606-0601

Kane, P., & Garber, J. (2004). The relations among depression in fathers, children's psychopathology, and father–child conflict: A meta-analysis. *Clinical Psychology Review, 24,* 339–360. doi: 10.1016/j.cpr.2004.03.004

Kapoor, S. (2006). Alternate care for infants of employed mothers. Unpublished doctoral dissertation of the Department of Child and Family Development, Lady Irwin College, University of Delhi, India.

Kato, K., Ishii-Kuntz, M., Makino, K., & Tsuchiya, M. (2002). The impact of parental involvement and maternal childcare anxiety on sociability of three-year-olds: Two cohorts comparison. *Japanese Journal of Developmental Psychology, 13,* 30–41.

Kato, K., & Kondo, K. (2007). A comparison between fathers and mothers in a play situation with three-year olds. *Japanese Journal of Developmental Psychology, 18,* 35–44.

Kaur, J. S. (2018). Children's narratives on the father–child relations. In R. Sriram (Ed.), *Fathering in India: Images and realities.* New York: Springer.

Kaye, D. K., Kakaire, O., Nakimuli, A., Osinde, M. O., Mbalinda, S. N., & Kakande, N. (2014). Male involvement during pregnancy and childbirth: Men's perceptions, practices and experiences during the care for women who developed childbirth complications in Mulago Hospital, Uganda. *BMC Pregnancy Childbirth, 31(14),* 54. doi: 10.1186/1471-2393-14-54

Keizer, R., Lucassen, N., Jaddoe, V., & Tiemeier, H. (2014). A prospective study on father involvement and toddlers' behavioral and emotional problems: Are sons and daughters differentially affected? *Fathering, 12*(1), 38–51. doi: 10.3149/fth.1201.38

Keller, H., Borke, J., Chaudhary, N., Lamm, B., & Kleis, A. (2010). Continuity in parenting strategies: A cross-cultural comparison. *Journal of Cross-Cultural Psychology, 41*(3), 391–409.

Khaleque, A. (2017). Perceived parental hostility and aggression, and children's psychological maladjustment, and negative personality dispositions: A meta-analysis. *Journal of Child and Family Studies, 26*(4), 977–988. doi: 10.1007/s10826-10016-0637-0639

Khaleque, A., & Rohner, R. P. (2011). Pancultural associations between perceived parental acceptance and psychological adjustment of children and adults: A meta-analytic review of worldwide research. *Journal of Cross-Cultural Psychology, 43*(5), 784–800.

Khaleque, A., & Rohner, R. P. (2012). Transnational relations between perceived parental acceptance and personality dispositions of children and adults: A meta-analytic review. *Personality and Social Psychology Review, 16,* 103–115. doi: 10.1177/1088868311418986

Khaleque, A., & Rohner, R. P. (2013). Effects of multiple acceptance and rejection on adult's psychological adjustment: A multi-cultural study. *Social Indicators, 113,* 393–399.

Khanobdee, C., Sukratanachaiyakul, V., & Gay, J. T. (1993). Couvade syndrome in expectant Thai fathers. *International Journal of Nursing Studies, 30*(2), 125–131.

Kiernan, K. (2006). Non-residential fatherhood and child involvement: Evidence from the Millennium Cohort Study. *Journal of Social Policy, 35,* 651–669.

Kim, N. H. (2011). Early childhood parents' perceptions of good father's roles and social roles for good fathering. *Journal of Future Early Childhood Education, 18*(2), 79–98.

Kim, S., & Queck, K. M. (2013). Transforming fatherhood: Reconstructing fatherhood through faith-based father school in South Korea. *Review of Religious Research, 55*(2), 231–250.

Kim, S. W., & Hill, N. E. (2015). Including fathers in the picture: A meta-analysis of parental involvement and students' academic achievement. *Journal of Educational Psychology, 107*(4), 919–934. doi: 10.1037/edu0000023

Kim, Y-I, & Jang, S. J. (2018). *A randomized controlled trial of the effectiveness of a responsible fatherhood program: The case of tyro dads.* Report prepared for the Fatherhood Research and Practice Network.

Kimber, M., Henriksen, C. A., Davidov, D. M., Goldstein, A. L., Pitre, N. Y., Tonmyr, L., & Afifi, T. O. (2015). The association between immigrant generational status, child maltreatment history and intimate partner violence (IPV): Evidence from a nationally representative survey. *Social Psychiatry and Psychiatric Epidemiology, 50*(7), 1135–1144. doi: 10.1007/s00127-014-1002-1

Kirwil, L. (2009). Parental mediation of children's internet use in different European countries. *Journal of Children and Media, 3*(4), 394–409. doi: 10.1080/17482790903233440

Kitzmann, K. M., Gaylord, N. K., Holt, A. R., & Kenny, E. D. (2003). Child witnesses to domestic violence: A meta-analytic review. *Journal of Consulting and Clinical Psychology, 71*(2), 339–352.

Knoester, C., & Eggebeen, D. J. (2006). The effects of the transition to parenthood and subsequent children on men's well-being and social participation. *Journal of Family Issues, 27*, 1532–1560.

Knoester, C., Petts, R. J., & Eggebeen. D. J. (2007). Commitments to fathering and the well-being and social participation of new, disadvantaged fathers. *Journal of Marriage and Family, 69*, 991–1004.

Kocak, A. A. (2004). *Evaluation report of the Father Support Programme.* ACEV Mother–Child Education Foundation.

Kokkinaki, T. (2009). Emotional expressions during early infant – father conversations. *European Journal of Developmental Psychology, 6*(6), 705–721.

Kokkinaki, T., & Vasdekis, V. S. (2015). Comparing emotional coordination in early spontaneous mother–infant and father–infant interactions. *European Journal of Developmental Psychology, 12*(1), 69–84. doi: 10.1080/17405629.2014.950220

Koslowski, A., Blum, S., & Moss, P. (2016). *International review of leave policies and research 2016.* Available at: www.leavenetwork.org/lp_and_r_reports/

Kotasadam, A., & Finseraas, H. (2011). The state intervenes in the battle of the sexes: Causal effects of paternity leave. *Social Science Research, 40*, 1611–1622.

Kouvo, A. M., Voeten, M., & Silvén, M. (2015). Fathers' and mothers' attachment representations as predictors of preadolescents' attachment security: A ten-year follow-up of Finnish families. *Scandinavian Journal of Psychology, 56*(5), 527–536. doi: 10.1111/sjop.12224

Kramer, K. Z., & Kramer, A. (2016). At-home father families in the United States: Gender ideology, human capital, and unemployment. *Journal of Marriage and Family, 78*(5), 1315–1331. doi: 10.1111/jomf.12327

Kravchenko, Z., & Robila, M. (2015). Fatherhood and fathering in Eastern Europe. In J. Roopnarine (Ed.), *Fathers in cultural perspectives* (pp. 108–132). Santa Barbara, CA: Praeger/ABC-Clio.

Kroll, M. E., Carson, C., Redshaw, M., & Quigley, M. A. (2016). Early father involvement and subsequent child behaviour at ages 3, 5 and 7 years: Prospective analysis of the UK Millennium Cohort Study. *PLoS ONE, 11*(9), e0162339. doi: 10.1371/journal.pone.0162339

Kurtz, S. N. (1992). *All the mothers are one: Hindu India and the cultural reshaping of psychoanalysis.* New York: Columbia University Press.

Kutahyalioglu, N. S. (2017). Turkish immigrant fathers' pre-birth support with their spouses and post-birth involvement with their infants. Unpublished thesis. Syracuse University.

Laflamme, D., Pomerleau, A., & Malcuit, G. (2002). A comparison of fathers' and mothers' involvement in childcare and stimulation behaviors during free-play with their infants at 9 and 15 months. *Sex Roles, 47,* 507–518.

Laflamme, L., Månsdotter, A., & Lundberg, M. (2012). Dangerous dads? Ecological and longitudinal analyses of paternity leave and risk for child injury. *Journal of Epidemiology and Community Health, 66,* 1001–1004.

Lamb, M. E. (Ed.) (1976). *The role of the father in child development.* New York: Wiley.

Lamb, M. (1977). Father–infant and mother–infant interaction in the first year of life. *Child Development, 48,* 167–181.

Lamb, M. E. (2002). Infant – father attachments and their impact on child development. In C. S. Tamis-LeMonda & N. Cabrera (Eds.), *Handbook of father involvement: Multidisciplinary perspectives* (pp. 93–117). Mahwah, NJ: Erlbaum.

Lamb, M. E. (Ed.) (2010). *The role of the father in child development* (5th ed.). New York: Wiley.

Lamb, M. E. (2013). The changing faces of fatherhood and father–child relationships: From fatherhood as status to father as dad. In M. A. Fine & F. D. Fincham (Eds.), *Handbook of family theories: A content-based approach* (pp. 87–102). New York: Routledge.

Lamb, M. E., & Lewis, C. (2010). The development and significance of father–child relationships in two-parent families. In M. E. Lamb (Ed.), *The role of the father in child development* (5th ed.) (pp. 94–153). New York: Wiley.

Lamb, M. E., & Lewis, C. (2013). Father–child relationships. In N. Cabrera & C. S. Tamis-LeMonda (Eds.), *Handbook of father involvement* (2nd ed.) (pp. 119–134). New York: Routledge.

Lamb, M. E., Pleck, J. H., Charnov, E. L., & Levine, J. A. (1985). Paternal behavior in humans. *American Zoologist, 25,* 883–894.

Lamb, M. E., Pleck, J. H., Charnov, E. L., & Levine, J. A. (1987). A biosocial perspective on paternal behavior and involvement. In J. B. Lancaster, J. Altmann, A. S. Rossi & L.R. Sherrod (Eds.), *Parenting across the lifespan: Biosocial dimensions* (pp. 111–142). Hawthorne, NY: Aldine.

Lancy, D. F. (2007), Accounting for variability in mother–child play. *American Anthropologist, 109,* 273–284. doi: 10.1525/aa.2007.109.2.273

Lansford, J. E., Alampay, L., Bacchini, D., Bombi, A. S., Bornstein, M. H., Chang, L., & Zelli, A. (2010). Corporal punishment of children in nine countries as a function of child gender and parent gender. *International Journal of Pediatrics,* 1–12.

Lawrence, P. J., Davies, B., & Ramchandani, P. G. (2013). Using video feedback to improve early father–infant interaction: A pilot study. *Clinical Child Psychology and Psychiatry, 18*(1), 61–71. doi: 10.1177/1359104512437210.

Laxman, D. J., McBride, B. A., Jeans, L. M., Dyer, W. J., Santos, R. M., Kern, J. L., & . . . Weglarz-Ward, J. M. (2015). Father involvement and maternal depressive symptoms in families of children with disabilities or delays. *Maternal and Child Health Journal, 19*(5), 1078–1086. doi: 10.1007/s10995-014-1608-7

Lee, B., Keown, L. J., & Brown, G. L. (2016). Relationships between parenting practices and perceptions of child behaviour among Korean immigrant mothers and fathers. *International Journal of Psychology.* doi: 10.1002/ijop.12398

Lee, S. J., Taylor, C. A., & Bellamy, J. L. (2012). Paternal depression and child neglect in father – involved families of young children. *Child Abuse and Neglect, 36,* 461–469.

Lee, T., Wang, M., Lin, K., & Kao, C. (2012). The effectiveness of early intervention on paternal stress for fathers of premature infants admitted to a neonatal intensive care unit. *Journal of Advanced Nursing, 69*(5), 1085–1095. doi: 10.1111/j.1365-2648.2012.06097.x

Leonard , W., Pitts, M., Mitchell, A., Lyons, A., Smith, A., Patel, S., Couch, M., & Barrett, A. (2012). *Private Lives 2: The second national survey of the health and wellbeing of gay, lesbian, bisexual and transgender (GLBT) Australians*. Melbourne: Australian Research Centre in Sex, Health and Society, LaTrobe University.

Leo-Rhynie, E., & Brown, J. (2013). Child rearing practices in the Caribbean in the early childhood years. In C. Logie & J. L. Roopnarine (Eds.), *Issues and perspectives in early childhood education in the Caribbean*. La Romaine, Trinidad and Tobago: Caribbean Publishers.

Levine, E., Kaufman, R., Hammar, C., & Fagan, J. (2015). *How involved are fathers with their children? A study of fatherhood programs*. Fatherhood Research and Practice Network. Retrieved from www.frpn.org/asset/frpn-research-brief-how-involved-are-fathers-their-children-study-fatherhood-programs

LeVine, R. (1974). Parental goals: A cross-cultural view. *Teacher's College Record, 76*(2), 226–239.

LeVine, R. A., Dixon, S., LeVine, S., Richman, A., Leiderman, P. H., Keefer, C. H., & Brazelton, T. B. (1996). *Child care and culture: Lessons from Africa*. New York: Cambridge University Press.

Levtov, R., van der Gaag, N., Greene, M., Kaufman, M., & Barker, G. (2015). *State of the world's fathers*. Washington, DC: Prumondo, Rutgers, Save the Children, Sonke Justice Centre, and the Engage Alliance.

Li, X. [Xuan] & Lamb, M. E. (2013). Fathers in Chinese culture: From stern disciplinarians to involved parents. In D. Shwalb, B. Shwalb & M. E. Lamb (Eds.), *Fathers in cultural contexts* (pp. 15–41). New York: Routledge.

Li, X. [Xuan] & Lamb, M. E. (2015). Fathers in Chinese culture: Traditions and transitions. In J. L. Roopnarine (Ed.), *Fathers across cultures: The importance, roles, and diverse practices of dads* (pp. 273–306). Santa Barbara, CA: Praeger/ABC-Clio.

Liang, Z., Zhang, G., Deng, H., Song, Y., & Zheng, W. (2013). A multilevel analysis of the developmental trajectory of preschoolers' effortful control and prediction by parental parenting style. *Acta Psychologica Sinica, 45*(5), 556–567. doi: 10.3724/sp.j.1041.2013.00556

Liu, J. [Jinhua] (1995). An intergenerational comparison of paternal child-rearing attitudes and ideas in Shanghai. *Psychological Science, 4*, 211–215, 255.

Liu, L., & Li, Y. (2013). Fuqin canyujiaoyang zhuangkuang dui xueqian ertong shehuijineng de zuoyong [The effects of fathers' involvement and parenting on children's early social skills]. *Psychological Development and Education, 2013*(1), 38–45.

Liu, X., & Zhao, N. (2006). Fuqin juese touru yu ertong de chengzhang [The role of the father and child development]. *Studies of Foreign Education, 33*(197), 13–18.

Livingstone, S., & Haddon, L. (2009). *EU Kids Online: final report 2009*. London: EU Kids Online Network.

Lloyd, A. B., Lubans, D.R., Plotnikoff, R.C., & Morgan, P. L. (2014). Impact of the "Healthy Dads, Healthy Kids" lifestyle programme on the activity- and diet-related parenting practices of fathers and mothers. *Pediatric Obesity, 9*, e149 – e155.

Loper, A. B., & Tuerk, E. H. (2007). Parenting programs for incarcerated parents: Current research and future directions. *Criminal Justice Policy Review, 17*(4), 407–427. doi: 10.1177/0887403406292692

Loue, S. (2006). *Sexual partnering, sexual practices, and health*. New York: Springer.

Low, B. (1990). Marriage systems and pathogen stress in human societies. *American Zoologist, 30*(2), 325–340.

Lozoff, B. (1983). Birth and "bonding" in non-industrial societies. *Developmental Medicine and Child Neurology, 25*(5), 595–600.

Lu, Y., & Zhang, Y. (2008). Chuzhongsheng yiyu yu yilian, ziwoxiaonenggan de guanxi yanjiu [Researches into the relationships among attachment, general self-efficacy and depressive symptoms in junior middle school students]. *Psychological Development and Education, 2008*(1), 55–60.

Lucassen, N., Tharner, A., van IJzendoorn, M. H., Bakermans-Kranenburg, M. J., Volling, B. L., Verhulst, F. C., Lambregtse-Van den Berg, M. P., & Tiemeier, H. (2011). The association between paternal sensitivity and infant – father attachment security: A meta-analysis of three decades of research. *Journal of Family Psychology, 25*(6), 986–992.

Lucassen, N. , Kok, R. , Bakermans-Kranenburg, M. J., van IJzendoorn, M. H., Jaddoe, V. W., Hofman, A. , Verhulst, F. C., Lambregtse-Van den Berg, M. P., & Tiemeier, H. (2015). Executive functions in early childhood: The role of maternal and paternal parenting practices. *British Journal of Developmental Psychology, 33*(4), 489–505. doi: 10.1111/bjdp.12112

Lundquist, E., Hsueh, J., Lowenstein, A. E., Faucetta, K., Gubits, D., Michalopoulos, C., & Knox, V.(2014). *A family-strengthening program for low-income families: Final impacts from the Supporting Healthy Marriage Evaluation. OPRE Report 2014–2009A.* Washington, DC: Office of Planning, Research and Evaluation, Administration for Children and Families, U.S. Department of Health and Human Services.

Lundy, B. L. (2002). Paternal socio-psychological factors and infant attachment: The mediating role of synchrony in father–infant interactions. *Infant Behavior and Development, 25*(2), 221–236. doi: 10.1016/S0163–6383(02)00123–00126

Luz, R., George, A., Vieux, R., & Spitz, E. (2017). Antenatal determinants of parental attachment and parenting alliance: How do mothers and fathers differ? *Infant Mental Health Journal, 38*, 183–197. doi: 10.1002/imhj.21628

Maccoby, E. E., & Martin, J. A. (1983). Socialization in the context of the family: Parent–child interaction. In P. Mussen (Ed.), *Handbook of child psychology vol. 4.* New York: Wiley.

Maccoby, E. E., & Mnookin, R. H. (1992). *Dividing the child: Social and legal dilemmas of custody.* Cambridge, MA: Harvard University Press.

MacDonald E. E., & Hastings R. P. (2010) Fathers of children with developmental disabilities. In M. E. Lamb (Ed.), *The role of the father in child development* (5th ed.) (pp. 486–516). Hoboken, NJ: Wiley.

MacKenzie, M. J., Nicklas, E., Waldfogel, J., & Brooks-Gunn, J. (2013). Spanking and child development across the first decade of life, *Pediatrics, 1227.* doi: 10.1542/peds. 2013–1227

Madhavan, S., & Roy, K. (2012). Securing fatherhood through kin work a comparison of black low-income fathers and families in South Africa and the United States. *Journal of Family Issues, 33*, 801–822.

Madsen, S. A., Lind, D., & Munck, H. (2007). Men's abilities to reflect their infants' states of mind: Interviews with 41 new fathers on experiences of parenthood. *Nordic Psychology, 59*(2), 149–163. doi: 10.1027/1901–2276.59.2.149

Main, M. (1995). Recent studies in attachment: Overview, with selected implications for clinical work. In S. Goldberg, R. Muir & J. Kerr (Eds.), *Attachment theory: Social, developmental, and clinical perspectives* (pp. 407–474). Hillsdale, NJ: Analytic Press.

Main, M., & Cassidy, J. (1988). Categories of response to reunion with the parent at age 6: Predictable from infant attachment classifications and stable over a 1-month period. *Developmental Psychology, 24*, 415–426.

Main, M., & Solomon, J. (1990). Procedures for identifying infants as disorganized/disoriented during the Ainsworth Strange Situation. In M. T. Greenberg, D. Cicchetti & E. M. Cummings (Eds.), *Attachment in the preschool years* (pp. 121–160). Chicago: University of Chicago Press.

Main, M., & Weston, D. R. (1981). The quality of the toddler's relationship to mother and to father: Related to conflict behavior and the readiness to establish new relationships. *Child Development, 52*(3), 932–940. doi: 10.2307/1129097

Makusha, T., & Richter, L. (2015). Black fathers in South Africa. In J. L. Roopnarine (Ed.), *Fathers across cultures: The importance, roles, and diverse practices of dads* (pp. 391–409). Santa Barbara, CA: Praeger/ABC-CLIO.

Makusha, T., Richter, L., & Chikovore, J. (2013). Fatherhood and masculinities in South Africa. In D. Glennrich (Ed.), *Men and masculinities in South Africa*. Pietermaritzburg: PACSA and Sonke Gender Justice Network.

Malik, N. M., Boris, N. W., Heller, S.S ., Harden, B.J ., Squires, J., & Chazan-Cohen, R. (2007). Risk for maternal depression and child aggression in Early Head Start families: A test of ecological models. *Infant Mental Health Journal, 28*, 171–191.

Malphurs, J. E., Field, T. M., Larraine, C., Pickens, J., Pelaez-Nogueras, M., Yando, R., & Bendell, D. (1996). Altering withdrawn and intrusive interaction behaviors of depressed mothers. *Infant Mental Health Journal, 17*(2), 152–160.

Malphurs, J. E., Raag, T., Field, T., Pickens, J., Yando, R., & Bendell, D. (1996). Touch by intrusive and withdrawn mothers with depressive symptoms. *Early Development and Parenting, 5*, 111–115.

Månsdotter, A., Fredlund, P., Hallqvist, J., & Magnusson, C. (2010). Who takes paternity leave? A cohort study on prior social and health characteristics among fathers in Stockholm. *Journal of Public Health Policy, 31*(3), 324–341.

Marcus, R. F., & Mirle, J. (1990). Validity of a child interview measure of attachment as used in child custody evaluations. *Perceptual and Motor Skills, 70*, 1043–1054.

Maridaki-Kassotaki, K. (2000). Understanding fatherhood in Greece: How involved are Greek fathers in the care of their young children? *Psicologia: Teoria e Pesquisa, 16*(3), 213–219.

Marlowe, F. (1999). Showoffs or providers? The parenting effort of Hadza men. *Evolution and Human Behavior, 20*, 391–404.

Marlowe, F. (2005). Who tends Hadza children? In B. S. Hewlett & M. E. Lamb (Eds.), *Hunter-gatherer childhoods: Evolutionary, developmental, and cultural perspectives* (pp. 175–213). New Brunswick, NJ: Aldine Transaction.

Marotto-Navarro, G., Pastor-Moreno, G., Ocaña-Riola, R., Benítez-Hidalgo, V., García-Calvente, M. D., Gutiérrez-Cuadra, M. D., Gijón-Sánchez, M. T., Río-Lozano, M. D., & Marcos-Marcos, J. (2013). Male and female involvement in the birth and child-rearing process. *Journal of Clinical Nursing, 22*, 3071–3083. doi: 10.1111/jocn.12153

Marsiglio, W. (2009). Healthy dads, healthy kids. *Contexts, 8*, 22–27.

Marsiglio, W., & Pleck, J.H. (2005). Fatherhood and masculinities. In M. Kimmel, J. Hearn & R. W. Connell (Eds.), *Handbook of studies on men and masculinities* (pp. 249–269). Thousand Oaks, CA: Sage.

Martin, B., Hewitt, B., Yerkes, M., Xiang, N., Rose, J. and Coles, L. (2014). *Paid parental leave evaluation, phase 3 report*. Canberra: Australian Government Department of Social Security.

Martin, J. A., Hamilton, B. E., Osterman, M., Driscoll, A. K., & Drake, P. (2018). Births: Final data for 2016. *National Vital Statistics Reports, 67*(1), Hyattsville, MD: National Center for Health Statistics.

Martini, F., & Sénéchal, M. (2012). Learning literacy skills at home: Parent teaching, expectations, and child interest. *Canadian Journal of Behavioural Science, 44*(3), 210–221. doi: 10.1037/a0026758

Masten, A. S., & Cicchetti, D. (2010). Developmental cascades. *Development and Psychopathology, 22*, 491–495. doi: 10.1017/S0954579410000222

McAllister, F., Burgess, A., Kato, J., & Barker, G. (2012). *Fatherhood: Parenting programmes and policy: A critical review of best practice*. Washington, DC: The Fatherhood Institute/Promundo/MenCare.

McCrudden, E., Braiden, H. J., Sloan, D., McCormack, P., & Treacy, A. (2014). Stealing the smile from my child's face: A preliminary evaluation of the "Being a Dad" programme in a Northern Ireland prison. *Child Care in Practice, 20*(3), 301–312. doi: 10.1080/13575279.2013.865592

McMunn, A., Martin, P., Kelly, Y., & Sacker, A. (2015). Fathers' involvement: Correlates and consequences for child socioemotional behavior in the United Kingdom. *Journal of Family Issues, 38*(8), 1109–1131.

McWayne, C., Downer, J. T., Campos, R., & Harris, R. D. (2013). Father involvement during early childhood and its association with children's early learning: A meta-analysis. *Early Education and Development, 24*(6), 898–922. doi: 10.1080/10409289.2013.746932

Melnyk, B. M., Feinstein, N. F., Alpert-Gillis, L., Fairbanks, E., Crean, H. F., Sinkin, R. A., & . . . Gross, S. T. (2006). Reducing premature infants' length of stay and improving parents' mental health outcomes with the creating opportunities for parent empowerment (COPE) neonatal intensive care unit program: A randomized, controlled trial. *Pediatrics, 118*(5), e1414 – e1427. doi: 10.1542/peds.2005–2580

Melnyk, B. M., Fineout-Overholt, E., & Mays, M. Z. (2008). The evidence-based practice beliefs and implementation scales: Psychometric properties of two new instruments. *Worldviews on Evidence-Based Nursing, 5*, 208–216. doi: 10.1111/j.1741–6787.2008.00126.x

Menashe-Grinberg, A., & Atzaba-Poria, N. (2017). Mother–child and father–child play interaction: The importance of parental playfulness as a moderator of the links between parental behavior and child negativity. *Infant Mental Health Journal, 38*(6), 772–784.

MenEngage Africa & Sonke Gender Justice. (2015). *MenEngage Tri-country Project review: Kenya, Rwanda and Sierra Leone.* Cape Town, South Africa: Sonke Gender Justice.

Metindogan, A. (2015). Fathering in Turkey. In J. L. Roopnarine (Ed.), *Fathers across cultures: The importance, roles, and diverse practices of dads* (pp. 327–349). Santa Barbara, CA: Praeger/ABC-Clio.

Mikelson, K. S. (2008). He said, she said: Comparing mother and father reports of father involvement. *Journal of Marriage and Family, 70*(3), 613–624. doi:10.1111/j.1741–3737.2008.00509.x

Mincy, R. B., Garfinkel, I., & Nepomnyaschy, L. (2005). In-hospital paternity establishment and father involvement in fragile families. *Journal of Marriage and Family, 67*(3), 611–626.

Ministry of Health and Social Affairs. (2009). *Never violence: Thirty years on from Sweden's abolition of corporal punishment.* Stockholm: Save the Children Sweden and Swedish Ministry of Health and Social Affairs.

Minuchin, S., Rosman, B. L., & Baker, L. (1978). *Psychosomatic families: Anorexia nervosa in context.* Cambridge, MA: Harvard University Press. doi: 10.4159/harvard.9780674418233

Mirnia, K., Bostanabad, M, A., Asadollahi, M., & Razzaghi, H. (2016). Paternal skin-to-skin care and its effect on cortisol levels of the infants. *Iranian Journal of Pediatrics, 27*(1), e8151. doi: 10.5812/ijp.8151

Miyake, K., Chen, S-J., & Campos, J. (1985). Infant temperament and mother's mode of interaction and attachment in Japan: An interim report. In I. Bretherton & E. Waters (Eds.), *Growing points of attachment theory and research. Monographs of the Society for Research in Child Development, 50*(209), 276–297.

Modecki, K. L., Hagan, M., Sandler, I., & Wolchik, S. (2015). Latent profiles of non-residential father engagement six years after divorce predict long-term offspring outcomes. *Journal of Clinical Child and Adolescent Psychology, 44*(1), 123–136. doi: 10.1080/15374416.2013.865193

Mol, S. E., & Bus, A. G. (2011). To read or not to read: A meta-analysis of print exposure from infancy to early adulthood. *Psychological Bulletin, 137*(2), 267–296. doi: 10.1037/a0021890

Monteiro, L., Veríssimo, M., Vaughn, B.E., Santos, A., Torres, N., & Fernandes, M. (2010). The organization of children's secure base behaviour in two-parent Portuguese families and father's participation in child-related activities. *European Journal of Developmental Psychology, 7*(5), 545–560. doi: 10.1080/17405620902823855

Morrow, L. (1985). Retelling stories: A strategy for improving young children's comprehension, concept of story structure, and oral language complexity. *Elementary School Journal*, *85*, 647–661.

Murphey, D., & Mae Cooper, P. (2015). *Parents behind bars: What happens to their children*. Washington, DC: Child Trends.

Murray, J., Bijleveld, H. J., Farrington, D. P., & Loeber, R. (2014). *Effects of incarceration on children: Cross cultural comparative studies*. Washington, DC: APA.

Murray, J., Farrington, D. P., & Sekol. I. (2012). Children's antisocial behavior, mental health, drug use, and educational performance after parental incarceration: A systematic review and metaanalysis. *Journal of the American Psychological Association*, *138*, 175–210.

Mwoma, T. B. (2009). Paternal involvement in children's education: An implication of children's performance in preschool in Gucha district Kenya. Unpublished doctoral dissertation, Kenyatta University, Nairobi.

Mwoma, T. B. (2014). Fathering among different communities in Kenya. Unpublished research findings. Nairobi, Kenya.

Mwoma, T. B. (2015). Fathering in Kenya. In J. L. Roopnarine (Ed.), *Fathers across cultures: The importance, roles, and diverse practices of dads* (pp. 410–428). Santa Barbara, CA: Praeger.

Naito, T., & Gielen, U. P. (2005). The changing Japanese family: A psychological portrait. In J. L. Roopnarine & U. P. Gielen (Eds.), *Families in global perspective* (pp. 63–84). Boston: Allyn & Bacon.

Nakamichi, K., & Nakazawa, J. (2003). Maternal/paternal childrearing style and young children's aggressive behavior. *Chiba University Faculty of Education Bulletin*, *51*, 173–179.

Nakazawa, J. (2015). Fathering in Japan. In J. L. Roopnarine (Ed.), *Fathers across cultures: The importance, roles, and diverse practices of dads* (pp. 309–324). Santa Barbara, CA: Praeger/ABC-Clio.

Namy, S., Heilman, B., Stich, S., Crownover, J., Leka, B., & Edmeades, J. (2014). Changing what it means to "become a man": Participants' reflections on a school-based programme to redefine masculinity in the Balkans. *Culture, Health and Sexuality*, *17*(2), 206–222.

National Institute of Population and Social Security Research. (2010). *The 14th national basic birth research, 2010*. Available at www.ipss.go.jp/ps-doukou/j/doukou14/doukou14.asp

Nepomnyaschy, L., & Garfinkel, I. (2010). Child support enforcement and fathers' contributions to their nonmarital children. *Social Service Review*, *84*(3), 341–380. doi: 10.1086/655392

Neshteruk, C. D., Nezami, B. T., Nino-Tapias, G., Davison, K. K., & Ward, D. S. (2017). The influence of fathers on children's physical activity: A review of the literature from 2009 to 2015. *Preventive Medicine: An International Journal Devoted to Practice and Theory*, 10212–10219. doi: 10.1016/j.ypmed.2017.06.027

Neumann, M. M., Hood, M., & Neumann, D. L. (2009). The scaffolding of emergent literacy skills in the home environment: A case study. *Early Childhood Education Journal*, *36*(4), 313–319. doi: 10.1007/s10643–008–0291-y

Newman, C., Fowler, C., & Cashin, A. (2011). The development of a parenting program for incarcerated mothers in Australia: A review of prison-based parenting programs. *Contemporary Nurse*, *39*(1), 2–11. doi: 10.5172/conu.2011.39.1.2

NICHD Early Child Care Research Network. (2009). Family–peer linkages: The mediational role of attentional processes. *Social Development*, *18*(4), 875–895.

Nobes, G., & Smith, M. (1997). Physical punishment of children in two-parent families. *Clinical Child Psychology and Psychiatry*, *2*(2), 271–281. doi: 10.1177/1359104597022007

Nobes, G., Smith, M., Upton, P., & Heverin, A. (1999). Physical punishment by mothers and fathers in British homes. *Journal of Interpersonal Violence*, *14*(8), 887–902. doi: 10.1177/088626099014008006

Nomaguchi, K. M., & Milkie, M. A. (2003). Costs and rewards of children: The effects of becoming a parent on adults' lives. *Journal of Marriage and Family, 65*(2), 356–374. doi: 10.1111/j.1741–3737.2003.00356.x

Noor, N. (1999). Roles and women's well-being: Some preliminary findings from Malaysia. *Sex Roles, 41,* 123–145.

Obokata, A., & Muto, T. (2005). Regulatory and preventive factors for mild delinquency of junior high school students: Child–parent relationships, peer relationships, and self-control. *Japanese Journal of Developmental Psychology, 16,* 286–299.

O'Brien, M., & Moss, P. (2010). Father work and family policies in Europe. In M. E. Lamb (Ed.), *The role of the father in child development* (5th ed.) (pp. 551–577). New York: Wiley.

OECD. (2010). *OECD Family Database, child support, no: PF1.5.* Available at www.oecd.org/els/family/41920285.pdf

OECD. (2014). *OECD Family Database, SF2.4: Share of births outside of marriage.* Available at www.oecd.org/els/family/SF_2_4_Share_births_outside_marriage.pdf

OECD. (2016a). Parental leave: Where are the fathers? OECD/Policy Briefs. Available at www.oecd.org/policy-briefs/parental-leave-where-are-the-fathers.pdf

OECD. (2016b). *OECD Family Database.* Available at www.oecd.org/els/family/database. htm

Oelofsen, N., & Richardson, P. (2006) Sense of coherence and parenting stress in mothers and fathers of preschool children with developmental disability. *Journal of Intellectual and Developmental Disability, 31,* 1–12.

O'Halloran, M. S., Rizzolo, S., Cohen, M. L., & Wacker, R. (2013). Assessing the impact of a multiyear marriage education program. *The Family Journal, 21,* 328–334. doi: 10.1177/1066480713476849

Oláh, L. Sz. (2001). Gender and family stability: Dissolution of the first parental union in Sweden and Hungary. *Demographic Research, 4*(2).

Olayemi, O., Bello, F. A., Aimakhu, C. O., Obajimi, G. O., & Adekunle, A. O. (2009). Male participation in pregnancy and delivery in Nigeria: A survey of antenatal attendees. *Journal of Biosocial Science, 41*(4), 493–503. doi: 10.1017/S0021932009003356

Oldrup, H., Frederiksen, S., Henze-Pedersen, S., & Olsen, R. F. (2016). Indsat Far – Udsat Barn? Hverdagslivog Trivsel Blandt Børn af Fængslede [Imprisoned father – exposed child?]. *Det Nationale Forskningscenter for Velfard.* Available at https://pure.sfi.dk/ws/files/473564/1617_Indsat_far_udsat_barn.pdf

Olsson, M. B., & Hwang, C. P. (2006) Well-being, involvement in paid work and division of child-care in parents of children with intellectual disabilities in Sweden. *Journal of Intellectual Disability Research, 50,* 963–969.

Opondo, C., Redshaw, M., & Quigley, M. A. (2017). Association between father involvement and attitudes in early child-rearing and depressive symptoms in the pre-adolescent period in a UK birth cohort. *Journal of Affective Disorders, 22,* 1115–1122. doi: 10.1016/j. jad.2017.06.010

Opondo, C., Redshaw, M., Savage-McGlynn, E., & Quigley, M. A. (2017). Father involvement in early child-rearing and behavioural outcomes in their pre-adolescent children: Evidence from the ALSPAC UK birth cohort. *BMJ Open, 6*(11), e012034. doi: 10.1136/bmjopen-2016–012034

Oshima, K. (2013). Parents' marital trust, positive parenting, and young adults' mental health. *Japanese Journal of Developmental Psychology, 24,* 55–65.

Ouellet-Morin, I., Fisher, H. L., York-Smith, M., Fincham-Campbell, S., Moffitt, T. E., & Arseneault, L. (2015). Intimate partner violence and new-onset depression: A longitudinal study of women's childhood and adult histories of abuse. *Depression and Anxiety, 32*(5), 316–324.

Oyserman, D., Coon, H. M., & Kemmelmeier, M. (2002). Rethinking individualism and collectivism: Evaluation of theoretical assumptions and meta-analyses. *Psychological Bulletin*, *128*, 3–72. doi: 10.1037/0033–2909.128.1.3

Ozdemir, F. K., & Alemdar, D. K. (2017). Supporting of the fathers to visit their infants in neonatal intensive care unit decreases their stress level: A pretest-posttest quasi-experimental study. *Community Mental Health Journal*, *4*(51).

Ozgün, O., Çiftçi, M. A., & Erden, Ş. (2013). The meaning of fatherhood as perceived by Turkish police fathers and their young children. *Educational Research and Reviews*, *8*(21), 1966–1978.

Ozkan, M., Altindag, A., Oto, R., & Sentunali, E. (2006). Mental health aspects of Turkish women from polygamous versus monogamous families. *International Journal of Social Psychiatry*, *52*(3), 214–220. doi: 10.1177/0020764006067207

Paige, K. E., & Paige, J. M . (1981). *The politics of reproductive ritual.* Berkeley: University of California Press.

Palkovitz, R. (2002). Involved fathering and child development: Advancing our understanding of good fathering. In C. Tamis-LeMonda & N. Cabrera (Eds.), *Handbook of father involvement: Multidisciplinary perspective* (pp. 119–140). Mahwah, NJ: Lawrence Erlbaum Associates.

Pancsofar, N., & Vernon-Feagans, L. (2006). Mother and father language input to young children: Contributions to later language development. *Journal of Applied Developmental Psychology*, *27*(6), 571–587. doi: 10.1016/j.appdev.2006.08.003

Pandya, V. (1992). Gukwelonone: The games of hiding fathers and seeking sons among the Ongee of Little Andaman. In B. S. Hewlett (Ed.), *Father–child relations: Cultural and biosocial contexts.* (pp. 263–279). New York: Aldine De Gruyter.

Panter-Brick, C., Burgess, A., Eggerman, M., McAllister, F., Pruett, K., & Leckman, J. F. (2014). Practitioner review: Engaging fathers: Recommendations for a game change in parenting interventions based on a systematic review of the global evidence. *Journal of Child Psychology and Psychiatry*, *55*(11), 1187–1212. doi: 10.1111/jcpp.12280

Papp, L. M., Goeke-Morey, M. C., & Cummings, E. M. (2007). Linkages between spouses' psychological distress and marital conflict in the home. *Journal of Family Psychology*, *21*(3), 533–537.

Paquette, D. (2004a). Dichotomizing paternal and maternal functions as a means to better understand their primary contributions. *Human Development*, *47*, 237–238.

Paquette, D. (2004b). Theorizing the father–child relationship: Mechanisms and developmental outcomes. *Human Development*, *47*, 193–219. doi: 10.1159/000078723

Paquette, D., & Bigras, M. (2010). The risky situation: A procedure for assessing the father–child activation relationship. *Early Child Development and Care*, *180*(1–2), 33–50. doi: 10.1080/03004430903414687

Paquette, D., & Dumont, C. (2013). Is father–child rough-and-tumble play associated with attachment or activation relationships? *Early Child Development and Care*, *183*(6), 760–773. doi: 10.1080/03004430.2012.723440

Parfitt, Y., Pike, A., & Ayers, S. (2013). The impact of parents' mental health on parent–baby interaction: A prospective study. *Infant Behavior and Development*, *36*(4), 599–608.

Parsons, T., & Bales, R. F. (1955). *Family, socialization and interaction process.* Glencoe, IL: Free Press.

Patnaik, A., & Ankita, P. (2014). Making leave easier: Better compensation and "daddy-only" entitlements. *SSRN Electronic Journal.* Available at https://pdfs.semanticscholar.org/60ec/1b6aa533de09649c5 c8867cb0e9fc41b3a e2.pdf

Pattnaik, J. (Ed.) (2013). *Father involvement in young children's lives: A global analysis.* New York: Springer Science.

Paulson J. F., Dauber, S., & Leiferman, J. A. (2006). Individual and combined effects of postpartum depression in mothers and fathers on parenting behavior. *Pediatrics*, *118*(2), 659–668. doi: 10.1542/peds.2005–2948

Pestvenidze, E., & Bohrer, M. (2007). Finally, daddies in the delivery room: Parents' education in Georgia. *Global Public Health, 2*(2), 169–183. doi: 10.1080/17441690601054330

PEW Research Center (2013). *Modern parenthood: Roles of moms and dads converge as they balance work and family.* Washington, DC: Pew Research Center.

PEW Research Center (2014). *Growing number of dads home with the kids: Biggest increase among those caring for family.* Washington, DC: Pew Research Center.

PEW Research Center (2015). *Parenting in America: Outlook, worries, aspirations are strongly linked to financial situation.* Washington, DC: Pew Research Center.

PEW Research Center (2017). *As U.S. marriage rate hovers at 50%, education gap in marital status widens.* Washington, DC Pew Research Center.

Phares, V. (2010). Where have all the fathers gone? Fathers' involvement in child and family therapy. *New Therapist, 65,* 11–17.

Phares, V., & Compas, B. E. (1992). The role of fathers in child and adolescent psychopathology: Make room for daddy. *Psychological Bulletin, 111*(3), 387–412. doi: 10.1037/0033-2909.111.3.387

Phares, V., Rojas, A., Thurston, I. B., & Hakinson, J. C. (2010). Including fathers in clinical interventions for children and adolescents. In M. E. Lamb (Ed.), *The role of the father in child development* (pp. 459–485). Hoboken, NJ: Wiley.

Plantin, L. (2001). *Män, familjeliv och föräldraskap* [Men, family life, and parenthood]. Umeå, Sweden: Boréa.

Plantin, L. (2015). Contemporary fatherhood in Sweden: Fathering across work and family life. In J. L. Roopnarine (Ed.), *Fathering across cultures: The importance, roles, and diverse practices of dads* (pp. 91–107). Santa Barbara, CA: Praeger/ABC-Clio.

Plantin, L., Olukoya, A., & Ny, P. (2011). Positive health outcomes of fathers' involvement in pregnancy and childbirth paternal support: A scope study literature review. *Fathering, 9*(1), 87–102. doi: 10.3149/fth.0901.87

Pleck, J. H. (2010). Paternal involvement: Revised conceptualization and theoretical linkages with child outcomes. In M. E. Lamb (Ed.), *The role of the father in child development* (5th ed.) (pp. 58–93). Hoboken, NJ: Wiley.

Poh, H. L., Koh, S. S., Seow, H. C., & He, H. G. (2014). First-time fathers' experiences and needs during pregnancy and childbirth: A descriptive qualitative study. *Midwifery, 30*(6), 779–787. doi: 10.1016/j.midw.2013.10.002

Portu-Zapirain, N. (2013). Attachment relationships with fathers and mothers during early childhood. *Psychology, 4*(3), 254–260.

Potter, C. A. (2016). "I accept my son for who he is – he has incredible character and personality": Fathers' positive experiences of parenting children with autism. *Disability and Society, 31*(7), 1–18. doi: 10.1080/09687599.2016.1216393

Primus, M. (2018). Parental warmth and physical punishment and their associations with children's social and academic skills in Trinidad and Tobago. Unpublished doctoral dissertation, Syracuse University.

Promundo. (2015). *Promundo's 2015 annual report.* Rio de Janeiro and Washington, DC: Promundo. Available at https://promundoglobal.org/resources/annual-report-2015/

Promundo, Instituto PAPAI, Salud y Género, and ECOS. (2013). *Program H/M/D: A toolkit for action: Engaging youth to achieve gender equity.* Rio de Janeiro and Washington, DC: Promundo.

Pudasainee-Kapri, S., & Razza, R. A. (2015). Associations among supportive coparenting, father engagement and attachment: The role of race/ethnicity. *Journal of Child and Family Studies, 24*(12), 3793–3804. doi: 10.1007/s10826-015-0187-6

Puhlman, D. J., & Pasley, K. (2013). Rethinking maternal gatekeeping. *Journal of Family Theory and Review, 5*(3), 176–193.

Pulerwitz, J., Barker, G., Segundo, M., & Nascimento, M. (2006). *Promoting more gender-equitable norms and behaviors among young men as an HIV/AIDS prevention strategy: Horizons final report*. Washington, DC: Population Council.

Pulerwitz, J., Hughes, L., Mehta, M., Kidanu, A., Verani, F., & Tewolde, S. (2015). Changing gender norms and reducing intimate partner violence: Results from a quasi-experimental intervention study with young men in Ethiopia. *American Journal of Public Health, 105*(1), 132–137. doi: 10.2105/AJPH.2014.302214

Putnick, D. L., Bornstein, M. H., Lansford, J. E., Chang, L., Deater-Deckard, K., & . . . Bombi, A. S. (2012). Agreement in mother and father acceptance-rejection, warmth, and hostility/rejection/neglect of children across nine countries. *Cross-Cultural Research, 46*, 191–223.

Putnick, D. L., Bornstein, M. H., Lansford, J. E., Malone, P. S., Pastorelli, C., & . . . Oburu, P. (2015). Perceived mother and father acceptance-rejection predict four unique aspects of child adjustment across nine countries. *Journal of Child Psychology and Psychiatry, 56*(8), 923–932.

Qian, Y., & Sayer, L. C. (2016). Division of labor, gender ideology, and marital satisfaction in East Asia. *Journal of Marriage and Family, 78*(2), 383–400.

Quellet-Morin, I., Fisher, H., York-Smith, M., Fincham-Campbell, S., Moffitt, T. E., & Arseneault, L. (2015). Intimate partner violence and new-onset depression: A longitudinal study of women's childhood and adult histories of abuse. *Depression and Anxiety, 33*, 316–324.

Raikes, H. H., & Bellotti, J. (2006). Two studies of father involvement in Early Head Start programs: A national survey and a demonstration program evaluation. *Parenting: Science and Practice, 6*, 229–242. doi: 10.1080/15295192.2006.9681307

Raikes, H. H., Summers, J. A., & Roggman, L. A. (2005). Father involvement in Early Head Start Programs. *Fathering, 3*(1), 29–58. doi: 10.3149/fth.0301.29

Rambaut, R. G. (1994). The crucible within: Ethnic identity, self-esteem, and segmented assimilation among children of immigrants. *The International Migration Review, 28*(4), 748–794

Ramchandani, P., Stein, A., Evans, J., & Boyce O'Connor, T. G. (2005). Paternal depression in the postnatal period and child development: A prospective population study. *Lancet, 365*(9478), 2201–2205. doi: 10.1016/S0140–6736(05)66778–5

Ramchandani, P. G., & Psychogiou, L. (2009). Paternal psychiatric disorders and children's psychosocial development. *Lancet, 374*(9690), 646–653.

Ramchandani, P. G., Psychogiou, L., Vlachos, H., Iles, J., Sethna, V., Netsi, E., & Lodder, A. (2011). Paternal depression: An examination of its links with father, child and family functioning in the postnatal period. *Depression and Anxiety, 28*(6), 471–477.

Ramchandani, P. G., O'Connor, T. G., Evans, J., Heron, J., Murray, L., & Stein, A. (2008). The effects of pre- and postnatal depression in fathers: A natural experiment comparing the effects of exposure to depression on offspring. *Journal of Child Psychology and Psychiatry, and Allied Disciplines, 49*(10), 1069–1078.

Ramkissoon, M. W. (2002). The psychology of fathering in the Caribbean: An investigation of the physical and psychological presence of the Jamaican father. Unpublished Thesis, University of West Indies, Mona, Jamaica.

Rebhun, L. A. (2005). Families in Brazil. In J. L. Roopnarine & U. P. Gielen (Eds.), *Families in global perspective* (pp. 330–343). Boston: Allyn and Bacon.

Redshaw, M., & Henderson, J. (2013). Fathers' engagement in pregnancy and childbirth: evidence from a national survey. *BMC Pregnancy and Childbirth, 13*, 70.

Rege, M., & Solli, I. F. (2013). The impact of paternity leave on fathers' future earnings. *Demography, 50*, 2255–2277. doi: 10.1007/s13524-13013-0233-0231

Richter, L., Chikovore, J., & Makusha, T. (2010). The status of fatherhood and fathering in South Africa. *Childhood Education, 86*, 360–365.

Richter, L. & Smith, W. (2006). Children's views of fathers. In L. Richter & R. Morell (Eds.), *Baba: Men and fatherhood in South Africa* (pp. 155–172). Cape Town: HSRC Press.

Rienks, S. L., Wadsworth, M. E., Markman, H. J., Einhorn, L., & Etter, E. M. (2011). Father involvement in urban low-income fathers: Baseline associations and changes resulting from preventive intervention. *Family Relations, 60,* 191–204.

Rinaldi, C. M. & Howe, N. (2012). Mothers' and fathers' parenting styles and associations with toddlers' externalizing, internalizing, and adaptive behaviors. *Early Childhood Research Quarterly, 27* (2), 266–273.

Ríos-Salas, V., & Meyer. D. R. (2014). Single mothers and child support receipt in Peru. *Journal of Family Studies, 20*(3), 298–310.

Rodriguez, E. T., & Tamis-LeMonda, C. S. (2011). Trajectories of the home learning environment across the first 5 years: Associations with children's vocabulary and literacy skills at prekindergarten. *Child Development, 82*(4), 1058–1075. doi: 10.1111/j.1467–8624. 2011.01614.x

Rogoff, B., Mistry, J. J., Goncu, A., & Mosier, C. (1993). Guided participation in cultural activity by toddlers and caregivers. *Monographs of the Society for Research in Child Development, 58* (7).

Rohner, R. P. (1986). *The warmth dimension: Foundations of parental acceptance-rejection theory.* Beverly Hills, CA: Sage.

Rohner, R. P. (2016). Introduction to interpersonal acceptance rejection theory (IPAR theory) and Evidence. *Online Readings in Psychology and Culture, 6*(1). doi: 10.97072307–0919.1055

Rohner, R. P., & Khaleque, A. (Eds.) (2005). *Handbook for the study of parental acceptance and rejection* (4th ed.). Storrs, CT: Rohner Research Publications.

Rohner, R. P., & Khaleque, A. (2013). Parenting essentials: Parental warmth, behavioral control, and discipline. In K. D. Keith (Ed.), *Encyclopedia of cross-cultural psychology.* Malden, MA: Wiley.

Romero-Balsas, P. (2015). Consecuencias del permiso de paternidad en el reparto de tareas y cuidados en la pareja [Consequences of paternity leave on allocation of childcare and domestic tasks]. *Reis: Revista Española de Investigaciones Sociológicas, 149,* 87–109.

Romero-Balsas, P., Muntanyola-Saura, D., & Rogero-Garcia, J. (2013). Decision-making factors within paternity and parental leaves: Why Spanish fathers take time off from work. *Gender, Work and Organization, 20*(6), 678–691. doi: 10.1111/gwao.12004

Roney, R. C. (1996). Storytelling in the classroom: Some theoretical thoughts. *Storytelling World, 9,* 7–9.

Roopnarine, J. L. (2004). African American and African Caribbean fathers: Level, quality, and meaning of involvement. In M. E. Lamb (Ed.), *The role of the father in child development* (pp. 58–97). Hoboken, NJ: Wiley.

Roopnarine, J. L. (2011). Cultural variations in beliefs about play, parent–child play, and children's play: Meaning for childhood development. In A. Pellegrini (Ed.), *The Oxford handbook of the development of play.* New York: Oxford University Press.

Roopnarine, J. L. (2013). Fathers in Caribbean cultural communities. In D. Shwalb, B. Shwalb, & M. E. Lamb (Eds.), *Fathers in cultural perspectives* (pp. 203–227). New York: Routledge.

Roopnarine, J. L. (Ed.) (2015). *Fathers across cultures: The importance, roles, and diverse practices of dads.* Santa Barbara, CA: Praeger/ABC-Clio.

Roopnarine, J. L., Brown, J., White, P. S., Riegraf, N. B., Crossely, D., Hossain, Z., & Webb, W. (1995). Father involvement in childcare and household work in common-law low income dual-earner and single-earner Jamaican families. *Journal of Applied Developmental Psychology, 16,* 35–52.

Roopnarine, J. L., & Dede Yildirim, E. (2017). The moderating role of relationship skills education on depressive symptoms in fathers with young children. *American Journal of Orthopsychiatry, 87*(4), 402–413. doi: 10.1037/ort0000230

Roopnarine, J. L., & Dede Yildirim, E. (2018). Influence of relationship skills education on pathways of associations between paternal depressive symptoms and IPV and childhood behaviors. *Psychology of Men and Masculinity, 19*(2), 223–233. doi: 10.1037/men0000100

Roopnarine, J. L., Dede Yildirim, E., & Davidson, K. (2019). Mother–child and father–child play in different cultural contexts and childhood development. In P. Smith & J. L. Roopnarine (Eds.), *The Cambridge handbook of play: Developmental and disciplinary perspectives.* London: Cambridge University Press.

Roopnarine, J. L., Evans, M., & Pant, P. (2011). Parenting and socialization practices among Caribbean families: A focus on fathers. In D. Chadee & J. Young (Eds.), *Current themes in social psychology.* Mona, Jamaica: University of the West Indies Press.

Roopnarine, J. L., Fouts, H. N., Lamb, M. E., & Lewis-Elligan, T. Y. (2005). Mothers and fathers behaviors toward their 3–4 month-old infants in low-, middle-, and upper-socioeconomic African American families. *Developmental Psychology, 41,* 723–732.

Roopnarine, J., & Hossain, Z. (2013). African American and African Caribbean fathers. In N. Cabrera & C. Tamis-Lemonda (Eds.), *Handbook of father involvement* (pp. 223–243), New York: Routledge.

Roopnarine, J. L., Hossain, Z., Gill, P., & Brophy, H. (1994). Play in the East Indian context. In J. L. Roopnarine, J. Johnson and F. Hooper (Eds.), *Children's play in diverse cultures.* Albany: State University of New York Press.

Roopnarine, J. L., & Jin, B. (2016). Family socialization practices and childhood development in Caribbean cultural communities. In J. L. Roopnarine & D. Chadee (Eds.), *Caribbean psychology: Indigenous contributions to a global discipline* (pp. 71–96). Washington, DC: American Psychological Association.

Roopnarine, J. L., Krishnakumar, A., Logie, C., Narine, L., & Davidson, K. (2017). Moderating role of neighbourhood factors on the associations between parenting practices and children's early language skills in Trinidad and Tobago. *Caribbean Journal of Psychology, 9*(1), 24–45.

Roopnarine, J. L., Krishnakumar, A., Metindogan, A., & Evans, M. (2006). Links among parenting styles, academic socialization, and the early academic and social skills of pre-kindergarten and kindergarten-age children of English-speaking Caribbean immigrants. *Early Childhood Research Quarterly, 21,* 238–252.

Roopnarine, J. L., Krishnakumar, A., & Vadgama, D. (2013). Indian fathers: Family dynamics and investment patterns. *Psychology and Developing Societies, 25,* 223–247.

Roopnarine, J. L., Krishnakumar, A., & Xu, Yi-Li (2009). Beliefs about mothers' and fathers' roles and the division of childcare and household labor in Indo Caribbean immigrants with young children. *Cultural Diversity and Ethnic Minority Psychology, 15,* 173–182.

Roopnarine, J., Lu, M., & Ahmeduzzaman, M. (1989). Parental reports of early patterns of caregiving, play, and discipline in India and Malaysia. *Early Child Development and Care, 50,* 109–120.

Roopnarine, J. L., & Mounts, N. S. (1985). Mother–child, father–child play. *Early Child Development and Care, 20,* 157–169.

Roopnarine, J. L., Talukder, E., Jain, D., Joshi, P., & Srivastav, P. (1990). Characteristics of holding, patterns of play and social behaviors between parents and infants in New Delhi, India. *Developmental Psychology, 26,* 667–673.

Roopnarine, J. L., Talukder, E., Jain, D., Joshi, P., & Srivastav, P. (1992). Personal well-being, kinship tie, and mother–infant and father–infant interactions in single-wage and dual-wage families in New Delhi, India. *Journal of Marriage and the Family, 54,* 293–301.

Roopnarine, J. L., Yang, Y., Krishnakumar, A., & Davidson, K. L. (2013). Parenting practices in Guyana and Trinidad and Tobago: Connections to preschoolers' social and cognitive skills. *Interamerican Journal of Psychology, 47*(2), 313–328.

Roskos, K. (2019). Play and literacy: Knowns and unknowns in a changing world. In P. Smith & J. L. Roopnarine (Eds.), *The Cambridge handbook of play: Developmental and disciplinary perspectives* (pp. 528–545). Cambridge: Cambridge University Press. doi: 10.1017/9781108131384.029

Rossin, M. (2011). The effects of maternity leave on children's birth and infant health outcomes in the United States. *Journal of Health Economics, 30*, 221–239.

Roy, K. (2008). A life course perspective on fatherhood and family policies in the United States and South Africa. *Fathering, 6*(2), 92–112.

Roy, K. M., & Dyson, O. (2010). Making daddies into fathers: Community-based fatherhood programs and the construction of masculinities for low-income African American men. *American Journal of Community Psychology, 45*(1–2), 139–154. doi: 10.1007/s10464-009-9282-4

Roy, K., & Smith, J. (2013). Nonresident fathers, kin, and intergenerational parenting. In N. J. Cabrera & C. S. Tamis-LeMonda (Eds.), *Handbook of father involvement: Multidisciplinary perspectives* (pp. 320–337). New York: Routledge.

Ruhm, C. J. (2000) Parental leave and child health. *Journal of Health Economics, 19*(6), 931–960.

Ruiz, M. R., Holgado-Tello, F. P., & Carrasco, M. Á. (2017). The relationships between father involvement and parental acceptance on the psychological adjustment of children and adolescents: The moderating effects of clinical status. *Psychiatry Research*, 25688–25695. doi: 10.1016/j.psychres.2017.06.022

Sagi, A., Koren-Karie, N., Gini, M., Ziv, Y., & Joels, T. (2002). Shedding further light on the effects of various types and quality of early childcare on infant–mother attachment relationship: The Haifa Study of Early Child Care. *Child Development, 73*(4), 1166–1186. doi: 10.1111/1467-8624.00465

Salway, S. Chowbey P., & Clarke, L. (2009) *Parenting in modern Britain: Experiences of Asian fathers in the UK.* York Publishing.

Sam, D. L., & Berry, J. W. (2018). *Cross-cultural psychology.* Abingdon: Routledge.

Sanders, M. R., Kirby, J. N., Tellegen, C. L., & Day, J. J. (2014). The Triple P-Positive Parenting Program: A systematic review and meta-analysis of a multi-level system of parenting support. *Clinical Psychology Review, 34*(4), 337–357.

Sanghavi, T. (2010). Factors influencing Asian Indian American children's academic performance. Unpublished doctoral dissertation, Syracuse University.

Sansiriphun, N., Kantaruksa, K., Klunklin, A., Baosuang, C., & Jordan, P. (2010). Thai men becoming a first-time father. *Nursing and Health Sciences, 12*, 403–409. doi: 10.1111/j.1442-2018.2010.00549.x

Sapountzi-Krepia, D., Lavdaniti, M., Dimitriadou, A., Psychogiou, M., Sgantzos, M., He, H. G., Faros, E., & Vehviläinen-Julkunen, K. (2010). Fathers' feelings and experience related to their wife/partner's delivery in northern Greece. *Open Nursing Journal, 4*, 48–54. doi: 10.2174/1874434601004010048

Saraff, A., & Srivastava, H. C. (2008). Envisioning fatherhood: Indian fathers' perceptions of an ideal father. *Population Review, 47*(1), 45–59.

Saraff, A., & Srivastava, H. C. (2010). Patterns and determinants of paternal involvement in childcare: An empirical investigation in a metropolis of India. *Population Research and Policy Review, 29*(2), 249–273. doi: 10.1007/s11113-11009-9139-9134

Saraswathi, T. S., & Dutta, R., (2010). India. In M. Bornstein (Ed.), *Handbook of cultural development science.* New York: Psychology Press.

Sarkadi, A., Kristiansson, R., Oberklaid, F., & Bremberg, S. (2008). Fathers' involvement and children's developmental outcomes: A systematic review of longitudinal studies. *Acta Paediatrica, 97*(2), 153–158. doi: 10.1111/j.1651–2227.2007.00572.x

SCB. (2011). Barns sociala relationer. *Levdansforhallanden*, rapport 119. www.scb.se

Schaffer, H. R., & Emerson, P. E. (1964). The development of social attachments in infancy. *Monographs of the Society for Research in Child Development*, 1–77.

Schermerhorn, A. C., & Cummings, E. M. (2008).Transactional Family Dynamics: A new framework for conceptualizing family influence processes. *Advances in Child Development and Behavior, 36*, 187–250. doi: 10.1016/S0065–2407(08)00005–0

Schneider, B. H., Atkinson, L., & Tardif, C. (2001). Child–parent attachment and children's peer relations: A quantitative review. *Developmental Psychology, 37*(1), 86–100.

Scott, K. L., & Crooks, C. V. (2007). Preliminary evaluation of an intervention program for maltreating fathers. *Brief Treatment and Crisis Intervention, 7*(3), 224–238. doi: 10.1093/brief-treatment/mhm007

Scourfield, J., Culpin, I., Gunnell, D., Dale, C., Joinson, C., Heron, J., & Collin, S. M. (2016). The association between characteristics of fathering in infancy and depressive symptoms in adolescence: A UK birth cohort study. *Child Abuse and Neglect, 58*, 119–128.

Secret, M. (2012). Incarcerated fathers: Exploring the dimensions and prevalence of parenting capacity of non-violent offenders. *Fathering, 10*(2), 159–177.

Sejourne, N., Vaslot, V., Beaume, M., Goutaudier, N., & Chabrol, H. (2012). The impact of paternity leave and paternal involvement in child care on maternal postpartum depression. *Journal of Reproductive and Infant Psychology, 30*(2), 135–144. doi: 10.1080/02646838.2012.693155

Shannon, J. D., Tamis-LeMonda, C. S., & Cabrera, N. (2006). Fathering in infancy: Mutuality and stability between 6 and 14 months. *Parenting, 6*, 167–188.

Sharma, D. (2000) Infancy and childhood in India: A critical review. *International Journal of Group Tensions, 29*, 219–251.

Shen, H., Magnusson, C., Rai, D., Lundberg, M., Lê-Scherban, F., Dalman, C., & Lee, B. (2016). Associations of parental depression with child school performance at age 16 years in Sweden. *JAMA Psychiatry, 73*(3), 239–246. doi: 10.1001/jamapsychiatry.2015.2917

Shen, J., Wu, H., & Zhao, M. (2006). Fumu yangyufangshi dui ertong xingwei he xinlijiankang yingxiang de yanjiu [Study of the effect of parental rearing pattern on the children's behavior and mental health]. *Chinese Journal of Children's Health, 14*(2), 133–135.

Shloim, N., Edelson, L. R., Martin, N., & Hetherington, M. M. (2015). Parenting styles, feeding styles, feeding practices, and weight status in 4–12 year-old children: A systematic review of the literature. *Frontiers in Psychology, 6*. doi: 10.3389/fpsyg.2015.01849

Shonkoff, J. P. (2010). Building a new biodevelopmental framework to guide the future of early childhood policy. *Child Development, 81*(1), 357–367. doi:10.1111/j.1467–8624.2009.01399.x

Shonkoff, J. P., & Phillips, D. A. (2000). *From neurons to neighborhoods: The science of early childhood development*. Washington, DC: National Academy Press.

Shorey, S., Hong-Gu, H., & Morelus, E. (2016). Skin-to-skin contact by fathers and the impact on infant and paternal outcomes: An integrative review. *Midwifery, 40*, 207–217. doi: 10.1016/j.midw.2016.07.007

Shukla, A. (1987). Decision making in single- and dual-career families in India. *Journal of Marriage and the Family, 49*, 621–629.

Shwalb, D., Shwalb, B., & Lamb, M. E. (2013). (Eds.) *Fathers in cultural context.* New York: Routledge.

Shwalb, D. W., & Hossain, Z. (2018). *Grandparents in cultural context.* New York: Routledge.

Sigel, I. E., & McGillicuddy-De Lisi, A. V. (2002). Parent beliefs are cognitions: The dynamic belief systems model. In M. H. Bornstein (Ed.), *Handbook of parenting: Being and becoming a parent* (pp. 485–508). Mahwah, NJ: Lawrence Erlbaum Associates.

Silverstein, L. B., & Auerbach, C. F. (1999). Deconstructing the essential father. *American Psychologist, 54*(6), 397–407. doi: 10.1037/0003–066X.54.6.397

Simmerman S., Blacher J., & Baker B. L. (2001). Fathers' and mothers' perceptions of father involvement in families with young children with a disability. *Journal of Intellectual and Developmental Disability 26*, 325–338.

Singer, D. G., Singer, J. L., D'Agostino, H., & DeLong, R. (2009). Children's pastimes and play in sixteen nations. *American Journal of Play, 1*(3), 283–312.

Singh, A., & Ram, F. (2009). Men's involvement during pregnancy and childbirth: Evidence from rural Ahmadnagar, India. *Population Review Publication, 48*(1), 83–102.

Singh, D., Lample, M., & Earnest, J. (2014). The involvement of men in maternal health care: Cross-sectional, pilot case studies from Maligita and Kibibi, Uganda. *Reproductive Health, 11*(1). doi: 10.1186/1742-4755-11-68

Skevik, A. (2006). Fairness in child support assessments: The views of non-resident fathers in Norway. *International Journal of Law, Policy and the Family, 20*(1), 181–200. doi: 10.1093/lawfam/ebl012

Skinner, C., Cook, K., & Sinclair, S. (2017). The potential of child support to reduce lone mother poverty: Comparing population survey data in Australia and the UK. *Journal of Poverty and Social Justice, 25*(1), 79–94. doi: 10.1332/175982717X14860543256937

Slagt, M., Deković, M., de Haan, A. D., van den Akker, A. L., & Prinzie, P. (2012). Longitudinal associations between mothers' and fathers' sense of competence and children's externalizing problems: The mediating role of parenting. *Developmental Psychology, 48*(6), 1554–1562. doi: 10.1037/a0027719

Sleigh, H., Barker, G., Toliver, M., Bah, A., & Keita, M. (2013). *Men, gender equality and gender relations in Mali: Findings from the International Men and Gender Equality Survey*. Mali: CARE International.

Smith, L. E., & Howard, K. S. (2008). Continuity of paternal social support and depressive symptoms among new mothers. *Journal of Family Psychology, 22*(5), 763–773. doi: 10.1037/a0013581

Smith, P. K., & Roopnarine, J. L. (2019). (Eds.) *The Cambridge handbook of play: Developmental and disciplinary perspectives*. Cambridge: Cambridge University Press.

Smith, R. (1996). *The matrifocal family*. New York: Routledge.

Sobel, D. M., & Weisberg, D. S. (2014). Tell me a story: How children's developing domain knowledge affects their story construction. *Journal of Cognition and Development, 15*(3), 465–478. doi: 10.1080/15248372.2012.736111

Sonke Gender Justice. (2015). *MenEngage Africa: Building on solid foundations: Strengthening and deepening the impact of work with men and boys for gender equality across Sub-Saharan Africa through the MenEngage Network: Year one report: July '14 – June '15*. South Africa: Sonke Gender Justice.

Sorkhabi, N. (2005). Applicability of Baumrind's parent typology to collective cultures: Analysis of cultural explanations of parent socialization effects. *International Journal of Behavioral Development, 29*(6), 552–563. doi: 10.1080/01650250500172640

Southern Africa Labour and Development Research Unit. (2011). *National Income Dynamics Study 2010–2011, Wave 2, Version 3.1*. Cape Town: Southern Africa Labour and Development Research Unit. Cape Town: DataFirst.

Southern Africa Labour and Development Research Unit. (2012). *National income dynamics study 2012, Wave 3, Version 2.1*. Cape Town: Southern Africa Labour and Development Research Unit. Cape Town: DataFirst.

Southern Africa Labour and Development Research Unit. (2016). *National Income Dynamics Study 2008, Wave 1, Version 6.1*. Cape Town: Southern Africa Labour and Development Research Unit. Cape Town: DataFirst.

Spjeldnaes, I. O., Moland, K. M., Harris, J., & Sam, D. L. (2011). "Being man enough": Fatherhood experiences and expectations among teenage boys in South Africa. *Fathering, 9*(1), 3–21. doi: 10.3149/fth.0901.3

Springer, L. (2009). *Fatherhood in the neighborhood.* USA: Xulon Press.

Sriram, R. (Ed.) (2019). *Fathering in India: Images and realities:* New York: Springer.

Sriram, R., Dave, P., Khasgiwala, A., & Joshi, A. (2006). Women and families in households in Gujarat. In P. Dave (Ed.), *A profile of women in Gujarat* (pp. 195–218). Vadodara, India: Women's Studies Research Centre, Maharaja Sayajiaro University of Baroda.

Sriram, R., & Navalkar, P. G. (2012). Who is an "ideal" father? Fathers, mothers and children's views. *Psychology and Developing Societies, 24*(2), 205–237.

Sriram, R., & Sandhu, G. K. (2013). Fathering to ensure child's success: What urban Indian fathers do. *Journal of Family Issues, 34*(2), 161–183.

Sroufe, L. A., & Rutter, M. (1984). The domain of developmental psychopathology. *Child Development, 55*(1), 17–29. doi: 10.2307/1129832

Stanley, S. M., Rhoades, G. K., Loew, B. A., Allen, E. S., Carter, S., Osborne, L. J., . . . Markman, H. J. (2014). A randomized controlled trial of relationship education in the U.S. Army: 2-year outcomes. *Family Relations, 63*, 482–495. doi: 10.1111/fare.12083

Statistical Handbook of Japan (2018). Statistics Bureau, Ministry of Internal Affairs and Communications. Japan.

Statistics South Africa (2011). *Census 2011 Statistical release – P0301.4.* Pretoria: Statistics South Africa.

Stearns, J. (2015). The effects of paid maternity leave: Evidence from temporary disability insurance. *Journal of Health Economics, 43*, 85–102.

Stemmler, M., Beelmann, A., Jaursch, S., & Lösel, F. (2007). Improving parenting practices in order to prevent child behavior problems: A study on parent training as part of the EFFEKT program. *International Journal of Hygiene and Environmental Health, 210*, 563–570. doi: 10.1016/j.ijheh.2007.08.007

St George, J., & Freeman, E. (2017). Measurement of father–child rough-and-tumble play and its relations to child behavior. *Infant Mental Health Journal, 38*(6), 709–725.

Strier, R. (2014). Unemployment and fatherhood. *Gender, Work and Organization, 21*, 395–410. doi: 10.1111/gwao.12044

Strier, R. (2015). Fathers in Israel: Contextualizing images of fatherhood. In J. L. Roopnarine (Ed.), *Fathers across cultures: The importance, roles, and diverse practices of dads* (pp. 350–367). Santa Barbara, CA: Praeger/ABC-Clio.

Stryker, S. (1968). Identity salience and role performance. *Journal of Marriage and Family, 4*, 558–564.

Stutz, M., & Schwarz, B. (2014). Effects of different facets of paternal and maternal control behaviour on early adolescents' perceived academic competence. *European Journal of Developmental Psychology, 11*(2), 227–241. doi: 10.1080/17405629.2013.867846

Su, L. P., Kubricht, B., & Miller, R. (2017). The influence of father involvement in adolescents' overall development in Taiwan. *Journal of Adolescence, 59*, 35–44. doi: 10.1016/j.adolescence.2017.05.010

Sun, L., & Roopnarine, J. L. (1996). Mother–infant and father–infant interaction and involvement in childcare and household labor among Taiwanese families. *Infant Behavior and Development, 19*, 121–129.

Super, C., & Harkness, S. (1997). The cultural structuring of child development. In J. Berry, P. Dasen & T. Saraswathi (Eds.), *Handbook of cross-cultural psychology: Basic processes and human development* (pp. 1–39). Needham, MA: Allyn & Bacon.

Super, C. M., & Harkness, S. (2002). Culture structures the environment for development. *Human Development, 45*(4), 270–274.

Suppal, P., & Roopnarine, J. (1999). Parental involvement in child care as a function of maternal employment in nuclear and extended families in India. *Sex Roles, 40*(9/10), 731–744.

Suppal, P., Roopnarine, J. L., Buesig, T., & Bennett, A. (1996). Ideological beliefs about family practices: Contemporary perspectives among north Indian families. *International Journal of Psychology, 31*, 29–37.

Swartz, S., & Bhana, A. (2009). *Teenage tata: Voices of young fathers in South Africa.* Cape Town: Human Sciences Research Council.

Swartz, S., Bhana, A., Richter, L., & Versfeld, A. (2013). Promoting young fathers' positive involvement in their children's lives. HSRC Policy Brief. Available at http://repository. hsrc.ac.za/bitstream/handle/20.500.11910/3140/7546.pdf?sequence=1

Sweeney, S., & MacBeth, A. (2016). The effects of paternal depression on child and adolescent outcomes: A systematic review. *Journal of Affective Disorders, 20*, 544–559. doi: 10.1016/j.jad.2016.05.073

Takehara, K., Suto, M., Kakee, N., Tachibana, Y., & Mori, R. (2017). Prenatal and early postnatal depression and child maltreatment among Japanese fathers. *Child Abuse and Neglect, 70*, 231–239. doi: 10.1016/j.chiabu.2017.06.011

Tam, V. C. (2009). A comparison of fathers' and mothers' contributions in the prediction of academic performance of school-age children in Hong Kong. *International Journal of Psychology, 44*(2), 147–156. doi: 10.1080/00207590801910242

Tam, V. C., & Lam, R. S. (2003). Parenting style of Chinese fathers in Hong Kong: Correlates with children's school-related performance. *International Journal of Adolescent Medicine and Health, 15*(1), 51–62.

Tamis-LeMonda, C., Baumwell, L. B., & Cabrera, N. J. (2013). Fathers' role in children's langugage development. In N. J. Cabrera & C. S. Tamis-LeMonda (Eds.), *Handbook of father involvement: Multidisciplinary perspectives* (2nd ed.) (pp. 135–150). New York: Taylor and Francis.

Tamis-LeMonda, C.S., Baumwell, L., & Cristofaro, T. (2012). Parent–child conversations during play. *First Language, 32*, 413–438. doi: 10.1177/0142723711419321

Tamis-LeMonda, C. S., Kahana-Kalman, R., & Yoshikawa, H. (2009). Father involvement in immigrant and ethnically diverse families from the prenatal period to the second year: Prediction and mediating mechanisms. *Sex Roles, 60*(S.I. 7–8), 496–509. doi: 10.1007/s11199-11009-9593-9599

Tamis-LeMonda, C. S., Shannon, J. D., Cabrera, N., & Lamb, M. E. (2004). Fathers and mothers at play with their 2- and 3-year-olds: Contributions to language and cognitive development. *Child Development, 75*, 1806–1820.

Tanaka, S. (2005). Parental leave and child health across OECD countries. *The Economic Journal, 115*(501), F7 – F28.

Tanskanen, A., & Erola, J. (2017). Do nonresident fathers compensate for a lack of household resources? The associations between paternal involvement and children's cognitive and educational assessments in the UK. *Research on Social Stratification and Mobility, 48*(1), 32–40.

Tautolo, E., Schluter, P. J., & Paterson, J. (2015). Pacific father involvement and early child behaviour outcomes: Findings from the Pacific Islands families study. *Journal of Child And Family Studies, 24*(12), 3497–3505. doi: 10.1007/s10826-015-0151-5

Thomson, E., Winkler-Dworak, M., & Kennedy, S. (2013). The standard family life course: An assessment of variability in life course pathways. In A. Evans and J. Baxter (Eds.), *Negotiating the life course: Stability and change in life pathways* (pp. 35–52). Dordrecht: Springer.

Thullen, M. J., McMillin, S. E., Korfmacher, J., Humphries, M. L., Bellamy, J., Henson, L., & Hans, S. (2014). Father participation in a community-doula home-visiting intervention with young, African American mothers. *Infant Mental Health Journal, 35*, 422–434. doi: 10.1002/imhj.21463

Thulstrup, S. H., & Karlsson, L. E. (2017). Children of imprisoned parents and their coping strategies: A systematic review. *Societies, 7*(15), 1–16. doi: 10.3390/soc7020015

Tomlinson, M., Cooper, P., & Murray, L. (2005). The mother–infant relationship and infant attachment in a South African peri-urban settlement. *Child Development, 76*(5), 1044–1054.

Tornello, S. L., Sonnenberg, B. N., & Patterson, C. J. (2015). Division of labor among gay fathers: Associations with parent, couple, and child adjustment. *Psychology of Sexual Orientation and Gender Diversity, 2*(4), 365–375. doi: 10.1037/sgd0000109

Trautmann, J., Alhusen, J., & Gross, D. (2015). Impact of deployment on military families with young children: A systematic review. *Nursing Outlook, 63*(6), 656–679.

Travis, J. & Waul, M. (2003). Prisoners once removed: The children and families of prisoners. In J. Travis & M. Waul (Eds.), *The impact of incarceration and reentry on children, families, and communities* (pp. 1–29). Washington, DC: The Urban Institute Press.

True, M. M., Pisani, L., & Oumar, F. (2001). Infant – mother attachment among the Dogon of Mali. *Child Development, 72*(5): 1451–1466.

Trute, B. (1990). Child and parent predictors of family adjustment in households containing young developmentally disabled children. *Family Relations, 39*, 292–297.

Tsai, S., & Chen, C. (1997). Somatic symptoms, stress and social support of expectant fathers [Chinese]. *Nursing Research, 5*(5), 439–451.

Tudge, J. (2008). *The everyday life of young children: Culture, class and childrearing in diverse societies.* New York: Cambridge University Press.

Tulananda, O., & Roopnarine, J. L. (2001). Mothers' and fathers' interactions with preschoolers in the home in Northern Thailand: Relationships to teachers' assessments of children's social skills. *Journal of Family Psychology, 14*, 676–687.

Tuli, M., & Chaudhary, N. (2010). Elective interdependence: Understanding individual agency and interpersonal relationships in Indian families. *Culture and Psychology, 16*(4), 477–496. doi: 10.1177/1354067X10380157

Tully, L. A., Piotrowska, P. J., Collins, D. A. J., Mairet, K. S., Black, N., Kimonis, E. R., . . . Dadds, M. R. (2017). Optimising child outcomes from parenting interventions: Fathers' experiences, preferences and barriers to participation. *BMC Public Health, 17*, 550. doi: 10.1186/s12889-12017-4426-4421

Turan, T., Basbakkal, Z., & Ozbek, S. (2008). Effect of nursing interventions on stressors of parents of premature infants in neonatal intensive care unit. *Journal of Clinical Nursing, 17*(21), 2856–2866. doi: 10.1111/j.1365–2702.2008.02307.x

Tynkkynen, L., Vuori, J., & Salmela-Aro, K. (2012). The role of psychological control, socioeconomic status and academic achievement in parents' educational aspirations for their adolescent children. *European Journal of Developmental Psychology, 9*(6), 695–710. doi: 10.1080/17405629.2012.671581

Umemura, T., Jacobvitz, D., Messina, S., & Hazen, N. (2013). Do toddlers prefer the primary caregiver or the parent with whom they feel more secure? The role of toddler emotion. *Infant Behavior and Development, 36*(1), 102–114. doi: 10.1016/j.infbeh.2012.10.003

United Nations. (2016). *Global sustainable development report 2016.* Department of Economic and Social Affairs. Available at https://sustainabledevelopment.un.org/content/documents/2328Global%20Sustainable%20development%20report%202016%20(final).pdf

United Nations Children's Fund (UNICEF). (2015). *Monitoring the situation of children and women for 20 years: The multiple indicator cluster surveys (MICS) 1995–2015.* New York: UNICEF. Available at http://mics.unicef.org/publications/reportsandmethodological-papers

United Nations Children's Fund (UNICEF). (2016). *The state of the world's children 2016.* New York: UNICEF.

United Nations Children's Fund (UNICEF). (2018). *The multiple indicator cluster surveys (MICS) 1995–2015.* New York: UNICEF.

United Nations Development Fund for Women (UNIFEM). (2008). *Progress of the world's women 2008/2009.* New York: UNIFEM. Available at www.unifem.org/progress/2008

United Nations Population Fund (UNFPA). (2006). *State of world population 2006.* New York: UNFPA.

U.S. Bureau of Labor Statistics. (2015). *Labor force characteristics by race and ethnicity.* Available at www.bls.gov/opub/reports/race-and-ethnicity/2015/home.htm

U.S. Census Bureau. (2014). *The survey of income and program participation (SIPP) Wave 1.* Washington, DC.

U.S. Census Bureau. (2015). *Current population survey, annual social and economic supplement, Table SHP-1.* Washington, DC.

U.S. Census Bureau. (2016). *Selected social characteristics, 2012–2016 American Community Survey 5-year estimates.* Washington, DC.

Van Belle, J. (2016). *Paternity and parental leave policies across the European Union.* European Commission. Available at www.rand.org/pubs/research_reports/RR1666.html

van Bertalanffy, L. (1972). The history and status of general systems theory. *The Academy of Management Journal, 15*(4), 407–426.

Van der Pal,S. M.,Maguire, C. M.,Cessie,S.,Wit, J. M.,Walther,F. J.,& Bruil, J. (2007). Parental experiences during the first period at the neonatal unit after two developmental care interventions. *Acta Pediatrica, 96*(11), 1611–1616. doi: 10.1111/j.1651–2227.2007.00487.x

van IJzendoorn, M. H., & De Wolff, M. S. (1997). In search of the absent father: Meta-analysis of infant – father attachment: A rejoinder to our discussants. *Child Development, 68*(4), 604–609. doi: 10.2307/1132112

van IJzendoorn, M. H., & Sagi, A. (1999). Cross-cultural patterns of attachment: Universal and contextual dimensions. In J. Cassidy & P. R. Shaver (Eds.), *Handbook of attachment: Theory, research, and clinical applications* (pp. 713–734). New York: Guilford Press.

van IJzendoorn, M. H., & Sagi-Schwartz, A. (2008). Cross-cultural patterns of attachment: Universal and contextual dimensions. In J. Cassidy & P. R. Shaver (Eds.), *Handbook of attachment: Theory, research, and clinical applications* (pp. 880–905). New York: Guilford Press.

van IJzendoorn, M. H., Sagi, A., & Lamberman, M. E. (1992). The multiple caretaker paradox: Data from Holland and Israel. In R. C. Pianta (Ed.), *Beyond the parent: The role of other adults in children's lives* (pp. 5–24). San Francisco: Jossey-Bass.

Varghese, C., & Wachen, J. (2016). The determinants of father involvement and connections to children's literacy and language outcomes: Review of the literature. *Marriage and Family Review, 52*(4), 331–359. doi: 10.1080/01494929.2015.1099587

Velázquez, A. S. (2015). Fathering in México. In J. L. Roopnarine (Ed.), *Fathers across cultures: The importance, roles, and diverse practices of dads* (pp. 63–87). Santa Barbara, CA: Praeger/ABC-Clio.

Verhoeven, M., Bögels, S. M., & van der Bruggen, C. C. (2012). Unique roles of mothering and fathering in child anxiety: Moderation by child's age and gender. *Journal of Child and Family Studies, 21*(2), 331–343. doi: 10.1007/s10826–011–9483-y

Verissimo, M., Santos, A. J., Vaughn, B. E., Torres, N., Monteiro, L., & Santos, O. (2011). Quality of attachment to father and mother and number of reciprocal friends. *Early Child Development and Care, 181*(1), 27–38. doi: 10.1080/03004430903211208

Verma, R. K., Pulerwitz, J., Mahendra,V., Khandekar S., Barker, G., Fulpagare, P., & Singh, S. K. (2006). Challenging and changing gender attitudes among young men in Mumbai, India. *Reproductive Health Matters, 14*(28), 135–143.

Verschueren, K., & Marcoen, A. (1999). Representation of self and socioemotional competence in kindergartners: Differential and combined effects of attachment to mother and father. *Child Development, 70*(1), 183–201. doi: 10.1111/1467–8624.00014

von Bertalanffy, L. (1965). Zür Geschichte theoretischer Modelle in der Biologie. *Studium Generale, 18,* 290–298.

von Bertalanffy, L. (1968). *General system theory: Foundations, development, applications.* New York: George Braziller.

von Wyl, A., Perren, S., Braune-Krickau, K., Simoni, H., Stadlmayr, W., Burgin, D., & von Klitzing, K. (2008). How early triadic family processes predict children's strengths and difficulties at age three. *European Journal of Developmental Psychology, 5,* 466–491. doi: 10.1080/17405620600989701

Wagner, A., Predebon, J., Mosmann, C., & Verza, F. (2005) Compartilhar tarefas? Papéis e funções de pai e mãe na sociedade contemporânea [Sharing tasks? Fathers' and mothers' roles and functions in the contemporary society]. *Psicologia, Teoria e Pesquisa, 21*(2), 181–186.

Wall, K. (2015). Fathers in Portugal: From old to new masculinities. In J. L. Roopnarine (Ed.), *Fathers across cultures: The importance, roles, and diverse practices of dads* (pp. 132–154). Santa Barbara, CA: Praeger/ABC-Clio.

Wanjiku, N. R. (2016). Influence of paternal involvement on children's performance in number work and language activities in public preschools in Starehe subcounty, Kenya. Unpublished doctoral dissertation, Kenyatta University, Nairobi.

Ward, C. (1996). Acculturation. In D. Landis & R. Bhagat (Eds.), *Handbook of intercultural training* (pp. 124–147). Thousand Oaks, CA: Sage.

Wartella, E., Rideout, V., Lauricella, A. R., & Connell, S. L. (2014). *Parenting in the age of digital technology: A national survey (revised).* Evanston, IL: Center on Media and Human Development, Northwestern University. Available at http://cmhd.northwestern.edu/wp-content/uploads/2015/06/ParentingAgeDigitalTechnology.REVISED.FINAL.2014.pdf

Waterman A. S. (1984). Identity formation: discovery or creation? *Journal of Early Adolescence, 4,* 329–341. doi: 10.1177/0272431684044004

Waters, E. (1987). *Attachment Q-set (Version 3).* Available from www.johnbowlby.com

Weisner, T. S. (1997). The ecocultural project of human development: Why ethnography and its findings matter. *Ethos, 25*(2), 177–190.

Weitzman, M., Rosenthal, D.G., & Liu, Y.H. (2011). Paternal depressive symptoms and child behavioral or emotional problems in the United States. *Pediatrics, 128*(6), 1126–1134. doi: 10.1542/peds.2010-3034

Wenger, E., White, N., Smith, J. D., & Rowe, K. (2005). *Technology for communities.* Available at http://technologyforcommunities.com/CEFRIO-Book_Chapter_v_5.2.pdf

Whitehouse, G., Baird, M., Brennan, D. and Baxter, J. A. (2017). Australia country note. In S. Blum, A. Koslowski, & P. Moss (Eds.), *International review of leave policies and research.* Available at: www.leavenetwork.org/lp_and_r_reports/

Whiting, B. B. (Ed.). (1963). *Six cultures: Studies of child rearing.* New York: John Wiley.

Whiting, B. B., & Whiting, J. W. M. (1975). *Children of six cultures: A psycho-cultural analysis.* Cambridge, MA: Harvard University Press.

Widarsson, M., Engström, G., Tydén, T., Lundberg, P., & Hammar, L. M. (2015). "Paddling upstream": Fathers' involvement during pregnancy as described by expectant fathers and mothers. *Journal of Clinical Nursing, 24*(7–8), 1059–1068.

Wielgos, M., Jarosz, K., Szymusik, I., Myszewska, A., Kaminski, P., Ziolkowska, K., & Przybos, A. (2007). Family delivery from the standpoint of fathers: Can stereotypes of participant or non-participant father be fully justified? *European Journal of Obstetrics, Gynecology and Reproductive Biology, 132*(1), 40–45.

Wilcox, W. B., Doherty, W., Glenn, N., & Waite, L. (2005). *Why marriage matters: Twenty-six conclusions from the social sciences* (2nd ed.). New York: Institute for American Values.

Wilder, S. (2014). Effects of parental involvement on academic achievement: a meta-synthesis. *Educational Review, 66*(3), 377–397. doi: 10.1080/00131911.2013.780009

Wilson, K. R., Havighurst, S. S., Kehoe, C., & Harley, A. E. (2016). Dads tuning in to kids: Preliminary evaluation of a fathers' parenting program. *Family Relations, 65*, 535–549. doi: 10.1111/fare.12216

Wilson, S., & Durbin, C. E. (2010). Effects of paternal depression on fathers' parenting behaviors: A meta-analytic review. *Clinical Psychology Review, 30*(2), 167–180. doi: 10.1016/j.cpr.2009.10.007

Woods, L. N., Lanza, A. S., Dyson, W., & Gordon, D. M. (2013). The role of prevention in promoting continuity of health care in prisoner reentry initiatives. *American Journal of Public Health, 103*(5), 830–838. doi: 10.2105/AJPH.2012.300961

Woolard, I., Buthelezi, T., & Bertscher, J. (2012). Child grants: Analysis of the NIDS wave 1 and 2 datasets. SALDRU working paper 84, NIDS discussion paper 2012/7. Cape Town: SALDRU, University of Cape Town.

World Health Organization. (2007). *Fatherhood and health outcomes in Europe: A summary report.* Copenhagen: WHO Regional Office for Europe. Available at www. euro.who. int/_data/assets/pdf_file/0019/69013/E91129sum.pdf

World Vision, Promundo, & MenCare. (2013). *A MenCare fathers' group manual for Sri Lanka.* Washington, DC.

Xie, J., Zhang, H., & Li, X. (2009). Fumu jiaoyangfangshi, ziwogainian yudaxuesheng wangluochengyin de guanxi [The relationship among parenting styles, self concept and internet addiction among university students]. *Studies on Ideological Education, 163*, 47–50.

Xu, A., & Zhang, L. (2007). Fuqin canyu: Hexie jiating jianshe zhong de shanghai chengxiang bijiao [Father involvement: A comparison between rural and urban families during the construction of harmonious families]. *Youth Studies, 6*, 41–48.

Xu, A., & Zhang, L. (2008). Nongcun fuqin de qinzhi canyu yiyuan, xingwei yu tiyan: Shanghai jiaoxian de jingyan yanjiu [Rural fathers' will, acts and experience of parenting: Experienced researcher of Shanghai's suburbs]. *Bulletin of Social Science, Hunan Normal University, 3*, 72–76.

Xu, L., Pirog, M.A., & Vargas, E. D. (2016). Child support and mixed-status families an analysis using the Fragile Families and Child Wellbeing Study. *Social Science Research, 60*, 249–265. doi: 10.1016/j.ssresearch.2016.06.005

Yang, G. (2010). Fumu jiaoyangfangshi dui zhongxuesheng zhuguan xingfugan de yingxiang [The impact of parent's upbringing modes on senior high school students' subjective well-being]. *Journal of Wuxi Institute of Technology, 19*(1), 93–96.

Yang, X., & Zhou, H. (2008). Qingshaonian qinzi goutong de tedian yanjiu [Characteristics of parent – adolescent communication]. *Psychological Development and Education, 2008*(1), 49–54.

Yargawa, J., & Leonardi-Bee, J. (2015). Male involvement and maternal health outcomes: Systematic review and meta-analysis. *Journal of Epidemiology and Community Health, 69*(6), 604–612. doi: 10.1136/jech-2014-204784

Yeh, K. H., Tsao, W. C., & Chen, W. W. (2009). Parent–child conflict and psychological maladjustment: A mediational analysis with reciprocal filial belief and perceived threat. *International Journal of Psychology, 45*(2), 131–139.

Yeung, W. J., Sandberg, J. F., Davis-Kean, P. E., & Hofferth, S. L. (2001). Children's time with fathers in intact families. *Journal of Marriage and Family, 63*, 136–154. doi: 10.1111/j.1741-3737.2001.00136.x

Yogman, M., & Garfield, C. F. (2016). Fathers' roles in the care and development of their children: The role of pediatricians. *Pediatrics, 138*(1), e1 – e15.

Young, D., & Roopnarine, J. L. (1994). Fathers' involvement with preschoolers in the home in families with typical children and in families with disabled children. *Topics in Special Early Childhood Education, 14,* 488–502.

Yu, C. Y., Hung, C. H., Chan, T. F., Yeh, C. H., & Lai, C. Y. (2012). Prenatal predictors for father–infant attachment after childbirth. *Journal of Clinical Nursing, 21,* 1577–1583. doi: 10.1111/j.1365–2702.2011.04003.x

Zevalkink, J., Riksen-Walraven, J. M., & Van Lieshout, C. F. (1999). Attachment in the Indonesian caregiving context. *Social Development, 8*(1), 21–40. doi: 10.1111/1467–9507.00078

Zhang, X. (2013). Bidirectional longitudinal relations between father–child relationships and Chinese children's social competence during early childhood. *Early Childhood Research Quarterly, 28,* 83–93. doi: 10.1016/j.ecresq.2012.06.005

Zhang, X., Chen, H., Zhang, G., Zhou, B., & Wu, W. (2008). Qinziguanxi yu wentixingwei de dongtai xianghuzuoyong moxing: Dui ertong zaoqi de zhuizongyanjiu [A longitudinal study of parent–child relationships and problem behaviors in early childhood: Transactional models]. *Acta Psychologica Sinica, 40*(5), 571–582.

Zreik, G., Oppenheim, D., & Sagi-Schwartz, A. (2017). Infant attachment and maternal sensitivity in the Arab minority in Israel. *Child Development, 88*(4), 1338–1349. doi: 10.1111/cdev

INDEX

Locators in *italics* refer to figures and those in **bold** to tables.